THE PORT OF HOUSTON

A HISTORY

THE PORT OF Houston

A HISTORY

Marilyn McAdams Sibley

UNIVERSITY OF TEXAS PRESS AUSTIN

Library of Congress Catalog Card No. 68–21251
Copyright © 1968 by Marilyn McAdams Sibley
All Rights Reserved

ISBN 978-0-292-74173-7

DEDICATED TO
WILLIAM NEAL BLANTON
1890–1967

FOREWORD

The Board of Navigation and Canal Commissioners of the Port of Houston has long believed that a definitive history should be written to chronicle the growth of the Port and record its contribution to the development of the city. Consequently, shortly after the observance of Houston's fiftieth anniversary as a deep-water port in November of 1964, the Board, encouraged by the unflagging interest of the late Commissioner W. N. Blanton during his more than a dozen years of service, commissioned Dr. Marilyn McAdams Sibley to prepare such a history, which is respectfully dedicated to Commissioner Blanton's memory.

This work is the result of Dr. Sibley's lengthy and exhaustive research, coupled with her own recognized ability as a narrator and historian. It presents for the first time the full and complete story of the nation's third largest port from the days it was little more than a steamboat landing on a shallow and tortuous bayou, down to the immensity of its present operation.

To those men of vision who foresaw and worked for this great potential, to those men who served before us on this Port Commission, to those hundreds who have labored to build and operate this Port and to those who have assisted in the publication of this history, we are, indeed, grateful.

Howard T. Tellepsen, *Chairman*
R. H. Pruett, *Commissioner*
E. H. Henderson, *Commissioner*
W. D. Haden II, *Commissioner*
W. C. Wells, *Commissioner*

ACKNOWLEDGMENTS

Like the Port of Houston, this book is the work of many people. In a special way it is the work of the late William N. Blanton, who as Port commissioner for thirteen years was fascinated by the history of the Port and felt that it should be recorded. Over a period of years Mr. Blanton collected material, and, after the Port Commission arranged for the history to be written, he made his collection available as the foundation for this work.

Many others have also contributed material or drawn upon their memories to make this history as complete as possible, and to all of them I am indeed grateful. They will find many evidences of my indebtedness to them in the pages of the book.

For professional assistance I am especially indebted to Dr. James A. Tinsley, executive director of the Texas Gulf Coast Historical Association, under whose auspices this book was written; and to Dr. Andrew Forest Muir of Rice University, who made his extensive notes and knowledge of early Houston available and who read the manuscript.

CONTENTS

ILLUSTRATIONS

1. Nicholas Clopper; Sidney Sherman; Thomas Wigg Grayson; Francis Richard Lubbock
2. Buffalo Bayou in Its Natural State; European Artist's Conception of Houston
3. San Jacinto Monument
4. John Kirby Allen; Augustus Chapman Allen; Original Plan of Houston
5. "Capital in Houston," Sketch by Mary Austin Holley; "Houston contains three hundred houses," Sketch by Mary Austin Holley
6. Main Street, Houston, 1856; Main Street, Houston, During Civil War
7. The Port of Houston, 1866; Main Street, Houston, 1885
8. John Thomas Brady; Charles Morgan; The Sidewheeler *Morgan*
9. Shooting Alligators on Buffalo Bayou
10. The Packet *St. Clair*; Steamboat *Lizzie*
11. Horace Baldwin Rice; Thomas H. Ball; Henry Martyn Robert; Joseph Chappell Hutcheson
12. Steamship *Dorothy*; Houston Delegation To Welcome Steamship *Dorothy*
13. The Steamer *Satilla*; The Turning Basin, 1913
14. J. Russell Wait; Benjamin Casey Allin; The *Merry Mount*

MAPS

THE PORT OF HOUSTON

A HISTORY

I. A PORT FIFTY MILES FROM THE SEA

~~~~~~

On a summer morning in 1966 the *Sam Houston*, inspection boat for the Port of Houston, took aboard some one hundred passengers for an excursion down the Houston Ship Channel. Twice and sometimes three times daily since 1958 the *Sam Houston* had made the cruise, showing to sightseers the wonders of Houston's manmade channel. From the Turning Basin, the head of deep water and the heart of Houston's waterfront, the channel stretched some fifty miles to meet the Gulf of Mexico at Bolivar Roads. For sixteen miles the channel followed the general course of historic Buffalo Bayou to its junction with the San Jacinto River, a point where General Sam Houston's army had won Texan independence in 1836. For nine additional miles the channel followed the San Jacinto River, cutting across Morgan's Point to enter Galveston Bay, thence twenty-five miles across the open bay to Bolivar Roads and the Gulf. Even before it reached the Gulf the channel made significant connections. Near Galveston Island it connected with the Gulf Intracoastal Waterway, an inland barge system that served the Gulf Coast and connected with the Mississippi system. Farther up the bay it was linked by way of Clear

Creek with the Manned Spacecraft Center of the National Aeronautics and Space Administration at Clear Lake; and by another tributary it served Bayport, an industrial park still in its early stages of development.

Although the ship channel followed the general course of natural streams, it was in fact a tribute to man's ingenuity and technical progress. The first generation of Anglo-American settlers in the area had dreamed of a channel that would bring ocean vessels across the shallow waters of Galveston Bay and inland to a point on meandering Buffalo Bayou. Later generations had inherited the dream, and late in the nineteenth century a group of practical dreamers had enlisted the assistance of the United States government. Throughout the twentieth century the United States Army Corps of Engineers had continually improved the waterway until it measured forty feet in depth for most of its length and from three to four hundred feet in width. In the same period first the City of Houston and then the Harris County Houston Ship Channel Navigation District had invested millions of dollars in Port facilities; and private interests had constructed industrial plants valued at an astronomical figure. Thus the waterway that the *Sam Houston*'s passengers saw in 1966 bore little resemblance to that known to nineteenth-century Texans.

As the inspection boat turned downstream, a voice over the loudspeaker called attention to the Port facilities. Clustered around the Turning Basin were facilities owned by the Harris County Houston Ship Channel Navigation District, a governmental agency created under the statutes of the State of Texas and administered by a five-man Board of Navigation and Canal Commissioners. The District's concrete wharves and warehouses lined the banks of the basin, and slightly downstream stood the public grain elevator, a facility constructed in the mid-1920's and enlarged time and again as Houston became one of the world's leading grain ports. Somewhat farther downstream and on the south bank stood Long Reach Docks, for decades the largest private terminal on the channel but purchased by the Navigation District in late 1965. Across the stream from Long Reach were several wharves constructed by the District in the previous decade. Adjoining these— and speaking significantly of the dynamic growth of the Port of Houston—the foundations for three additional wharves were being laid by workmen. By the 1960's these and other publicly owned Port facilities —among them, a bulk handling plant, a terminal railroad, and the World Trade Building—were yielding a profit of more than two million dollars annually.

As the *Sam Houston* moved downstream the voice over the speaker began pointing out the privately owned Port facilities. Four private terminals-for-hire supplemented the publicly owned facilities, and numerous private industrial wharves were scattered along the channel. In all, the Port had berthing space for almost a hundred ocean-going vessels and fifty barge docks. One hundred twenty steamship and ninety tanker lines made use of these facilities, transporting in 1965 almost sixty million tons of cargo valued at more than four billion dollars.[1]

On both sides of the channel adjacent to the docks were large industrial plants that accounted for much of the Port's tonnage. Among these were cement factories using oyster shell from Gulf reefs; oil refineries supplied by pipelines and tankers; chemical plants feeding on petroleum by-products; steel mills utilizing scrap iron and foreign ore; and a paper mill fed by the forests of East Texas. Economists hesitated even to estimate the value of this industrial complex, but when pressed for a figure they hazarded a guess of three billion dollars.[2]

The *Sam Houston* showed its passengers only a portion of the channel, but that portion was typical of the development of the channel's upper twenty-five miles. On isolated strips between large plants a few cows grazed under large trees, reminders that the industrial development was of recent origin and that there was still room for expansion. But at only one point on the upper channel was there no evidence of

---

[1] Harris County Houston Ship Channel Navigation District, *Port of Houston Annual Review*, 1965, pp. 1–9. The annual reports of the Navigation District on file at the administration office constitute the single most valuable source on the history of the Port after 1922. In references to these reports the Navigation District will hereinafter be cited as HCHSCND.

[2] Harris County Houston Ship Channel Navigation District, *A Brief Description of the Principal Industries, Port Facilities and Points of Interest Along the Houston Ship Channel*; Warren Rose, *Catalyst of an Economy: The Economic Impact of the Port of Houston, 1958–1963*, pp. 3, 15. For a description of the Port see Board of Engineers for Rivers and Harbors and the Maritime Administration, *The Port of Houston, Texas* (Port Series No. 24).

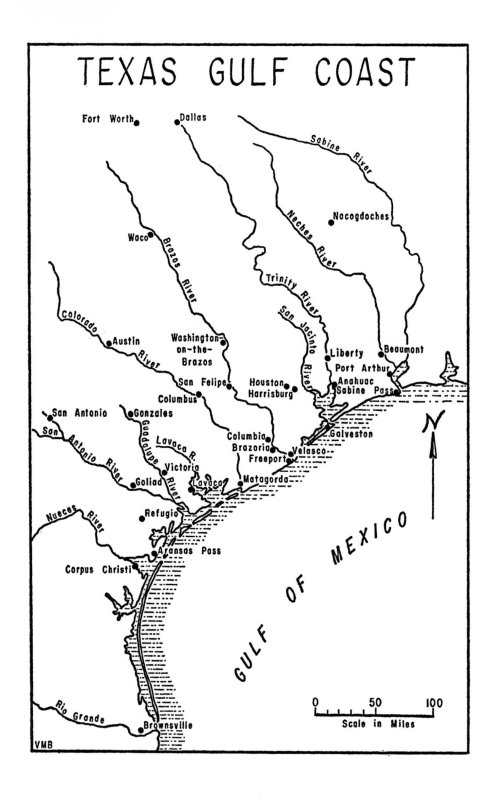

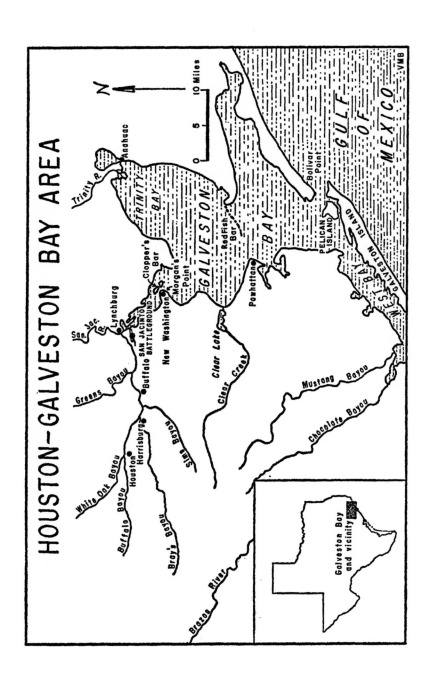

HOUSTON–GALVESTON BAY AREA

industry nor likely to be any, and that was at the San Jacinto Battleground, where a state park and impressive monument paid tribute to
pioneer Texans.

By the mid-1960's the Port of Houston and its related complex gave
direct or secondary employment to approximately 55,000 persons in
the Houston area and paid them about $320 million in wages annually.
If tertiary employment arising from Port activities were included, the
number of employed rose to approximately 100,000, with a consequent
increase in wages. For the period 1958–1963 the functional income
from all sources attributable to the Port—wages, proprietor's income,
corporate profits, interest, and rent—averaged almost $400 million per
year, or 11 per cent of all the income generated in Harris County.
If the multiplier and accelerator economic concepts were applied, the
total income from Port activities during that period varied from one-
half to one billion dollars annually, thus accounting for from 19 to 21
per cent of all the income generated in the county.[3]

The passengers who saw the channel on this particular morning
were typical of thousands of others who had seen it from the decks of
the *Sam Houston*. Among them were several Brazilian businessmen
guided by a representative from the Port's international relations department; a student from India who was studying in a local university;
a vacationing wheat farmer and his family from Kansas; a group of
cub scouts herded aboard by a den mother and a boy scout assistant;
a Sunday school class of young adults from a local church; and a group
from a civic club of a new residential development.

Of the passengers only the Brazilians were obviously interested in
the economic aspects of the channel. As the boat pulled away from
dock they talked with the Port's representative about the facilities for
handling coffee at the Port of Houston and the prospects of increased
coffee shipments.

The other passengers seemingly considered the cruise a pleasure
jaunt and took delight in the everyday sights of the ship channel. Some
exclaimed over the variety of vessels on the channel—large freighters

---

[3] Rose, *Catalyst of an Economy*, pp. 1–4, 19–41.

flying the flags of many countries; busy little tugs nosing heavy barges of sand upstream; a vessel carrying loaded truck trailers that needed only a motor to continue their journey by land; the bright red fireboat at dock near Brady Island; and squat oil barges en route to oil refineries. Others commented on the sights along the banks—ragged cotton bales and other commodities being loaded for shipment; the geometric designs of industrial plants against the sky; and the fields of oil storage tanks.

But as the ship proceeded downstream, it became apparent that most of the passengers had more at stake in the Port of Houston than they realized. When the vessel passed the grain elevator, the Kansas family gathered at ship's rail and discussed the possibility that grain from their own farm was stored there or even then being loaded aboard the Norwegian freighter at dock. The student from India joined the Kansans and voiced the hope that their grain and many other bushels from the elevator would eventually reach his country and relieve the hunger there.

Except for these sightseers, all those aboard had listed a local address when signing the guest register, and they were the ones who had most at stake in the Port. In the course of the cruise, however, it became evident that by far the majority of adults who signed in as local citizens had been born elsewhere and that they comprised a part of a great migration to Houston from other parts of Texas, neighboring states, the deep South, and other points that took place in the middle years of the twentieth century. Economic opportunity accounted for the migration —and for that opportunity the Port was in large measure responsible. Indeed, the tremendous growth in population had coincided with the development of the Port. In 1914, the year the Port obtained deep water, Houston had been a progressive but provincial city of about 100,000 people; by the mid-1960's it had grown into a metropolitan center of well over 1,000,000.

Whether newcomers or old, all local residents aboard the *Sam Houston* had more than a sightseer's interest in the Port. As federal taxpayers they had invested approximately $64 million in opening the channel to ocean vessels; and as local taxpayers they had invested an

additional $30 million in Port facilities. In return they were the bene-
ficiaries of some $150 million annually in taxes that the channel com-
plex paid to various governmental units.[4]

As private citizens they shared in other benefits that the Port and its
related activities brought to the area. The conversations of the passengers suggested some of those benefits. Two men, one a native of East
Texas and the other of Georgia, discussed the pay scales and fringe
benefits offered by various channel industries; a schoolteacher, originally from Arkansas, observed that a nearby community had one of the
best-paid school faculties in the South because of taxes paid by a single
oil refinery; a retail clerk, a native of the Middle West, spoke of a
record-breaking sale at the store where she worked. Some of those
aboard derived their livelihood directly from waterborne commerce,
that is, activities connected with the handling, transporting, and ware-
housing of cargo, or the construction and servicing of ships. Others
obtained employment in channel industries or with Port-dependent
companies. For others the benefits were less obvious, but whether engaged in trade, financing, or offering professional or personal services,
all shared in the general prosperity generated by the Port. Beyond this,
they shared in the social advantages—educational, cultural, and medi-
cal—that accrued to an affluent and growing community.

Of those aboard, the young scouts seemed least aware of the economic and social significance of the Port, but they were the ones who
most graphically illustrated its impact. In contrast to the adults, most
of the youngsters were native-born and were enrolled in schools enriched by industrial taxes. Of the nine boys, the father of one was employed at a channelside petrochemical plant, and the father of another
had been transferred to Houston by a company that did business with
the National Aeronautics and Space Administration. When questioned,
every boy in the group could name grandparents, relatives, friends, and
neighbors whose livelihood was closely associated with the Port. Thus
the boys brought to life an economist's statistics that almost one of
every nine workers in Houston was employed as a primary or secondary
result of the Port, and that if tertiary employment were included, the

---

[4] *Ibid.*, pp. 4-5.

number was increased to more than one in five.[5] In reality, however, the full impact of the Port on the area, state, and nation defied measurement. The channel's most spectacular development had occurred in the half century since the achievement of deep water, but for more than 130 years the waterway to the sea had been a vital factor in the settlement and development of the Texas Gulf Coast.

[5] *Ibid.,* pp. 1, i.

II. THE RIO BUFFALO:

"A BEAUTIFULLY MEANDERING RIVER"

THE POTENTIAL OF BUFFALO BAYOU WAS
not immediately apparent to the first white men who saw it. The first
European to set foot in Texas, the shipwrecked Spaniard Cabeza de
Vaca, probably passed in the vicinity. Yet, when Texas had been in the
possession of Spain for almost three hundred years, the bayou was still
an uncharted stream in a virtually unexplored wilderness. Indeed,
Spanish officials considered the entire Galveston Bay area a worthless
region, shot with marshes and scarcely worth defending from the tres-
passes of a few French and English traders who came to barter with the
Indians. In 1756 the Spanish established an outpost on the lower
Trinity River for the defense of the coast, but twelve years later an
inspection party that saw the area in a rainy season declared the post
superfluous. One member of the party, Nicolás de Lafora, assured his
superiors that no self-respecting nation would covet Galveston Bay,
much less attempt to take it. "We can sacrifice a certain Monsieur
Lampin who traded in a few hides on that unhabitable coast," he

wrote, "secure in the belief that no nation would attempt to form a colony there."[1]

Because of this belief and because of the Napoleonic Wars at home, Spain all but abandoned sovereignty of the Texas coast in the early nineteenth century. Indeed, her very sovereignty was called into question in 1803 when the United States purchased Louisiana from France and President Thomas Jefferson, looking at old maps, suggested that the newly acquired territory extended to the Rio Grande. But if Spain, a senile power, was unprepared to defend Texas, the United States, still a young republic, was equally unprepared to take it. Thus, from 1803 until a treaty settled the issue in 1819, both nations claimed the land without either exercising effective authority. As a result, the Texas coast became the special province of renegades and outcasts, and by 1818 Galveston Bay was the center of two thriving—but illegal— commercial activities, both directed by Jean Laffite. From his base on Galveston Island, Laffite preyed on Gulf shipping and engaged in the smuggling of contraband, primarily human, into Louisiana. Of the two activities the smuggling was by far the more profitable, for, although the importation of slaves was illegal in the United States after 1808, the planters of the lower South still needed laborers for their cane and cotton fields. This need Laffite and others of his ilk proposed to fill by bringing African Negroes to Galveston by way of the West Indies, then slipping them into the United States by way of the Sabine River or other inlets along the Texas-Louisiana coast.

The rival sovereigns of Texas chose to ignore the operations of Jean Laffite when possible, but early in 1818 both nations were goaded into action by another activity on Galveston Bay. A group of Napoleonic exiles, attracted by the power vacuum, landed on the Trinity River with the announced intention of establishing a colony there. Although Napoleon was safely incarcerated at Saint Helena, his name still had the power to terrify, and both Spain and the United States were filled with uneasiness at the idea of his followers entrenching themselves in Texas. Thus, Spain mustered a force to dislodge the intruders while

---

[1] Nicolás de Lafora, *The Frontiers of New Spain: Nicolás de Lafora's Description, 1766–1768*, Lawrence Kinnaird, ed., pp. 184–185.

the United States sent an emissary, George Graham, to warn them that they were trespassing on United States territory.

Graham, whose report of his mission stands as the first Anglo-American account of a sea journey to Texas, encountered considerable difficulty in reaching Galveston. He was advised in the United States to take the land route, following the Old San Antonio Road from Natchitoches to Nacogdoches, thence due south to the coast. But upon reaching the Sabine River, he was told that this route was impractical, that the best way to reach Galveston was to catch a smuggling boat on Lake Calcasieu. Swallowing any qualms he may have had about the propriety of an agent of the United States traveling by such means, Graham acted on this advice, and, after being tossed by a Gulf storm and enduring "a most unpleasant passage of eight days," he arrived at Galveston on August 24.

The French colony had already disintegrated when he arrived, but he took the occasion to confer at length with Laffite. Graham was surprised at the extent of the contraband trade with Louisiana. It was the "most extensive & illegal system of Smuggling" that had ever been carried on in the United States, he reported. Not only pirates but the "whole country" was engaged in it, many otherwise respectable planters entering the trade in the first instance to obtain Negroes for themselves and then remaining in it because of the profits.

Because of this trade, Graham concluded that the United States had underestimated the importance of the Texas Gulf Coast, and he took a long, hard look at it. As Spain had never charted the coast in detail and had forbidden the ships of other nations to venture there, he was dependent on sketchy maps and corsairs for his information. His geography was thus inexact, but, even so, he gave a perceptive appraisal of the hazards and potentials of navigation there. The chief obstacle, he noted, was a series of shifting sand bars that blocked the mouths of the principal streams and the entrances to most of the harbors. At Galveston, the best harbor in Texas, the bar afforded from ten to twelve feet of water according to the tide, while at the mouths of the Trinity, San Jacinto, and Brazos rivers there was only about four feet of water. In spite of the sand bars, Graham took a sanguine view of navigation in Texas and especially of the potential of Galveston Bay. The bay extended northeastward toward the Sabine, he reported, and southwestward toward the Brazos. Several major streams, among them the Trinity and San Jacinto, emptied into it, affording access to the interior and watering the best part of the province. In addition, southwesterly from Galveston to the Rio Grande stretched a chain of islands that suggested the possibility of a coastal canal, protected from Gulf storms. Graham recommended that the United States occupy Galveston Island without further quibbling with Spain. "Galveston is a position of much more importance than the Government has hitherto supposed," he informed the Secretary of State. "It is the key to the greatest & best part of the province of Texas."[2]

Except for freebooters, Graham was the first man to recognize the commercial potential of Galveston Bay, and history has proved him an astute observer. Somewhat more than a century after his visit, the bay had become the center of commerce on the Texas Gulf Coast, and the coastal canal envisioned by him had taken form as the Gulf Intracoastal Waterway. But perceptive as he was, Graham did not mention the stream that was destined to become the heart of navigation on Galveston Bay and one of the most fabulous waterways in the world. Indeed, at the time of Graham's visit, Buffalo Bayou was still an obscure stream, leading into an unknown interior. If he heard its name, there was no reason for him to think it worth mentioning in a discussion of Texas navigation.

Within four years after Graham's visit, the Mexican Revolution had driven Spain from Texas, and Mexico had granted Stephen Fuller Austin the right to locate colonists in the province. Austin's first grant encompassed the entire length of Buffalo Bayou, but still its importance was only slowly realized. In 1822 Nathaniel Lynch established himself at the confluence of the bayou and the San Jacinto River. Four years later John Richardson Harris founded Harrisburg farther upstream at the junction of Buffalo and Bray's bayous, and shortly thereafter he set up the first industry on Buffalo Bayou, a steam sawmill. A few other settlers, some legal and some otherwise, filtered into the area,

2 George Graham, "George Graham's Mission to Galveston in 1818: Two Important Documents Bearing upon Louisiana History," Walter Prichard, ed., *Louisiana Historical Quarterly*, XX (July, 1937), 619–650.

and Harris' schooner, *The Rights of Man,* and a few other small vessels began plying the bayou as far as Harrisburg, bringing in supplies for the colonists and taking out lumber, hides, and a few bales of cotton.[3]

Still, in comparison with the Brazos area, Buffalo Bayou developed slowly. Most of the early settlers came from the South with the idea of planting cotton and sugar cane, the staples of their native region. For these crops, the rich, deep soil of the Brazos bottoms seemed far more desirable than the soil that bordered Buffalo Bayou. Furthermore, during the 1820's and until after the Texan Revolution, most settlers expected the Brazos to become the great transportation artery of Texas. It was destined to be a small-scale Mississippi River, they assured each other. They would raise their crops on its banks and send their harvests to market on its waters. True, the Brazos posed problems in navigation. The shifting sand bar at its mouth afforded only from two to eight feet of water according to tide and weather, and, as Stephen F. Austin observed, the river opened "into the wild ocean without any bay."[4] Moreover, the Brazos, like other Texas rivers, was a meandering, tortuous stream, obstructed by snags, and in rainy seasons it carried too much water and in dry seasons too little. But with typical pioneer optimism, the settlers looked forward to the time when these obstacles would be overcome and when fortitude and enterprise would turn the Brazos into a little Mississippi.

From the beginning of Anglo-American colonization, settlers proposed schemes to tame the Brazos. Austin suggested digging a canal to open the river into nearby Galveston Bay; others suggested a system of pilings to direct the course of the river; still others suggested extensive dredging operations. Little came of these schemes, however, and by 1828 the river was still not navigable within sixty miles of San Felipe, the capital of Austin's colony. This circumstance caused several entrepreneurs, among them Nicholas Clopper, to cast about for means of reaching the Brazos markets without braving the river, and, in this connection the peculiar advantages of Buffalo Bayou first became apparent.

[3] Adele B. Looscan, "Harris County, 1822–1845," *Southwestern Historical Quarterly,* XVIII (October, 1914), 195–207.

[4] Eugene C. Barker, ed., *The Austin Papers,* II, 1239.

In contrast to most major Texas streams, the bayou ran in an east-west direction, pointing toward the Brazos River. Moreover, the bayou afforded better navigation than most Texas streams, being wide and deep from its junction with the San Jacinto River to Bray's Bayou and remaining deep though more narrow and tortuous from Bray's to White Oak Bayou. One had merely to look at the map to see what this meant in respect to the Brazos trade. Harrisburg, at the head of navigation on Buffalo Bayou, was only some twenty miles from the heart of the Brazos agricultural region and less than forty miles from San Felipe. Thus, goods destined for upstream points on the Brazos required a shorter overland haul if landed at Harrisburg than if landed at the head of navigation on the river.[5]

This realization excited Nicholas Clopper, a Yankee who had fallen on hard times at home and come to Texas to recoup his fortunes. Dreaming of trade with the interior, he bought half a league of land on the north side of Buffalo Bayou near Harrisburg in the fall of 1826. Then turning his eyes downstream, he decided upon a likely place for a city—a finger of land that separated San Jacinto and Galveston bays. Not only would traffic to the interior pass by this point, he reasoned, but it would be an ideal place to butcher cattle for shipment to the West Indies. Vessels bringing goods for the Brazos could take on a load of beef as they departed. In December, Clopper purchased the strip of land—to be known for almost a decade as Clopper's Point and thereafter as Morgan's Point—from the next owner. Then he returned to Ohio, there to organize the Texas Trading Company, composed of his three sons, Andrew May, Edward Nicholas, and Joseph Chambers, and three other men. In the fall of 1827 the associates of the new company set out from Cincinnati to Texas, taking passage from New Orleans to Harrisburg on the schooner *Little Zoe* and bringing with them an assortment of goods for pioneer Texas—whiskey, tobacco, hardware, glassware, dry goods, nails, flour, soap, combs, mirrors, snuff boxes, spices, medicines, and other items.[6]

Two of the Cloppers, Edward Nicholas and Joseph Chambers, kept

---

[5] Andrew Forest Muir, "The Destiny of Buffalo Bayou," *Southwestern Historical Quarterly*, XLVII (October, 1943), 91–106.

[6] Edward Nicholas Clopper, *An American Family*, pp. 130–131, 152.

journals of the voyage, telling how they spotted Galveston Island two days after Christmas, how they entered Galveston Bay at Bolivar Pass, and how they crossed the bay to enter Buffalo Bayou on January 3, 1828. The brothers were unaware, of course, that the route they followed from the pass to Harrisburg was destined for fame, or that they described in its natural state the waterway known to later generations as the Houston Ship Channel. Certainly, nothing about the route suggested that the largest vessels of the next century would travel there. Indeed, as the Cloppers crossed the bay they sighted the wrecks of two schooners, grim reminders that the few vessels of their own day that ventured there did so at great risk.[7]

The Cloppers, like George Graham of a decade earlier, were impressed by the advantages of the Galveston harbor. It afforded protection and good anchorage for shipping, and its channel from the sea varied from ten to thirty feet, they noted. But the channel was narrow in places, and the captain of the *Little Zoe* was unfamiliar with it. The schooner ran aground near the eastern tip of the island, and, while waiting for a high tide to put the ship afloat, the Cloppers went ashore, where they shot game birds and made a feast of oysters and redfish. Nearby, they recalled, Laffite had made his headquarters, and, across the pass at Bolivar Point, Jane Long had spent the winter of 1821 while her husband continued his filibustering expedition into Mexico.

Two days later, when the schooner was again afloat, the captain headed cautiously into the bay, sounding the channel as he went. "Sailed many miles through water of five feet depth, our schooner drawing upwards of four & a half," wrote Joseph. At one point they lost the channel and found themselves in shallow water. "We then cast anchor and sounded for the channel but found the water very shallow all around us," said Edward. "Our Captain returned in the jollyboat, almost discouraged from making any further attempts to find the channel. We however set sail again, and sailed about ten or twelve miles, with from five to seven feet of water, until we came to Red fish barr [*sic*]."

[7] The journals are printed *ibid.*, pp. 156–198. Joseph Chambers Clopper's journal is also printed as "J. C. Clopper's Journal and Book of Memoranda for 1828," *Southwestern Historical Quarterly*, XIII (July, 1909), 44–80.

Red Fish Bar, a reef of oyster shells stretching east and west across the middle of the bay, was the first of two major obstacles other than shallow water that blocked the Cloppers' way from Bolivar Pass to the mouth of Buffalo Bayou. Several channels crossed it, they observed, the main one being about a mile from the west shore and only fifty or sixty feet wide. This channel was deep, except for a narrow, hard shoal that afforded barely enough water for the *Little Zoe* to squeeze over. The Cloppers breathed in relief as they passed. "We struck in four & half feet water & dragged over," commented Joseph.

North of Red Fish Bar the water varied little from eight feet and gave the *Little Zoe* no problems in navigation until she reached the point of land owned by Nicholas Clopper that separated San Jacinto and Galveston bays. Here the second major obstacle obstructed the way, a shifting sand bar destined to acquire its permanent name, Clopper's Bar, from the passengers of *Little Zoe*. The captain would not attempt the bar without a pilot, so he anchored offshore and waited until three local men came aboard and piloted the vessel into San Jacinto Bay, thence to Lynchburg, where Buffalo Bayou met the San Jacinto River.

The Cloppers were pleasantly surprised at both the ease of navigation and the beauty of the bayou. "The Rio Buffalo is a beautifully meandering river, from sixty to a hundred yards wide and deep enough for schooner or steam boat navigation," wrote Edward. His brother was even more enthusiastic:

This is the most remarkable stream I have ever seen. At its junction with the San Jacinto [it] is about 150 yds. in breadth, having about three fathoms water with little variation in depth as high up as Harrisburg, 20 miles. The ebbing & flowing of the tide is observable about 12 miles higher, the water being of navigable depth close up to each bank, giving to this most enchanting little stream the appearance of an artificial canal. . . . Most of its course is bound in by timber & flowering shrubbery which overhang its grassy banks & dip & reflect their variegated hues in its unruffled waters. These impending shrubs are in places overtopped by the evergreen magnolia. . . . The banks of this stream are secured from the lavings of the water by what are here termed "cypress knees". . . . So closely & regularly

are they often found standing in lines as to resemble piles driven in pur-
posely as security against the innovation of the tides.

When the Cloppers reached Harrisburg, they unloaded their merchandise, set up a store, and made arrangements to build their city at
Clopper's Point. Then, leaving Andrew to oversee operations on Buffalo Bayou, the other members of the family and their associates loaded
an assortment of goods in wagons and headed for San Felipe and San
Antonio. They disposed of their goods with ease, but their expenses
were considerable and profits disappointing. Moreover, the overland
journey proved even more hazardous than the water route. Swollen
streams and boggy prairies impeded their progress; all members of the
party, unacclimated to Texas summers, fell ill; and Edward N. Clopper
died of fever at San Felipe. The grief-stricken father and brother continued their trip to San Antonio, then returned to Harrisburg with
little heart for further adventures in interior Texas. In the eyes of the
Cloppers their trading venture was a failure, but, as later developments
proved, they were only ahead of their time. In their account of their
failure, they described the dream of a route to the interior that others
would pursue more successfully, and they recorded the obstacles—
shallow water, Clopper's Bar, and Red Fish Bar—that blocked that
route to the sea.

Before the Texas Revolution few men dreamed Nicholas Clopper's
dream and even fewer pursued it. Even so, during the early 1830's
Galveston Bay attracted a number of settlers, some of them destined to
play crucial roles in its development. David Gouverneur Burnet, a pi-
ous adventurer who had married a kinswoman of the Cloppers, settled
near Lynchburg about 1830 and invested his capital in a steam sawmill. A few years later Lorenzo de Zavala, a Yucatán liberal who had
angered the Mexican dictator, Antonio López de Santa Anna, purchased land to the west of Burnet on Buffalo Bayou and brought his
young, second wife—an American—to live there. In the same period,
Augustus Chapman Allen, a Yankee land speculator, visited the bay
and looked at Buffalo Bayou with speculative eyes. Would the Cloppers, he inquired, be interested in selling their point? They would not
at the price he offered, so Allen turned his attention to Galveston

Island and talked of building a city there.[8] A short while later another newcomer, James Morgan, offered Nicholas Clopper a more attractive price, and, on December 22, 1834, Clopper sold the strip of land between San Jacinto and Galveston bays. Along with the land, Morgan acquired the dream of a city there. Backed by New York capitalists, he laid out the city of New Washington on newly renamed Morgan's Point. In 1835 he opened a store and built a warehouse to receive merchandise that he expected to arrive by schooner from New York.

In late 1830 the first steamboat on Texas waters, the *Ariel*, made its way up Buffalo Bayou, arriving at the Harrisburg landing on December 29. Henry Austin, a cousin of Stephen Fuller Austin, had brought the *Ariel* to Texas the previous year and placed it in operation on the lower Rio Grande. Disappointed in the prospects of profitable steamboat business there, he brought the vessel to the Brazos River in the summer of 1830. His observations convinced him that unless great improvements were made, that river too offered few inducements to the steamboat captain. Nevertheless, he was impressed by the rich land that bordered the Brazos and determined to make his home in his cousin's colony. In the fall he prepared to take the *Ariel* to New Orleans to obtain supplies for settling in Texas, but before the boat left the Texas coast it was beset by difficulties. Part of the crew deserted; some of the provisions spoiled; and the vessel was severely damaged in crossing the Brazos bar. After three unsuccessful efforts to reach New Orleans, Austin turned the *Ariel*, "leaking badly & her chimney blown away," into Galveston Bay and up Buffalo Bayou. By the time the boat reached Harrisburg, it was damaged beyond repair. Therefore, Austin pulled it out of the main channel and left it to rot.[9]

The next steamboat on Buffalo Bayou was the eighty-eight-ton *Cayuga*, brought to Texas with substantial encouragement from Brazos valley planters. In the fall of 1833 a group of these planters circulated a subscription list, promising five thousand acres of land and eight hundred dollars to Robert Wilson and William Plunkett Harris if they

[8] Clopper, *An American Family*, p. 279; William Fairfax Gray, *From Virginia to Texas . . .*, p. 157.

[9] William R. Hogan, "Henry Austin," *Southwestern Historical Quarterly*, XXXVII (January, 1934), 185–214.

would bring a steamboat to the river. By the following year Harris was operating the *Cayuga* on the Brazos and occasionally bringing it to Galveston Bay and Harrisburg.[10]

Despite this activity and the foresight of a few, the commerce of Galveston Bay on the eve of the Texan Revolution was still local in nature, and Buffalo Bayou led only to Harrisburg. Although Galveston harbor was considered the best in the country, the island seemed remote and undesirable to most settlers. Low, subject to overflow, and exposed to Gulf storms, it looked, one visitor observed, like "a piece of prairie that had quarrelled with the mainland and dissolved partnership."[11] Mary Austin Holley informed her readers in 1831 that Anahuac was the most promising town on Galveston Bay and that there was no settlement within forty miles of Galveston Island. The Brazos was "much the most eligible" entrance to Texas by sea, she said: "It is the route most frequented, and offers the best facilities for procuring the common necessaries that are needed on arrival, as well as the means of transportation into the interior."[12]

The revolution that created the Republic of Texas thrust Harrisburg and its route to the sea into sudden prominence. The first rumbles of revolt were sounded at Anahuac in 1832 when a government customs collector took his duties too seriously. Settlers of the area forced him to leave, then passed off their action as a part of another revolution then going on in Mexico, the revolution that brought Santa Anna to the Presidency. In early 1835 the Santanista government reopened the customshouse at Anahuac, and again violence erupted. DeWitt Clinton Harris and Andrew Briscoe, the son and future son-in-law, respectively, of the founder of Harrisburg, were arrested for refusing to pay duties. William Barret Travis led a force to release them; and, for a second time in three years, a Mexican customs collector was ejected from Texas. But these actions were only the preliminaries to revolu-

[10] William R. Hogan, *The Texas Republic . . .*, pp. 69–70; *Ship Registers and Enrollments of New Orleans, Louisiana*, III, 36.

[11] Francis C. Sheridan, *Galveston Island; or, A Few Months Off the Coast of Texas: The Journal of Francis C. Sheridan, 1839–1840*, Willis W. Pratt, ed., p. 32.

[12] Mary Austin Holley, *Texas: Observations, Historical, Geographical and Descriptive . . .*, in Mattie Austin Hatcher, *Letters of an Early American Traveller . . .*, p. 176.

tion. When the main show opened the spotlight fell first on San Antonio and then on Washington-on-the-Brazos before shifting to the junction of Buffalo Bayou and the San Jacinto River for the grand finale.

In late 1835 a ragtag collection of Texas rebels stormed San Antonio and forced a Mexican army to withdraw. Determined to teach the rebels a lesson, Santa Anna crossed the Rio Grande in February, 1836, with about seven thousand troops and headed for San Antonio, where fewer than two hundred men waited to stop him. While Santa Anna was beseiging San Antonio, Texan delegates met at Washington-on-the-Brazos. On March 2 they declared Texas independent, and they were in the process of drafting a constitution and forming a government when word came of the fall of the Alamo. When the first refugees arrived from the west, bringing rumors that the Texas army was retreating and the Mexicans advancing, the delegates were filled with an urgency to depart. "The members are now dispersing in all directions. A general panic seems to have seized them," wrote Colonel William Fairfax Gray, a Virginia land speculator who had ridden into Texas a few months earlier. "Their families are exposed and defenseless, and thousands are moving off to the east. A constant stream of women and children and some men, with wagons, carts and pack mules are rushing across the Brazos night and day."[13]

Some of the delegates departed without waiting to complete the business at hand. Others proposed adjourning the convention to Nacogdoches, but a hard core met on the night of March 16 in a session that lasted until four o'clock the next morning. They completed the constitution about midnight and in the early morning hours elected David G. Burnet President and Lorenzo de Zavala Vice President of an *ad interim* government. The choice of executives was portentous insofar as Buffalo Bayou was concerned, for within hours after the formation of the new government the Cabinet decided to take refuge in a safe place. The road leading toward Nacogdoches and the Sabine River was the logical route of escape, but Burnet and Zavala had other ideas. Both were familiar with the route from Harrisburg to the sea, and both

[13] Gray, *From Virginia to Texas*, p. 134.

had wives and young children on its banks. "The new executives have determined to go to Harrisburg, on the Buffalo Bayou, as a place of more safety than this, and of easy communication with the seaboard, New Orleans, etc.," Colonel Gray wrote in his diary.[14]

Gray, being a newcomer, found nothing amiss in the executives' decision, but Texans of longer standing were taken back by it. To most of them Harrisburg was a remote village, far removed from the main thoroughfares. Some Nacogdoches citizens were so perturbed that they wrote Burnet protesting the location of the temporary seat of government and stressing the difficulties of communicating with it. The route from the United States by sea was "too precarious," they pointed out, "and the time consumed in going to Harrisburg and back is serious in its consequences. . . . In the Summer months Harrisburg and the Country about it is not considered healthy, and strangers would feel some apprehension in visiting you there on that account. Besides it appears to us that in the progress of the war, you may be cut off from communication with the army."[15]

Disregarding any advice to the contrary, Burnet and his government headed south along the Brazos to Jared Ellison Groce's plantation, thence eastward along the trail known by courtesy as the Harrisburg road. Following in their wake was a group of hangers-on and land speculators, among them Colonel Gray, who had neither families nor property in Texas and who hoped to gain concessions from the beleaguered government.

Their arrival created a flurry of activity on Galveston Bay. Long-neglected Galveston Island suddenly became a position of first importance. By its nature it could be held by a few men, Burnet's military advisers observed. If only it were fortified it would protect all the bay from invasion by sea and at the same time afford harbor and protection to the Texas navy and to vessels bringing supplies from New Orleans. When word came of the Fannin debacle and of the advance of the enemy to the Brazos, the island became even more important. If worst came to worst, the men told each other, Galveston Island would afford

[14] Ibid., p. 134.
[15] William C. Binkley, ed., Official Correspondence of the Texan Revolution, I, 593.

a place of last retreat—a place where the women and children could take passage to New Orleans and where the government and army could make a last-ditch stand. "If your army is defeated it [Galveston Island] is the only point to which it can retreat without the certainty of being disbanded—it is the only port by which you can receive supplies of men and provisions from the United States," one of the defenders wrote the President.[16]

Burnet gave his neighbor, James Morgan, the rank of colonel and assigned him the task of fortifying Galveston Island. The task was no easy one, for the island was destitute of timber and laborers were few. Morgan called for the assistance of the steamer *Cayuga* and discovered to his surprise and to that of Burnet that the vessel was already in the service of the government. The provisional government had rented it from its owner some months previously. During the next few weeks the *Cayuga* chugged up and down Buffalo Bayou and all about the bay, taking men and timber to Galveston, refugees to Anahuac, and supplies—including whiskey "suitable for genteel men to drink"—to the government at Harrisburg.[17] In mid-April two other steamers that customarily plied the Brazos, the *Laura* and *Yellow Stone*, joined the *Cayuga* in Galveston Bay. The 65-ton *Laura* arrived in time to take supplies to the victorious army after the Battle of San Jacinto. The *Yellow Stone*, a 144-ton vessel commanded by John E. Ross, had been at Groce's plantation taking on a load of cotton when the Texan army arrived there on March 31. During the second week in April the steamer ferried the Texas soldiers across the Brazos, then headed downstream, eluding the Mexican army and arriving at Galveston in time to take President Burnet to visit his victorious soldiers.[18]

There were other vessels on Galveston Bay in March and April. The schooners *Flash* and *Kosciusko* had recently brought merchandise to Morgan at New Washington. Another schooner, the *Shenandoah*, still remained in the bay after bringing African Negroes for Monroe Edwards, the notorious blackbirder who had taken up the slave trade where Laffite left off. Also in Galveston harbor were the *Independence*

[16] *Ibid.*, II, 644.
[17] *Ibid.*, pp. 528, 534, 545–546.
[18] *Ibid.*, pp. 577, 632, 984–985; *Ship Registers*, III, 121, 130.

and *Brutus* of the Texas navy, seeking refuge after adventures at sea with Mexican vessels. On April 7 a third naval vessel, the *Invincible*, arrived at Galveston with a prize, the brig *Pocket*. The prize was indeed welcome, for it carried large stores of food which were promptly sent up the bayou to Harrisburg, thence by land to the hungry army.[19]

Another welcome arrival in early April was the *Pennsylvania*, bringing two cannon, the famous Twin Sisters, as a gift from the people of Cincinnati. In a special way the cannon were the contribution of old Nicholas Clopper to the Revolution. He presided over the meeting that voted to collect the contributions. Because the United States was nominally neutral in revolution, the Cincinnati newspapers called the cannon Hollow Ware in the reports of the proceedings. Clopper's hollow ware, like the supplies from the *Pocket*, was shipped to Harrisburg by water, thence overland to the army.[20]

While cannon and supplies headed to the Brazos, panic-stricken settlers from that area converged on Galveston Bay en route to the Sabine and the safety of the United States. Rain-swollen streams slowed the refugees' progress from Buffalo Bayou eastward. The *Cayuga* ferried some of them to Anahuac. Others crossed by raft, flatboat, or other means. Still others congregated on the banks of streams waiting for transportation. By April 2, Colonel Gray was told, the prairie near Lynchburg resembled a camp-meeting ground, being covered with carts, tents, mules, women, children, baggage, slaves, and cattle. To alleviate the distress and to free men to join the army, Burnet designated a tract on the south side of the bayou as an encampment for refugees and appointed men to provide timber and food and to construct temporary shelters.[21]

During the weeks while the government was at Harrisburg, Burnet issued several proclamations to reassure the refugees and stop their flight, but at the same time both he and Zavala spent much time with their own families preparing them for evacuation. If the executives had

[19] Binkley, ed., *Official Correspondence*, I, 469–473, 477; II, 605; Gray, *From Virginia to Texas*, p. 148.

[20] Clopper, *An American Family*, pp. 259–260; Binkley, ed., *Official Correspondence*, II, 564, 612.

[21] *Ibid.*, p. 618; Gray, *From Virginia to Texas*, p. 151.

come to Harrisburg for that purpose, however, they might better have
taken another direction, for the very fact of their presence attracted the
Mexican army. When Santa Anna with the advance of his army
reached San Felipe on April 7, he found the Brazos impassable at that
point. He headed downstream to a more favorable crossing and learned
there that the rebel government—with his old enemy Zavala as Vice
President—had gone to Harrisburg. This circumstance seemed to offer
a rare opportunity to the Mexican dictator. Why not end the Revolution
with one stroke by capturing its civil leaders and at the same time take
revenge on his personal enemy? His main force was to his rear, but this
fact seemed unimportant at the time. The only Texan force of any size
was north on the Brazos and, to all appearances, in full retreat toward
the United States border. Santa Anna decided to pursue the fugitive
government. Sending word to his other forces to join him, he crossed
the Brazos with about 750 troops and descended on Harrisburg.

When he arrived at that place, he found it deserted except for three
printers who had recently come as refugees from San Felipe bringing
with them the press of the *Telegraph and Texas Register*. The government and other inhabitants had departed on the steamer *Cayuga* only
hours earlier, the printers informed Santa Anna. In hopes of intercept-
ing the steamer before it reached Galveston Bay, Santa Anna sent
Colonel Juan Nepomuceno Almonte with about fifty horsemen to
Morgan's Point. Their mission was almost successful. Burnet had
stopped at New Washington to pick up his family, and, as the Mexicans approached, he and his family jumped into rowboats and made
for the vessel anchored in the bay. If the Mexicans had known him by
sight, they could easily have taken him. "We just got started about 30
yards from the shore when the Mexican Cavalry appeared on the Bank
. . .," wrote Burnet's brother-in-law, who participated in the narrow
escape. "They could have shot him easy with a pistol, for he was standing up in the B[oa]t paddling with an oar, and two Black boys pulling
their oars just as hard as they could, to get out of the way."[22]

Although the rebel government eluded him, Almonte discovered
that Colonel Morgan's warehouse bulged with food and other supplies.

[22] Clopper, *An American Family*, p. 265.

This was of no small consequence, for the Mexican army was well in advance of its quartermaster. Upon hearing of the supplies, Santa Anna tossed the press of the *Telegraph and Texas Register* into Buffalo Bayou, set fire to Harrisburg, and joined Almonte at New Washington.

While these events were taking place, the Texas army faced a hard decision. The disasters of San Antonio and Goliad left Sam Houston with between seven and eight hundred men, roughly one-tenth the number Santa Anna had led into Texas. Houston, a man of more common sense than the luckless defenders of the Alamo, withdrew from the Colorado River to San Felipe in late March and then turned north along the Brazos to Groce's plantation, recently abandoned by the civil government. To all appearances Houston intended to retreat toward the Sabine, where General Edmund Pendleton Gaines waited with a United States army. Gaines held ambiguous orders from President Andrew Jackson, an old friend of Houston. If the Texas army had retreated far enough, all present evidence suggests, Gaines would have found some pretext to enter the fray. But Houston was not certain of this in April, 1836, and his men did not even suspect it. The Texan soldiers who had not already departed for safer locales belonged to the stand-and-die school of William Barret Travis. To them retreat seemed an admission of cowardice. From the time Houston ordered the retreat from the Colorado there were rumbles of mutiny; and when on the morning of April 16 he ordered his army eastward from Groce's the rumbles became ominous. Santa Anna had gone to Harrisburg, the soldiers knew, but where was the General taking them? A few miles east of Groce's the road forked, the left fork going toward Nacogdoches and the right to Harrisburg. Which fork, they asked each other, did the General intend to take? This question has yet to be satisfactorily answered, and Houston's intentions are still a matter of controversy. But whatever he intended, the first men to reach the fork turned toward Harrisburg and a shout went through the ranks as the others followed. At least one person thought Houston intended taking the army to Nacogdoches. Mrs. Pamela Mann had lent a yoke of oxen to draw the Twin Sisters. After the army turned to the right, she rode up to Houston. "General, you told me a damn lie," she said. "You said you was going on the Nacogdoches road. Sir, I want my oxen." With that she cut the oxen loose and departed, leaving the soldiers to get the cannon to Harrisburg as best they could over a prairie trail boot-deep in mud.[23] On several occasions the General himself put his shoulder to the wheel of the cannon and on others the men lifted them bodily over mud holes.

The army reached Buffalo Bayou on April 18, and for the first time Sam Houston saw the waterway that would one day be known as the Houston Ship Channel. Standing not far from the site of the future Turning Basin, he looked across at the smoldering ruins of Harrisburg, then ordered his weary men to make camp. A scout brought the information that the Mexican army lay downstream near Galveston Bay. Early the next morning Houston told his men that they would soon meet the enemy and in a rousing speech gave them their battlecry: "Remember the Alamo! Remember Goliad!" Then, sitting on the bank of the bayou, he wrote a note to an old friend. "This morning we are in preparation to meet Santa Anna. It is the only chance of saving Texas . . .," he said. "We shall use our best efforts to fight the enemy to such advantages as will insure victory, though the odds are greatly against us. I leave the result in the hands of a wise God, and rely upon his providence."[24] Breaking camp, he led his army a few miles down the bayou, crossed to its south side, and followed its general course to a prairie opposite the mouth of the San Jacinto.

When Santa Anna learned of the approach of the Texans, he turned his army upstream, where on April 21 it was virtually annihilated by a Texan army roughly three-fourths its size. The battle lasted about eighteen minutes, Sam Houston wrote in his official report; the Texans lost 9 killed or mortally wounded and 16 wounded; the Mexicans lost 630 killed, 208 wounded, and 730 taken prisoners. When this news spread eastward to the fleeing settlers, they were at first incredulous.

---

[23] Robert H. Hunter, *Narrative of Robert Hancock Hunter, 1813–1902*, p. 20.

[24] Eugene C. Barker and Amelia W. Williams, eds., *The Writings of Sam Houston*, I, 413.

Colonel Gray had almost reached the safety of United States soil when he heard the news, and he was frankly skeptical. "It is likely there has been a battle and victory," he wrote in his diary, "but the result is too much *wholesale*."[25]

But for once the shrewd Virginian was wrong. The results were even more *wholesale* than indicated by Houston's figures of those killed and wounded. A century later an inscription on the base of the San Jacinto Monument more accurately set forth the dimensions of the victory:

Measured by its results, San Jacinto was one of the most decisive battles of the world. The freedom of Texas from Mexico won here led to annexation and to the Mexican War, resulting in the acquisition by the United States of the states of Texas, New Mexico, Arizona, Nevada, California, Utah, and parts of Colorado, Wyoming, Kansas, and Oklahoma. Almost one-third of the present area of the American nation, nearly a million square miles of territory, changed sovereignty.

In addition to these far-reaching results, the battle had special significance for Buffalo Bayou. Never again could the stream be obscure, of course, for the battle had enrolled it in the annals of history. Future generations would roam along its bank, following the course of the two armies and pointing out their positions on the battlefield. But the San Jacinto campaign had done more for Buffalo Bayou than make it a historic site. The campaign had shown in bold relief the peculiar advantages of the bayou in relation to the Brazos River bottoms. By fleeing to Harrisburg and drawing the opposing armies after them, Burnet and Zavala had called attention to the bayou as a link between the interior and the sea and set it on its way to a commercial future as unlikely as Houston's victory at San Jacinto.

[25] Gray, *From Virginia to Texas*, p. 170.

III. "THE GREAT INTERIOR COMMERCIAL EMPORIUM"

~~~~~~

B̲EFORE THE LAST MEXICAN ARMY HAD WITH-
drawn from Texas soil, in 1836, men with an eye for business had
taken steps to exploit the water route from Galveston to the interior.
Even before the Battle of San Jacinto the speculators who followed
Burnet's government to Galveston Island began wrangling over the
confused land titles to the island and vying with each other for the
privilege of building a city there. Two associates of William Fairfax
Gray obtained a grant from Burnet for a section of land where Laffite's
fort had once stood, but when the first Texas Congress met in the fall
of 1836, this grant was disallowed. Instead, the Congress, after considerable haggling, conveyed the site to Michel Branamour Menard and
a group of associates on the basis of a prior claim and the promise of
fifty thousand dollars.[1]

Although Augustus Chapman Allen had talked of building a city at
Galveston and did invest in the Galveston City Company, he did not
wait for the titles to the island to be cleared to build his city. Instead,

[1] Dermot H. Hardy and Ingham S. Roberts, *Historical Review of South-East
Texas* . . ., I, 302–304.

he looked upstream and considered other likely sites. Morgan's Point, which he had tried to purchase a few years earlier, was in the hands of James Morgan and his New York backers, who still hoped to build their own city. That location being unavailable, Allen, in conjunction with his younger brother, John Kirby Allen, looked farther upstream. Harrisburg, at what was considered the head of navigation on Buffalo Bayou, was a logical site for a city, the Allens reasoned, for there land and water routes met. But when they tried to buy the site of Harrisburg, they discovered that it was involved in litigation due to the founder's death in 1829 and the conflicting claims of his widow and others. Here as at Galveston the impatient Allens could not wait on lengthy legal processes. If the Brazos River were made generally navigable—as many still expected it to be—then the Buffalo Bayou route to the interior would lose much of its significance. Thus, time was of the essence to the Allens. Looking still farther upstream, their eyes fell on a tract of land at the junction of Buffalo and White Oak bayous. Buffalo Bayou

This advertisement of the first steamboat to reach Houston appeared in the *Telegraph and Texas Register.*

narrowed above Bray's Bayou and turned and twisted so that a distance of some six or eight miles by land was fifteen by water. But the bayou was still deep above Harrisburg, and, after sounding it thoroughly, the Allens decided that White Oak rather than Bray's marked the head of navigation. Unlike the three other sites they had considered, that at the junction of Buffalo and White Oak bayous was available and the title was clear. John Austin had obtained title in 1824, and in 1836 his heirs were willing to sell. In August, 1836, the Allens acquired the tract, drew a paper city, and named it for General Sam Houston, then at the peak of his popularity as the wounded hero of San Jacinto.

The Allens were by no means the only hopeful city fathers on the banks of Buffalo Bayou and Galveston Bay during the 1830's. In addition to Lynchburg, Harrisburg, and New Washington, speculators laid out Powhattan, Scottsburg, Louisville, San Jacinto, Buffalo, Hamilton, and other cities with great expectations and few, if any, inhabitants. The proliferation of paper cities became a matter of jest to visitors in the area. Almost every enterprising man who came to Texas expected to make his fortune by founding a city, one anonymous visitor observed in 1837: "Should they all succeed, they will no doubt at some day make Texas as famous for her cities as Thebes was for her hundred gates."[2]

But while other founders contented themselves with acquiring a site and drawing a city on paper, the Allens showed themselves to be promoters par excellence. The site of Houston, the Allens' fourth choice, had little to recommend it above several others in the area and considerably less to recommend it than the site of Harrisburg. Yet, by sheer enterprise and by using promotional methods more common to the following century, the Allens made their paper city a reality. On August 30, only five days after they had acquired the site, they began advertising the city in the Columbia *Telegraph and Texas Register* and other newspapers, presenting as its first qualification the fact that it was at the head of navigation on Buffalo Bayou: "The town of Houston is located at a point on the river which must ever command the

[2] Andrew Forest Muir, ed., *Texas in 1837: An Anonymous, Contemporary Narrative*, pp. 12–13.

trade of the largest and richest portion of Texas . . .," read the advertisement, "and when the rich lands of this country shall be settled, a
trade will flow to it, making it, beyond all doubt, the great interior
commercial emporium of Texas."

Not only was Houston convenient to interior points, the Allens
pointed out, but it was connected by water with the coast and foreign
countries:

Tide water runs to this place and the lowest depth of water is about six feet.
Vessels from New Orleans or New York can sail without obstacle to this
place, and steamboats of the largest class can run down to Galveston Island
in 8 or 10 hours, in all seasons of the year. . . . Galveston harbor being the
only one to which vessels drawing a large draft of water can navigate, must
necessarily render the Island the great naval and commercial depot of the
country.

The Allens predicted a great future for their city: "As the country
shall improve rail roads will become in use, and will be extended from
this point to the Brazos, and up the same, also from this up to the head
waters of San Jacinto . . . and in a few years the whole trade of the
upper Brazos will make its way into Galveston Bay through the channel."

Such promotions were fairly common in the United States and later
became so in Texas, but the Allens' advertisement was the only one of
its kind that appeared in the *Telegraph* during August or for months
thereafter. As a consequence, Houston attracted considerable attention.
Colonel James Morgan, seeing the new town as a threat to his own
New Washington, was sarcastic in his comments to Andrew Briscoe of
Harrisburg: "The new town of Houston cuts a considerable swell in
the paper. . . . As for New Washington and Lynchburg, Scottsburg and
all the other burgs, not forgetting Powhattan, all must go down now.
Houstonburg must go ahead in the *newspaper at least*."[3]

But the Allens did not stop at newspaper promotion. One sentence
in their advertisement suggests another direction of their efforts: "Na-

[3] Morgan to Briscoe, September 30, 1836, in Adele B. Looscan, "Harris County,
1822–1845," *Southwestern Historical Quarterly*, XIX (July, 1915), 39–40.

ture appears to have designated this place for the future seat of Government." The selection of a capital city for the Republic was one of the pressing matters to come before the First Texas Congress in the fall of 1836, and John Kirby Allen, a member of the Congress, immediately put the claims of Houston before that body. One acquaintance described the younger Allen as "a very bright, quick man, with much magic about him."[4] All his brightness, quickness, and magic as well as his political wiles were needed to achieve his purpose, for there was much competition for the capital. Many towns, among them Nacogdoches, San Antonio, Goliad, Columbia, Washington, Matagorda, and Velasco, felt entitled to the honor, and, the first time the matter came before the Congress, the members could not agree on a place. When the matter was brought up a second time, on November 30, it was only after four ballots that Houston won the prize—and then by a slender majority, on a temporary basis, and on the promise of the proprietors to build a ten-thousand-dollar capitol building at their own expense.[5]

The Allens' choice of a name abetted their cause, for Sam Houston was elected President of the Republic of Texas in September, 1836. He was riding the crest of his popularity that fall, and the idea of a capital city on the banks of the stream that had seen his greatest victory tickled his vanity. The Allens achieved their purposes, too, disgruntled rivals charged, by dark machinations behind scenes. A Fayette County grand jury protested that the capital was located at Houston "to promote individual interest," while Anson Jones denounced the location as one of the three most "corrupt" acts of the First Congress, the other two being the sale of Galveston Island and the chartering of the Texas Railroad, Navigation and Banking Company. "Houston and Galveston were *pretty respectable* speculations by members of a legislature," he wrote in his memoirs, while the three acts together con-

[4] Francis Richard Lubbock, *Six Decades in Texas; or Memoirs of Francis Richard Lubbock*, C. W. Raines, ed., p. 45.

[5] Republic of Texas, *Journals of the House of Representatives*, 1 Cong., 1 Sess., pp. 39, 146, 150, 161, 169, 174, 211–212; H. P. N. Gammel, comp., *The Laws of Texas, 1822–1897*, I, 1138.

stituted "a perfect 'selling out' of Texas to a few individuals, or, at least of every thing that was available in 1836."[6]

The choice of Houston as temporary capital gave the town its first boost toward prominence, but that it should have been chosen when it was still only an idea in its founders' minds remains one of the unlikely circumstances that have marked the city's history. "The selection of the site, the naming of the place, the presentation of the advantages of the place, the success in securing the temporary location of the seat of government, constitute a high testimonial to the shrewdness, sagacity and enterprise of the promoters of the City of Houston," says a twentieth-century historian. "It marks the beginning of one of the few successful speculations of the kind, so numerous in that day."[7]

After the designation of Houston as the capital, the Allens changed the lead of their advertisement in the *Telegraph* to read "The City of Houston, the Present Seat of Government of the Republic of Texas," and other advertisements in the same paper told of a flurry of activity at the junction of Buffalo and White Oaks bayous. Thomas W. Ward, contractor for the capitol the Allens had promised, offered "immediate employment and liberal wages" to twenty carpenters and offered to furnish tools for those who did not have them. J. G. Welchmeyer advertised that stock of the Texas Railroad, Navigation and Banking Company would soon be sold in Houston, while later advertisements told of a theater and several land offices opening in Houston.[8]

But a few skeptics did not believe all they read in newspaper advertisements and began asking embarrassing questions about the location of the new capital. Was it really and truly at the head of navigation on Buffalo Bayou, they inquired, or was it a few miles—say twelve or fifteen—above the head? The questions were ones that would cause Houston city fathers to wince right up to the time when their sprawling city engulfed Harrisburg. The Allens heard the questions so many

6 Anson Jones, *Memoranda and Official Correspondence Relating to the Republic of Texas . . .*, pp. 18–19; see also, Hardy and Roberts, *South-East Texas*, I, 223–224.

7 Ernest W. Winkler, "The Seat of Government of Texas," Texas State Historical Association, *Quarterly*, X (October, 1906), 168–169.

8 Houston *Telegraph and Texas Register*, January 27, February 10, 14, 21, March 28, April 3, 1837.

times that in January, 1837, they felt compelled to prove that Houston was indeed at the head of navigation. Thus, they arranged for Captain Thomas Wigg Grayson to take the steamboat *Laura* from Columbia to Houston and persuaded a boatload of prominent citizens to make the trip. That the Allens chose the *Laura* for the demonstration suggests that they had a few reservations themselves, for the *Laura*, measuring 85 feet, was the smallest steamer in Texas waters. The next in length, the *Cayuga*, was 96 feet long, while the *Yellow Stone* was 122 and the *Constitution* 150.[9]

Among those who boarded the *Laura* for the trip were John Kirby Allen, the proprietor; Moseley Baker, a hero of San Jacinto; Benjamin C. Franklin, a distinguished lawyer; and Francis Richard Lubbock, then a young merchant but later a Civil War governor of Texas. Lubbock recalled in his memoirs that, after spending a few days aground in Galveston Bay, the *Laura* proceeded without difficulty to Harrisburg, finding navigation good "with plenty of water and breadth" to that point. But no boat had ever been above Harrisburg and the *Laura* was three days making the distance to Houston. "The slow time was in consequence of the obstructions we were compelled to remove as we progressed," Lubbock wrote:

We had to rig what were called Spanish windlasses on the shore to heave the logs and snags out of our way, the passengers all working faithfully. All hands on board would get out on the shore, and cutting down a tree would make of it a windlass by boring holes in it and placing it upon a support and throwing a bight of rope around it, secure one end to a tree in the rear and the other to the snags or fallen trees in the water. Then by means of the capstan bars we would turn the improvised capstan on land, and draw from the track of our steamer the obstructions. Capitalists, dignified judges, military heroes, young merchants in fine clothes from the dressiest city in the United States, all lent a helping hand.

This early project in bayou improvement was made more bearable by the fact that the *Laura* tied up at night and the passengers went ashore to dance and frolic with the settlers. Before reaching Houston, however, Lubbock and a few others remembered that the first town

---

[9] *Ship Registers and Enrollments of New Orleans, Louisiana,* III, 121, 36, 230, 48.

lots had gone on sale on January 19. Becoming impatient with their progress, they took a yawl and preceded the *Laura* upstream. "So little evidence could we see of a landing that we passed by the site and ran into White Oak Bayou, only realizing that we must have passed the city when we stuck in the brush," Lubbock wrote. "We then backed down the bayou, and by close observation discovered a road or street laid off from the water's edge. Upon landing we found stakes and footprints, indicating that we were in the town tract."[10]

Although the historic date of the *Laura*'s arrival at the Houston landing is somewhat uncertain, an early historian gives it as January 22, and that seems the most likely date.[11] Lubbock arrived in time to purchase land on January 21, but he preceded the steamer and possibly arrived a day earlier. By January 27 word of the *Laura*'s successful journey had reached Columbia, and the editor of the *Telegraph* hailed the news as proof positive that the contentions of his most faithful advertisers were correct. "The Fact Proved," read a notice in the *Telegraph*: "The steamboat *Laura*, Captain Grayson, arrived at the City of Houston some few days since without obstruction, thus it is proved that Houston will be a port of entry."

But when Francis Moore, Jr., new editor of the *Telegraph*, journeyed to Houston on the *Yellow Stone* in late April, he became doubtful of this fact. By then the schooner *Rolla* from Florida had gone up the bayou to Houston, arriving in time for the first-anniversary celebration of the Battle of San Jacinto, and the *Laura* had scheduled regular trips to Houston. Still, Moore's experiences led him to question that Buffalo Bayou was navigable as far as the new capital. The *Yellow Stone* spent one day aground at Clopper's Bar and arrived at Lynchburg on April 26. "A great part of the ensuing day was spent in groping (if a steamboat can grope) at the rapid rate of one or two miles an hour, to the very crown of the 'head of navigation of Buffalo Bayou' at the city of Houston," said Moore. Although he found the location of the capital "remarkably beautiful," and felt that the industry and enterprise of the founders would eventually make the city prominent, he risked an-

[10] Lubbock, *Six Decades in Texas*, pp. 45–46.
[11] Hardy and Roberts, *South-East Texas*, I, 226.

tagonizing a steady advertiser to express a frank opinion of the water-way: "The principal objection to this place is the difficulty of access by water; the bayou above Harrisburg being so narrow, so serpentine and blocked up with snags and overhanging trees that immense im-provements will be required to render the navigation convenient for large steamboats." Moore's opinion was possibly influenced by another matter. Although the Allens had promised him a house for the *Tele-graph,* he found "no building had ever been nearly finished in Houston intended for the press." "Like others who have confided in speculative things," he said, "we have been deceived."[12]

Stung by the editor's comments and still intent on proving their point, the Allens arranged for the *Constitution,* 262 tons and 150 feet long, to visit the capital. The steamboat—not to be confused with the frigate of the same name that was better known as *Old Ironsides*—ar-rived on June 1, and two days later editor Moore, still not quite con-vinced but in a better mood than the previous month, took note of the event: "We could hardly trust the testimony of our eyes on the morning of Thursday last on beholding the steamboat *Constitution* safely an-chored at the landing in this city . . .," he wrote. "We had harbored the impression that Houston was little above the head of navigation but this has *almost* convinced us to do what appears most advisable for the *Con-stitution*—that is, back out."[13]

Of necessity, the *Constitution* took the editor's suggestion, for she was too long to turn around at Houston. She backed down the bayou and turned at a bend near Harrisburg—a bend known thereafter as Constitution Bend until twentieth-century engineers made it into the Turning Basin of the Houston Ship Channel.

In spite of Francis Moore's doubts and the shortcomings of the bayou above Harrisburg, steamboats began paying regular visits to

[12] *Telegraph and Texas Register,* May 2, 1837.
[13] *Ibid.,* June 1, 1837. Because of the identical names, the steamboat and the frigate have often been confused. As a result it has been widely but erroneously published that the frigate visited Houston in 1837. *Old Ironsides* did come to Houston, but not until 1932, and then its visit was delayed because of doubts that its high masts would clear power lines over the channel. The old sailing vessel would have encountered insuperable difficulties in navigating the bayou overhung with trees in 1837.

Houston almost from the time the *Laura* made its first journey. By
March, 1838, Moore's paper reported that four steamboats—the
Branch T. Archer, the *Sam Houston*, the *Friendship*, and *Laura*—
were constantly plying between Houston and Galveston, and, within
the next few years Houston was visited more or less regularly by a
number of other steamboats, among them the *Emblem, Rodney, Rufus
Putnam, Correo, Trinity, Patrick Henry,* and *Dayton.* By 1840 the
Morning Star, a second Houston newspaper, carried a regular feature
entitled "The Port of Houston" which reported on vessels arriving and
departing and listed their passengers and the consignees of their cargoes.[14] The journey from Galveston to Houston took about ten hours,
and rates were set in May, 1840, at $5.00 for cabin passengers, $2.50
for deck passengers, and fifty cents per barrel for freight.

Of necessity the steamboats on the bayou were of the smaller class.
Most of them were sidewheelers with high-pressure engines and drew
very little water. The *Dayton,* for example, drew only two and a half
feet. The first Houston steamer one visitor saw reminded him of
Noah's ark "only it was built of live oak instead of gopher wood."[15]
The steamers also seemed odd to Matilda Charlotte Houstoun, a
wealthy Englishwoman who visited Houston in the early 1840's. "The
American river steamers differ very much in appearance from those to
which an European eye is accustomed," she wrote. "They have the
appearance of wooden houses, built upon a large raft; there is a bal-
cony or verandah, and on the roof is what is called the hurricane deck,
where *gentlemen* passengers walk and smoke."[16] The most remarkable
feature about the boats in the opinion of John Washington Lockhart,
who made the journey in late 1839 as a fifteen-year-old boy, was the
manner of lighting the way at night. Two big bonfires of pine knots
were built, one on either side of the bow. "These fires were made in
iron baskets, supported on iron rods attached to the bow, so that the

---

[14] *Ibid.,* March 17, 1838; Houston *Morning Star,* April 19, 1839; December 5, 6,
7, 8, 1839; January 10, 13, 29, 1840.

[15] Francis C. Sheridan, *Galveston Island; or, A Few Months Off the Coast of
Texas: The Journal of Francis C. Sheridan, 1839–1840,* Willis W. Pratt, ed., p. 33.

[16] Matilda Charlotte Houstoun, *Texas and the Gulf of Mexico; or, Yachting in
the New World,* II, 219.

boat in moving along carried its own light," he recalled. "These lights in straight parts of the bayou lit it up for some distance, but when the boat would have to make short curves in following the winding stream the bow would frequently appear to rest on one bank of the bayou and the stern on the other, and then the lights would make it appear as if we were about to take to the woods."[17]

A few critical visitors suggested that the steamboats on the bayou were discards from the Mississippi trade, and John Hunter Herndon, a young lawyer who took passage on the *Sam Houston* in early 1838, called that boat "a small filthy, horribly managed concern." After the boat had gone aground on both Red Fish and Clopper's bars, Herndon and some other passengers talked of going ashore and walking to Houston.[18] Passengers habitually shuddered at the thought of meeting another vessel after they entered the narrow channel above Harrisburg. "The Bayou became so narrow at last that I thought it would be no difficult matter to jump ashore from either side of the Boat," said Mrs. William Fairfax Gray, who, along with her husband, became a permanent resident of Houston after the Revolution:

And indeed I feared several times we should get aground. Once we were in an ugly situation, a snag having got entangled in one of the wheels. It caused some alarm & might have proved a dangerous accident. After seeing the number of floating logs etc. in the Bayou I ceased to wonder at the one wheeled Boats I had seen—my only wonder is how any escape.[19]

Despite these hazards, most visitors found the journey to Houston a memorable one. "The like of it is not to be found elsewhere in the world," wrote Gustav Dresel, a young German merchant who made the journey on the *Correo* in the late summer of 1838. Dresel, like other strangers, was impressed by the dense foliage that lined the banks, by the enormous trees whose branches sometimes met overhead, by the canal-like appearance of the stream, and especially by the size of

[17] Jonnie L. Wallis and Laurance L. Hill, eds., *Sixty Years on the Brazos: The Life and Letters of Dr. John Washington Lockhart, 1824–1900*, pp. 78–79.

[18] John Hunter Herndon, "Diary of a Young Man in Houston, 1838," Andrew Forest Muir, ed., *Southwestern Historical Quarterly*, LIII (January, 1950), 276–307.

[19] Mildred Stone Gray, quoted in Marguerite Johnston, *A Happy Worldly Abode*, p. 19.

the magnificent magnolia trees along the banks.[20] Customarily, as steamers passed up Galveston Bay, old Texans pointed out the San Jacinto Battleground to newcomers, and, more often than not in the early years of the Buffalo Bayou trade, some San Jacinto veteran was aboard to give an account of that historic day. Occasionally, the steamers stopped to make deliveries at private landings or to let perspiring Negroes load on firewood for the boiler. At other times the vessels stopped so that passengers could go ashore to shoot game; and when Mrs. Houstoun made the journey, her boat stopped while the cook went ashore to kill a beef for the passengers' dinner.[21]

Sometimes visitors found their fellow passengers as interesting as anything else about the trip. Mary Austin Holley traveled upstream with a group of German immigrants who entertained the passengers with their native folksongs,[22] while Mrs. Houstoun found an assortment of interesting individuals aboard her steamer. A Baptist preacher told her of his concern over the poor education and the rude companions that the new country afforded his children. Another of her fellow passengers, probably Stephen Pearl Andrews, spoke eloquently in favor of the abolition of slavery, and yet another made a stump speech saying that Texas should become a colony of Great Britain. Mrs. Houstoun heard the slap of cards from the game room and snatches of conversation as men talked business and of the future of the Republic. Above all these noises, she heard the sound of the high-pressure engine and the dismal, unearthly chant of Negro boatmen. The total effect was one of unreality. "I shall not easily forget the night I passed on the Buffalo river," she wrote.[23]

Other passengers found the landing at the foot of Main Street at Houston equally unforgettable. "Everything around the landing place was in a state of nature except a portion of the steep bluff had been scraped off sufficiently for a roadway for drays and carts to get to the

---

[20] Gustav Dresel, *Gustav Dresel's Houston Journal: Adventures in North America, 1837–1841*, Max Freund, ed., pp. 30–31.

[21] Houstoun, *Texas*, II, 220.

[22] Mattie Austin Hatcher, ed., *Letters of an Early American Traveller, Mary Austin Holley: Her Life and Her Works, 1784–1846*, p. 69.

[23] Houstoun, *Texas*, II, 222.

sand bar, which had been converted into a wharf," recalled John W. Lockhart. Because of the bluff, the buildings of the town could not be seen from the bayou, but customarily all persons in the vicinity, including businessmen, gathered at water's edge whenever a steamboat arrived. The sand bar, formed by the currents of Buffalo and White Oak bayous, served not only as a wharf but also as a place where stablemen watered their stock and where drivers of water carts filled their barrels with water, which, there being no good wells in town, they later peddled from house to house and sold by the bucket or barrel. When young Lockhart arrived at Houston, the captain tied his boat to a large cypress tree near the landing, but the boy thought of this as unnecessary labor, for it seemed to him that the boat could not possibly have gone farther upstream. In fact, the stream was so narrow that he doubted whether the boat could turn around and head back for Galveston; so he lingered curiously to watch as the captain performed this seemingly impossible feat by backing the stern of the boat far enough into White Oak Bayou so that the bow could be swung around.[24]

While seamen were bringing the first steamers to Houston, other pioneers were blazing trails from the interior. A copy of the *Telegraph* carrying the Allens' advertisement of Houston reached the Brazos River settlements near present-day Hearne in early 1837 and fell into the hands of Zachariah N. Morrell, a frontier Baptist preacher from Tennessee. Indians were threatening Morrell's settlement and there was a shortage of lead and powder as well as other necessities. Customarily, Morrell obtained such goods from Natchitoches, some 300 miles distant by way of the Old San Antonio Road; but, taking a quick look at his map, he realized that Houston was much closer—about 160 miles from him. No road led to Houston, of course, and the country between was beset with Indians, but, after reading the Allens' advertisement again, Morrell decided to chance the trip. On March 18 he yoked eight oxen to a wagon and, taking his twelve-year-old son, two horses, and a rifle, set out for Houston.

Using the Brazos River and a compass as guides, Morrell arrived at Buffalo Bayou opposite Main Street about two weeks later. There was

---

[24] Wallis and Hill, *Sixty Years on the Brazos*, pp. 79–80.

no bridge or ferry, but a small flatboat nearby was big enough to carry over a single horse or an empty wagon. Morrell took his wagon over on the boat, swam his team across, and then took a good look at the new metropolis. It was a "city of tents," he reported, with only one or two log cabins. A large round tent, resembling the enclosure of a circus, served as a drinking saloon and there was plenty of whiskey and cigars. In other tents nearby Morrell found a large assortment of goods that interested him more. No lead was available, but he found everything else he needed and learned where he could obtain lead on his way home. Stopping long enough to preach the first sermon in the town, Morrell loaded his wagon with two kegs of powder and supplies for his family and neighbors and headed for home.[25]

Ox wagons like Morrell's soon became a familiar sight in Houston as other settlers looked for the most convenient point to exchange their products for basic necessities. By early 1838 Gustav Dresel noted on the streets of Houston "tradesmen of all sorts" from the interior, among them many Mexican smugglers who came in search of tobacco and other contraband.[26] About the same time, Edward Stiff commented on the number of traders arriving and departing. They were "of every variety of colour, from snowy white to sooty, and dressed in every variety of fashion, excepting the savage Bowie-knife, which, as if by common consent, was a necessary appendage to all," he wrote. On one day in April, 1840, twenty-three wagons arrived from the Brazos region.[27]

Railroads later followed the general routes blazed by these early visitors, and even after rails had revolutionized interior travel many farmers continued to bring wagons laden with cotton to Houston and carry away merchandise brought up the bayou by riverboats. Late in the nineteenth century a wagon yard on the outskirts was still a standard feature of the town.

---

[25] Zachariah N. Morrell, *Flowers and Fruits in the Wilderness* . . . , p. 63.

[26] Dresel, *Houston Journal*, p. 37.

[27] Edward Stiff, *The Texan Emigrant* . . ., pp. 68–80; Lubbock, *Six Decades*, p. 45.

Although many early visitors came for commercial reasons, Houston began existence as a boom town because of its designation as temporary seat of government. In the two and a half years that it was the capital, many came there to do business with the government. Foreign diplomats, Indian chiefs, government personnel, office seekers, immigrants, settlers, lawyers, speculators, rascals—all made their way up the bayou or over prairie trails to Houston. The ornithologist John James Audubon, who had been watching birds on the lower bayou, visited the capital in May, 1837, and was unimpressed by its physical appearance. The government building had no roof, he reported; the President lived in a two-room log cabin; and the streets were deep in mud. But young Gustav Dresel, who visited somewhat later, found the spirit of the new town so invigorating that he forgot its rawness. It was "gay-colored," "wild," "interesting," "picturesque," he wrote, and all residents and visitors met on an equal footing. "Everyone threw the veil of oblivion over past deeds. Everyone stood on his own merit. No family connections, former fortune, rank, or claims had any influence on present civic position." During the winter of 1838, there were only three stoves in Houston, and, when northers came, Dresel joined the President and other male residents around open fires in front of the saloons at night, there to enjoy hot drinks and merry speeches.[28]

Business boomed during 1837 and 1838, and the population increased rapidly. "No place has ever within my knowledge improved as this has," President Houston wrote less than a year after the *Laura's* first visit. "I presume not less than one hundred souls arrive by sea each week that passes, and generally of the better sort of folks—bringing wealth, worth and intelligence into the country."[29] By April 19 of the following year the *Morning Star* gave the population as 2,073, of which 1,620 were male and 453 female. Francis Moore, Jr.—his first bad impressions of the town long forgotten—called Houston the "first city of the republic in regard to population and wealth" in a book pub-

[28] Dresel, *Houston Journal*, pp. 33–36.
[29] Eugene C. Barker and Amelia W. Williams, eds., *The Writings of Sam Houston*, II, p. 184.

lished in 1840, while Arthur Ikin estimated the population at 5,000 in a book published the following year.[30]

But Houston's first boom was short-lived. Before Moore's and Ikin's books were off the press, a series of circumstances had tested the merits of the town and the endurance of its inhabitants. Early in 1839 a new administration designated Austin, another unborn city and one on the distant Indian frontier, as the permanent capital, and that fall thirty wagons headed westward carrying the national archives. The move meant the end of Houston, many observers predicted. The town would lapse into obscurity without the capital.

But that was only one blow—and possibly not the worst one—that fell on Houston that year. During the summer yellow fever developed in epidemic proportions and decimated the population. Customers and merchants alike avoided the town, and, when Dresel returned after a nine months' absence, he found the formerly animated streets deserted and a pall of gloom hanging over them. Those who remained expressed amazement that he should return and entertained him by enumerating his acquaintances who had died. When he retired late that night he heard the moans of a fever victim from one room and the callous remarks of a group of card players from another. If they were to die, the card players vowed, they wanted at least to have some fun before the end. Worst of all, Dresel discovered by morning light that his bed had been previously occupied by a sick person and that the linens had not been changed.[31]

To add another threat to Houston's existence, the litigation that had stifled the development of Harrisburg was settled in 1839, and Andrew Briscoe began promoting the advantages of that place. In an advertisement reminiscent of the Allens' earlier promotion, Briscoe bore down on Houston's most vulnerable spot. Because of the difficulty in navigating above Harrisburg, he pointed out, the location of his town was far superior to that of Houston. Furthermore, the proprietors of

---

[30] Francis Moore, Jr., *Map and Description of Texas* . . ., p. 80; and Arthur Ikin, *Texas* . . ., p. 28.

[31] Dresel, *Houston Journal*, pp. 78–79.

Harrisburg proposed to organize "a great Importing Company" to trade directly with nations beyond the Atlantic.[32]

As if to prove Briscoe's allegations about navigation above Harrisburg, a series of steamboat disasters occurred between that point and Houston in early 1840. On February 6 the *Emblem* hit a snag about six miles below Houston and sank; four days later the *Rodney* was caught in a rise on the bayou and damaged; the next month the *Brighton* hit a snag and sank. Until this time there had been few accidents on the bayou, and the *Morning Star* took the first calmly, commenting, "This is the first instance of the kind that has occurred on this bayou." But after the second there was a note of alarm in the editor's comment: "This bayou has been navigated for three or four years almost without accident to a boat. Something strange has been happening to our steamboats lately." When by April 22 two sunken boats blocked traffic between Harrisburg and Houston, the editor spoke with a hint of desperation about the tremendous loss of trade and of "that terrible and abiding curse—the obstruction of the Bayou."[33]

To add to Houston's specific problems, the effects of the Panic of 1837 spread from the United States into Texas in the late 1830's, bringing a decade of hard times. Silver became nonexistent; Texas currency and bonds dropped in value; and business competition grew keen.

That the town survived this combination of adversities and did not become another of the many ghost towns that haunt Texas history can be attributed only to the enterprise of its inhabitants. John Kirby Allen, that bright, quick man with the touch of magic, died in 1838, but other Houstonians proved themselves worthy of being his successors. On January 28, 1840, when the future of the town looked darkest, a group of merchants who typified the leadership obtained a charter from the national government for a chamber of commerce. According to the charter, the purposes of the organization were to further the general and commercial interests of the Republic, to diminish litigation in the

[32] *Telegraph and Texas Register,* July 1, 1839.
[33] *Morning Star,* February 6, 10; April 22, 1840.

mercantile community, and to establish uniform and equitable charges. Those granted the charter were Thomas M. League, Henry Allen, William D. Lee, J. Temple Doswell, T. Francis Brewer, George Gazley, E. Osborne, Charles J. Hedenburg, John W. Pitkin, Charles Kesler, E. S. Perkins, and DeWitt Clinton Harris. The bill for the charter was introduced by Francis Moore, Jr., who had forgotten his early misgivings about the town's location to become its most enthusiastic booster and sometime mayor. The idea of a chamber of commerce was not a new one to Houstonians. In November, 1838, Robert Wilson, better known as "Honest Bob," a member of the Senate of the Third Congress, had presented their petition for such an organization. But before the bill could be put through Congress, Wilson was expelled from the Senate for using abusive language. When the bill was passed the following year, it simultaneously granted charters to Houston and Matagorda. Thus, Houston was denied the distinction of having the first chamber of commerce in Texas. At a meeting held at John Carlos' City Exchange on April 4, 1840, the Houston chamber was organized. E. S. Perkins was elected the first president, and the following names were added to those to whom the charter was granted: Francis R. Lubbock, Henry Kesler, Jacob DeCordova, J. Hart, Charles A. Morris, and John Carlos.[34]

At this crucial moment in Houston's existence, these men took the lead. Realizing that after the removal of the capital the town's very existence depended on the route to the sea, they applied their best efforts to clearing the bayou of wrecked boats in the spring of 1840. Within a week after the sinking of the *Emblem*, a public meeting was called to consider the matter. "It is a subject of vital interest to the prosperity of Houston," said the editor of the *Morning Star* in urging all citizens to attend.[35]

Aside from the immediate problem, the sunken boats brought a bigger question to the forefront. Whose responsibility was it to keep the bayou clear? As the city council pointed out, the stream was "one of

[34] *Telegraph and Texas Register*, November 28, December 29, 1838; January 2, 16, 1839; H. P. N. Gammel, comp., *The Laws of Texas, 1822–1897*, II, 448; *Morning Star*, April 6, 1840.

[35] *Morning Star*, February 12, 1840.

the natural highways of the Republic" and was theoretically the responsibility of the national government. But all citizens of the Republic of Texas knew that their poverty-stricken government had no funds to expend on rivers and harbors. From the time the *Laura*'s passengers made Spanish windlasses to clear a channel for their boat, the responsibility for Buffalo Bayou had fallen on those who used it. Houston merchants and boatowners assumed most of the burden, and in early 1839 a group of them organized the Buffalo Bayou Company to collect funds to clear the bayou as far as Harrisburg of overhanging limbs and snags. John D. Andrews was made president of the company; Henry Kesler, treasurer; William M. Bronaugh, secretary; and the actual work was placed under the supervision of L. J. Pilie. By April 19 five miles of channel had been cleared, and Francis Moore, Jr., predicted that soon steamboats could come from Galveston at night. "The fears which have been entertained by many persons, relative to the practicality of rendering the Bayou *permanently* navigable between Houston and Harrisburg will soon be dissipated by the successful labors of the enterprising projections of this undertaking," he wrote.[36]

But the obstructions of 1840 posed a more difficult problem than those of 1839. Snags and tree limbs were natural obstructions, but the wrecked boats were private property. Could individuals, a private company, or even the local government remove the boats from the bayou without being liable to damage suits from the owners, Houstonians asked; if so, how was the money to be raised to pay for the removal? In early March the city council appointed a committee to ask the chief justice of the Republic about the matter and see what legal steps could be taken to clarify the question.[37]

But the merchants could not wait for legal red tape. As the *Morning Star* pointed out, the trade lost in one week because of the obstructions was worth "half a dozen boats in such condition." At the meeting held after the sinking of the *Emblem*, a subscription was begun to obtain money to raise the boat. The first efforts to raise it were unsuccessful, however, and after the sinking of the *Brighton*, further voluntary con-

---

[36] *Ibid.*, April 12, 19, 1839; *Telegraph and Texas Register*, March 20, 1839.

[37] *Morning Star*, March 9, 1840; April 12, 19, 1839; *Telegraph and Texas Register*, March 20, 1839.

tributions were solicited. Because of the depression, money came in slowly. Thus, in late March one George Elgin proposed that a lottery be held to benefit the project. Elgin, who professed to have operated successful lotteries in other states, proposed that four drawings be held under the supervision of the mayor and aldermen of the city. Five per cent of the gross proceeds would go into the bayou-improvement fund, and a tempting grand prize of ten thousand dollars would be offered. The city council had some reservations about Elgin's scheme, but agreed to let him proceed with the lottery provided he keep an accurate account of the tickets sold and make returns to the mayor within two days after each drawing.[38] At about the same time that it accepted Elgin's proposal, the council appropriated a thousand dollars for the removal of the two boats, and shortly thereafter the county contributed five hundred.

The *Brighton* was finally raised in May, renamed the *General Houston,* and returned to the Buffalo Bayou trade. But in less than a year it had rejoined the *Emblem* at the bottom of the bayou. On March 1, 1841, the city council complained again of the wrecks of the steamers *Emblem* and *General Houston* in the stream and asked the owners once more to remove them.[39] At last, on January 29 of the following year, the city received relief in the form of permission from the Republic to clear away such obstructions. According to the new law, when a vessel sank in the bayou, three commissioners appointed by the mayor were to inspect it. If in their opinion the vessel was not likely to be raised so as to open the channel to navigation within twenty days, the mayor and aldermen could order the obstruction removed in any manner deemed proper without incurring penalty. The city was further given the power to preserve and improve navigation above Harrisburg and, best of all, to obtain funds for the purpose by levying a tax, not to exceed two and one-half cents per tonnage, on vessels coming to Houston. Thus was the improvement of the bayou above Harrisburg removed from the realm of individual effort, voluntary contributions, and lotteries and made the peculiar responsibility of the City of Houston. The coun-

---

[38] *Morning Star,* March 28, April 2, 22, 1840.

[39] Minutes of the City Council, City of Houston, Book A, 1840–1847, p. 78.

cilmen gave a contract for the maintenance of the bayou to Elam Stock-
bridge in 1843 and to the firm of Sterrett and Tichenor in 1844. After
1845 free wharfage was given to certain boatowners for keeping the
bayou clear.[40]

Below Harrisburg little was done during the era of the Republic or
for years thereafter to improve the channel. Red Fish and Clopper's
bars remained major obstacles, limiting the bayou trade to vessels of
extremely shallow draft. In the summers when the winds blew from the
south, plenty of water was usually over the bars, but during the winters
when winds blew from the north, commerce was sometimes halted for
days at a time. Josiah Gregg, the famous Western trader, found when
he arrived at Galveston in 1841 that he could not proceed to Houston
for four days because a stiff norther had lowered the water of Galveston Bay, and even then his boat went aground at Clopper's Bar.[41] The
delay of the mails because of shallow water at Clopper's Bar during
the winter of 1839 so provoked Francis Moore, Jr., that he launched
a one-man campaign for channel improvement. "We believe if the
owners of these steamboats would drop buoys just along the line of
the channel over this bar . . . all the boats would constantly pass over
it in the same track," he wrote, "and as much mud is raised by the
boats each time they pass, which is washed down by the current into
the bay below, the channel would thus be gradually deepened, so that
in a few months the boats could pass easily in low water." Moore
thought that a small piece of wood attached by six feet of string to a
brick or stone would serve as a buoy and that eight or ten of these
dropped from a boat at intervals of five or six rods would sufficiently
mark the channel.[42] Feeble though it was, Moore's suggestion represented as much effort as was expended to improve the lower channel
in the 1840's. Customarily, ship captains waited for favorable winds
and tides to carry them over the troublesome bars.

[40] Gammel, comp., *Laws of Texas*, II, 754–755; *Morning Star*, June 1, 1843; January 25, 1844; February 1, 1845; Minutes of City Council, City of Houston, Book
A, 1840–1847, pp. 192, 220, 260.

[41] Josiah Gregg, *Diary & Letters of Josiah Gregg . . .*, Maurice G. Fulton, ed.,
I, 102.

[42] *Telegraph and Texas Register*, November 4, 1839.

Along with sunken ships, civilization brought other problems in navigation to the strip of bayou for which Houstonians assumed special responsibility. In a natural state, the banks of the bayou were held firm by heavy vegetation and the water was deep and so clear that fish could be seen swimming at the bottom. Indeed, according to tradition, the stream was named for the myriads of Buffalo fish that inhabited it. Almost from the time the first dwelling was built and the first industry established, the problems of silting and water pollution appeared. Mrs. Gray commented on the muddy water at the time of her first visit in 1838, and shortly thereafter another observer noted with anxiety that large amounts of sand washed into the bayou at the foot of Main Street with every rain. Soon, he predicted, the landing would be so silted that steamboats could not get to White Oak Bayou to turn around. Even greater threats to navigation were sawmills that cut timber on the banks of the bayou and dumped the waste where rains washed it into the stream. The editor of the *Morning Star* discounted the dangers from silting by pointing out that the current swept the sand from the bayou during rainy seasons, but the dangers from the sawmills were not so easily dismissed. On March 8, 1841, the city council took its first action to prevent industrial wastes from endangering navigation. An ordinance was passed forbidding the deposit of sawdust on the banks of Buffalo or White Oak bayous, and thereafter the councilmen kept a sharp eye on the millowners, reminding them from time to time of the ordinance.[43] Such actions would become more frequent with increasing industrialization.

At the same time that they took responsibility for the channel above Harrisburg, Houstonians took steps to make the facilities of their town more attractive to commerce. In early 1840, Congress altered the city charter to permit the town to construct wharves on the banks of Buffalo Bayou within the city limits, to make other improvements for the convenience of landing crews and cargoes, and to collect wharfage to defray the expenses for doing so.[44] The city council immediately made grandiose plans to build "substantial wharves at the landing," these to

[43] *Morning Star*, April 9, 1839; Minutes of City Council, City of Houston, Book A, 1840–1847, pp. 81, 294.
[44] Gammel, comp., *Laws of Texas*, II, 411–413.

extend from Main Street to the lower side of Fannin, about five hundred feet, and to be twenty feet wide on top and six feet high from the low-water mark. The council discussed these wharves regularly at their meetings throughout the next two years and even let a contract to build them, but the prevailing hard times and the further disruption of commerce because of Mexican threats of invasion in 1842 delayed their construction. A visitor on the eve of annexation wrote that "the landing place was but an incline cut into the bank" of the stream.[45]

Although their grander construction plans did not take form, on June 10, 1841, the councilmen passed an ordinance establishing the Port of Houston and giving their waterfront a more ordered existence. According to the ordinance, the Port included all wharves, landings, slips, and roads on the banks of Buffalo and White Oak bayous within the city limits. The waterfront between Main and Fannin was reserved for steamboats and other large vessels, while smaller vessels were assigned to other positions. The rates of wharfage were set, ranging from one to six dollars per vessel according to size for the first day with lesser rates thereafter. The ordinance provided that a wharfmaster, to be selected by the city council, would have power to collect the wharfage and police the waterfront. Charles T. Gerlach, member of a prominent German merchant family, was appointed the first wharfmaster.[46]

Along with improving the channel and trade facilities, Houstonians worked diligently to improve the image of their town after the removal of the capital. Coastal areas were always considered unhealthful, and, after the epidemic year of 1839, Houston's reputation for sickliness threatened to drive customers away. Without knowing that mosquitoes caused yellow fever, the councilmen realized that stagnant water, filth, and lack of sanitation fostered disease. Thus, on March 7, 1840, the council created a board of health, with John D. Andrews as president. The members of the board were given the thankless task of inspecting their neighbors' premises and pointing out conditions dangerous to

[45] *Morning Star*, February 3, 20, 1840; Ferdinand Roemer, *Texas . . .,* Oswald Mueller, trans., p. 63; Minutes of City Council, City of Houston, Book A, 1840–1847, pp. 3, 49.

[46] *Morning Star*, June 10, 1841.

the general welfare. After several citizens had been irritated by the board's observations and defied its recommendations, the council passed an ordinance making the board the sole judge of what was a nuisance within the city limits and fining those who failed to comply with the board's recommendations.[47]

At about the same time that the board of health was created, the council passed an ordinance to prevent the sale of unwholesome or unfit food in the town. The ordinance provided, in addition, that the council would appoint a "market master and inspector of provisions" to keep the market in good order, to see that scales and weights were correct, and to inspect the brands on hogs and cattle slaughtered in the town in order to prevent thefts.[48]

Almost as detrimental to commerce as the town's reputation for poor health was its reputation for wickedness. "They have more of infidelity, subtle, organized and boldly blasphemous, than I have met in any place of its size in all my journeyings," said Methodist Bishop James Osgood Andrew after a visit to Houston. Another visitor called the town "the greatest sink of dissipation and vice that modern times have known," while yet another called it the "most uncivilized place in Texas."[49]

The more respectable elements tried to clean up the town in the early 1840's, and the editors of the two newspapers declared war on scoundrels. Occasionally, however, the *Morning Star* was put on the defensive. "Houston may not be remarkably moral, but it is more so, by far, than it has the reputation of being," wrote the editor.[50] Somewhat later Francis Moore, Jr., thought he saw signs of improvement in the general behavior. "For several months not a single serious quarrel or brawl has disgraced our streets, and drunkards are almost as rare as snow birds . . .," he wrote on one occasion. "The most delicate ladies can now promenade in all the principal streets and public squares, without the danger and mortification of hearing angry and

---

[47] *Ibid.*, March 7, 1840; June 17, 1841.

[48] *Ibid.*, March 28, 1840.

[49] James Osgood Andrew, *Miscellanies . . .*, p. 85; Herndon, "Diary," p. 284; Sheridan, *Galveston Island*, p. 112.

[50] *Morning Star*, January 20, 1840.

coarse wrangling or seeing miserable fools with bloody noses beating each others faces or hewing each other with bowie knives."[51]

As hard times pressed down and business rivalry grew keen, Houston merchants kept a close watch on their competition in other towns. At first they resented losing the capital to Austin, but they were soon mollified to discover that Houston lay across the most feasible route between the new capital and the sea. The Colorado River, on which Austin was located, was blocked by a raft, so it was navigable for only a short distance. Thus, Houstonians quickly pointed out, merchandise going to Austin by way of Houston required an overland journey only twenty miles longer than the route through the Colorado port of Matagorda—and the deep water afforded by Galveston harbor more than compensated for this extra distance. As the creation of a new capital on the frontier required the importation of building material, furnishings, and many other supplies, Houston merchants aggressively pursued the Austin market.

Indeed, Matagorda merchants charged that Houstonians were at times too aggressive. Some gentlemen en route to Matagorda, the *Colorado Gazette* reported, were told in Houston by "fellows whose ears should be nailed to a whipping post" that anyone going to Matagorda was likely to lose his scalp to hostile Indians, and furthermore that everyone had left Matagorda because of a raging yellow fever epidemic. "These falsehoods are not worth contradicting, as far as the effect on the business of our town is concerned," said the *Gazette*.[52]

The editor of the *Morning Star* replied blandly that "no one would rejoice more than ourselves to see the Colorado and other rivers of Texas rendered navigable." He more clearly portrayed his town's concern for the Austin market, however, when he heard that a stage line was to be established to Austin, but could not discover where the line would begin. "Can any one inform us of the 'whereabouts' of the route?" he demanded. "It should be from this city to Austin, as this is the route most travelled and the only one that would repay the expense of such an establishment."[53]

[51] *Telegraph and Texas Register*, April 13, 1842.
[52] *Morning Star*, January 31, 1840.
[53] *Ibid.*, January 31, 24, 1840.

Houston merchants looked beyond Austin to Santa Fe and visualized the rich trade of that area passing through their town and down Buffalo Bayou to the sea. In early 1840 a company of Santa Fe traders was organized in Houston, but this municipal project dissolved after the Republic sponsored the organization of the ill-fated Santa Fe expedition of 1841. Houstonians actively supported that expedition, and, when George Wilkins Kendall passed through en route to join the expedition in Austin, he found Houston in a bustle of preparation with every gunsmith and saddler busy. At Houston Kendall bought many of his own supplies for the journey.[54]

While Houstonians dreamed of Santa Fe gold, however, they realized that their continued prosperity depended in large measure on the Brazos market. In this respect the shortcomings of the Brazos River were as important as the virtues of Buffalo Bayou. Thus, Houstonians kept a watchful eye on navigation on the Brazos. What they saw was reassuring, for, although efforts were still made to navigate the river, it continued to be navigable only for short distances except during seasonal rises, and even then the river was hazardous and insurance rates high. "But one steamboat ever ascended the Brazos as high as Washington," the *Morning Star* reported with satisfaction in the spring of 1840:

Captain Harris commanded that one, and made a handsome speculation by the adventure. The planters all gave him a labor of land out of their leagues, along the river; and, he says, that being obliged to wait for three different rises in the river, in running up, and three in coming down, while waiting for each rise, *he cleared and planted with corn, five hundred acres of cane brake.*[55]

Because of the superior navigation on Buffalo Bayou as far as Harrisburg, Houstonians regarded that place as their chief rival in the Galveston Bay area during the Republican era. Despite the efforts of Andrew Briscoe, however, Harrisburg never recovered its position after its destruction by Santa Anna. While litigation was preventing

---

[54] *Ibid.*, January 24, 31, 1840; George Wilkins Kendall, *Narrative of an Expedition Across the Great South-Western Prairies, from Texas to Santa Fe*, I, 13.

[55] *Morning Star*, April 1, 1840.

its development, Houston merchants were establishing trade routes to their town, extending attractive credit to customers, and providing a good selection of goods at the best prices possible. By the time Harrisburg's litigants had settled their claims, the depression had descended. A visitor who passed by the town in 1842 called it "a deserted village."[56] Even so, Houstonians kept a wary eye on this potential rival.

Ironically, in view of the later rivalry that developed between the two towns, Houston and Galveston considered themselves business associates rather than competitors during the early 1840's. At the time Houston was founded, there was no town on Galveston Island. Although Michel B. Menard and his associates made plans for a city immediately after the Revolution, a severe storm inundated the island in the fall of 1837, and the town was not begun until the following year. As a consequence, Houstonians during the first years of their town's development took a possessive view of Galveston, regarding the harbor as peculiarly their own and the island as a depot where merchandise destined for Houston was reshipped. In spite of the Allens' predictions and the early visit of the *Rolla,* ocean vessels did not customarily go to Houston. Red Fish and Clopper's bars and the narrow bayou above Harrisburg precluded such travel except for the smallest sea vessels and then only on rare occasions when the wind and water permitted. As a rule, ocean vessels unloaded their cargoes at Galveston for reshipment by riverboat to Houston, thence by freight wagon to the interior.

Galveston entered its own boom period at about the time Houston's ended, but even then Houstonians continued to look at the island with a proprietary air. Indeed, merchants often had business interests in both towns and considered the two as terminal points of a single trade route rather than competitors. Houston papers took as much interest in the arrival of large vessels at Galveston as in the arrival of steamboats at their own landing and spoke of new wharves in Galveston in the same paragraph as the continued prosperity of Houston. When the *Fils Unique,* the first French vessel to sail directly to Texas, arrived at

[56] William Bollaert, *William Bollaert's Texas,* W. Eugene Hollon and Ruth Lapham Butler, eds., p. 108.

Galveston with a cargo of wines, brandy, fruit, and other luxuries, the *Morning Star* hailed the event as a momentous one, knowing full well that much of the cargo would soon be on its way to Houston. The arrival at Galveston of a large British vessel, the 350-ton *Ironsides,* was greeted in a similar manner, and the editor urged planters to send cotton to Galveston for the *Ironsides* to take back to Liverpool. Most of the cotton, it was understood, would come from the Brazos bottoms by way of Houston and Buffalo Bayou. The *Morning Star* also lobbied for a lighthouse at Galveston, vigorously defended the Galveston harbor against criticism, and commended the Charles Morgan ship line for maintaining service to Galveston even in off seasons.[57]

By the time of annexation, Galveston had outstripped Houston, being approximately twice as large in population and relatively even more prosperous. An 1845 guidebook called Galveston the "great commercial emporium" of Texas, a title the Allens had coveted for Houston. But even then Houstonians considered Galveston as their own ocean port, and Galvestonians took an equally benign view of Houston. Because the island was accessible only by water and Buffalo Bayou was its major highway to inland markets, Galveston merchants considered Houston their inmost distribution point. Only later, when Houston began pushing for direct deep-water navigation and Galveston began working for direct connections with the interior, did the bitter and classic rivalry develop between the two towns.

After Houston's first two years of phenomenal growth, the population stood still for a decade. According to the United States Census of 1850 the population was 2,397, only 324 more than the *Morning Star*'s figures for 1839. Even so, the town ranked third in size in Texas, being surpassed only by Galveston and San Antonio. Sketchy commercial statistics suggest that in addition a large transient population was usually in town in connection with trade. One account says that in 1839 only eight bales of cotton were shipped from Houston. For the year ending in May, 1842, the figure was 4,260 and for the following year 4,336. By 1844 the editor of the *Telegraph and Texas Register* noted a promising boom in trade. In the three weeks prior to May 22, 1844,

[57] *Morning Star,* January 11, 13, 15; February 18, 29; April 20, 1840.

approximately 1,000 bales of cotton were brought to Houston by wagon. Wharfmaster Daniel G. Wheeler reported that in that year 6,892 bales passed over the Houston wharves and that in 1845 a total of 11,359 bales was handled.[58] By the time Texas became a state, Buffalo Bayou was the only stream in Texas that was dependably navigable, and Houston was permanently established as a way station where water and land routes met. The town owed its existence "entirely to its location on Buffalo Bayou," observed a perceptive visitor on the eve of annexation. "This circumstance will always assure it an important position in the future."[59]

[58] *Telegraph and Texas Register*, March 26, October 8, 1845; July 19, 1843; May 22, 1844; *Morning Star*, May 12, 1842.
[59] Roemer, *Texas*, p. 63.

IV. THE COMING OF THE RAILROADS

~~~~~~

DURING THE REPUBLICAN PERIOD AND FOR the first decade after annexation the use of Buffalo Bayou was limited more by the dirt roads that led to it than by problems of navigation. Although boats often went aground at Red Fish or Clopper's bars, and occasionally hit snags above Harrisburg, these difficulties were minor when compared to those encountered by freight wagons. Roads were the responsibility of the county government during the Republican and early statehood periods, and, as funds and labor were always in short supply, all roads in Texas remained in a primitive condition. Crossings at streams were usually fixed, and private ferries operated at the most frequently used crossings, but travelers customarily proceeded across the country by routes as distinguished from roads. Blazed trees marked their way in the woods, and they "plumbed the track," that is, followed the path of their predecessors in open areas. If no trail was discernible, experienced travelers guided themselves by a compass.

In dry weather the dirt roads radiating from Houston were fairly good and wagons made their way across the flat prairies with little difficulty, but in rainy seasons the story was a far different one. Roads became quagmires, and freight wagons laden with cotton bogged so deep in mud that in extended periods of bad weather teamsters sometimes dumped bales of cotton by the wayside and left them to rot. A visitor during Houston's first boom predicted that the town's growth would be hindered by the interior roads: "It is scarcely accessible by land in the rainy season, being surrounded by low, wet prairies to a considerable extent," he wrote.[1] Another visitor of the same period concurred in this opinion. "Unless the roads are infinitely better than when I last passed over them, no wagon can be drawn over them," he wrote:

> They were then impassable,
> Not even Jack-assable.[2]

Although roads were a problem throughout Texas in wet weather, the Brazos prairie west of Houston became especially notorious. Ferdinand Roemer noted that in bad weather much of it flooded, presenting so dismal a sight that many immigrants who intended to settle in Texas returned home after seeing it.[3] Bishop James Osgood Andrew, who visited in the middle 1840's, found the roads to the north almost as bad. In traveling horseback from Houston to Montgomery, he passed wagons at Little Cypress Creek that had been waiting two weeks to cross. When he returned nine days later, the wagons were still there. "The roads during the winter are scarcely passable at all for heavily loaded cotton wagons," he wrote. "The streams are not bridged, so that the people in the interior are seeking new channels of communication with the coast."[4]

Because wagon freighting was slow at all times and almost impossible in bad weather, freight rates were high and merchandise sold in the interior at high and often exorbitant prices. Conversely, freighting charges cut heavily into the profits on cotton and other Texas exports. Texans realized that if they competed in the world market and rose

---

[1] Chester Newell, *History of the Revolution in Texas . . .*, p. 35.
[2] Charles A. Gulick, Jr., and others, eds., *The Papers of Mirabeau Buonaparte Lamar*, III, 38
[3] Ferdinand Roemer, *Texas . . .*, Oswald Mueller, trans., pp. 69–90.
[4] James Osgood Andrew, *Miscellanies . . .*, pp. 83–116.

above a self-sufficient economy they must reduce transportation costs. Thus, in the first decade after annexation the economic and political life of the state centered around transportation problems.

Railroads, of course, were the obvious answer to the problem of overland transportation in Texas, and the Republic granted charters to four railroad companies. None of these companies put a locomotive into operation, however, and only one actually began construction on a road. All failed primarily because of the lack of capital and the fact that even had capital been available the scanty population did not justify its investment.

The first charter to build a railroad in Texas was granted by the First Congress of the Republic to the Texas Railroad, Navigation and Banking Company. After stirring up considerable controversy because of its banking provisions, this company disintegrated. The next three efforts at railroad building centered around Galveston Bay and were aimed at tapping the Brazos market. The Brazos and Galveston Railroad Company, chartered May 24, 1838, proposed reaching the Brazos and Colorado rivers by a system of turnpikes, canals, and railroads. The Houston and Brazos Rail Road Company, chartered January 26, 1839, planned a road toward the Brazos near present Hempstead, while the Harrisburg Rail Road and Trading Company received a charter on January 9, 1841, with the intention of building toward the Brazos at Richmond.[5]

The last of these to receive a charter was the only one to begin actual construction. Conceived by Andrew Briscoe as part of his campaign to make his town the commercial emporium of Buffalo Bayou in the late 1830's, the Harrisburg railroad was begun in the spring of 1840 before receiving a charter. By March 13 the survey for the road was completed, and it was routed so that it passed within three miles of Houston. By May 16 a number of laborers were preparing the roadbed for rails.[6] Although the *Morning Star* hopefully suggested that the Harrisburg and Houston projects, as they tapped different portions of

---

[5] Andrew Forest Muir, "Railroad Enterprise in Texas, 1836–1841," *Southwestern Historical Quarterly*, XLVII (April, 1944), 337–370; S. G. Reed, *A History of Texas Railroads*, pp. 30–38.

[6] Houston *Morning Star*, March 13; May 16, 1840.

the Brazos, would supplement rather than compete with each other, most Houstonians saw the Harrisburg railroad as a direct threat to their commerce. Not to be outdone, they broke ground for their railroad in a festive ceremony on July 25, 1840. The Masons, Odd Fellows, and Milam Guards paraded; Sam Houston and others made speeches; and a stone was laid commemorating the occasion. The promoters apparently used all their energy on this ceremony, however, for they never began construction. Work on the Harrisburg project continued for several months. Then it, too, quietly passed into limbo because of lack of capital and population and threats of a renewal of the war with Mexico. Not until 1853 did the successor to the Harrisburg company, the Buffalo Bayou, Brazos and Colorado, put the first locomotive into operation in Texas.[7]

While waiting for the railroad era to begin, Houstonians made spasmodic efforts to improve their wagon roads. As the route west led to both the Brazos and Austin markets, they expended on it their best efforts at road building. This road was also regarded as the route toward the Santa Fe and Chihuahua trade, and, during the Gold Rush of 1849, Francis Moore, Jr., promoted it as the best and most economical route to California. Because the charter of the Houston and Brazos Rail Road Company authorized the building of turnpikes as well as railroads, practical men suggested even before the groundbreaking ceremony for the railroad that the company build a turnpike to Austin before attempting a railroad. If ditched on both sides, a wagon road would be almost as good as a railroad, the *Morning Star* suggested, and in time the wagon road could form the bed of the railroad. Such a turnpike "would soon form the main channel of communication with the upper country and tend to divert the whole trade of the upper Brazos and Colorado" to Houston.[8]

When the company failed to build either a railroad or a turnpike, the people at Austin and points between there and Houston became impatient. Mail sometimes took four weeks to reach Austin from the coast; twenty days was considered good time for freight wagons travel-

[7] *Ibid.*, April 23, 25; May 1, 1839; Houston *Telegraph and Texas Register*, July 29, 1840; Muir, "Railroad Enterprise," pp. 337–370.
[8] *Morning Star*, March 13, 1840.

ing from Houston to Austin; and freight rates for the trip ran about
thirty dollars per hundred pounds.[9] In hopes of alleviating these conditions, citizens from Houston, Galveston, Bastrop, LaGrange, and
Austin, none of whom were associated with the railroad projects of the
period, obtained a charter for the Houston and Austin Turnpike Company on January 19, 1841. This turnpike, too, remained a paper one.
A new route was laid out to Austin in mid-1840, but little was done to
improve it until much later when wharfage fees collected at the Port of
Houston were applied to grading it in the immediate vicinity of Houston. These fees were originally levied to clear the bayou above Harrisburg and build wharves at Houston. After these tasks were accomplished, surplus funds were applied to the Austin road.[10]

By 1852 this road was graded for twenty-three miles from Houston.
By that time wagon freighting had become big business in Houston;
the ox wagon was fondly called the "peculiar institution" of the town;
and many merchants specialized in supplying teamsters. Because of
vested interests in freighting, Houston was accused of opposing railroad construction in this period. Francis Moore, Jr., denied this charge,
but he saw the building of a plank road for wagons as a more practical
and immediate solution to Houston's problems than railroads. He supported a plan to put plank over the twenty-three miles of graded road
and with several Houston merchants—among them, Paul Bremond
and William Marsh Rice—organized the Brazos and Houston Plank
Road Company in 1852.[11] Before plank could be laid, however, the
Buffalo Bayou, Brazos and Colorado Railroad Company from Harrisburg showed signs of eventual success, and planters to the north of
Houston began agitating for a railroad. Bremond became interested in
the latter project, and began construction on the line that later became
famous as the Houston and Texas Central. This renewed interest in
railroads diverted energy and capital from the plank-road project,
which dropped into obscurity. At the advent of the railroad era, roads
leading to Houston—with the exception of the few miles improved by

9 *Ibid.*, March 14, 1840.
10 *Ibid.*, July 1, 1840.
11 *Democratic Telegraph and Texas Register*, July 2, 16, 1852.

wharfage fees—were still much the same as when Sam Houston's army had brought the Twin Sisters through boot-deep mud to Harrisburg.

As Bishop Andrew had predicted, the bad roads leading to Houston caused people on the interior to seek new channels to the coast after annexation. In the late 1840's planters on the Trinity and Brazos joined with Galveston interests in a determined effort to bypass Houston, an effort that marked the beginning of the Houston-Galveston rivalry. If the rivers were made navigable, the Galvestonians pointed out, planters would not only avoid the wagon haul to Houston, but could also eliminate the extra handling charges incurred in loading their produce on steamboats for Galveston and then reloading it on sea vessels for world markets. Moreover, by shipping direct to Galveston the planters could avoid the wharfage fees at Houston.

Some Galveston factors backed enterprising men who cut trees along the riverbanks and made rafts to bring cotton downstream to Galveston. As steamboats of lighter and lighter draft were developed, Galveston capitalists sent these to collect produce along the rivers. Still other Galveston capital went into a canal to link the Brazos River with Galveston Bay. Envisioned by Stephen F. Austin as early as 1822, this canal was the persistent dream of entrepreneurs throughout the 1830's and 1840's. The Galveston and Brazos Navigation Company was chartered on February 8, 1850, to build the waterway, which, when completed in 1855, was fifty feet wide, three and one-half feet deep, and large enough to handle steamboats, rafts, and other small craft. The canal was successful at first, but the expense of dredging proved more than the profits of the company would bear, and the canal was unable to compete with rail transportation.[13]

Houston interests countered the Galveston competition by attempting to bypass the island city in getting goods to market. From the time the Allen brothers wrote the first advertisement for their unborn city, men had dreamed of bringing ocean vessels directly to Houston. This

[12] Louis Sterne, *Seventy Years of an Active Life*, pp. 27–30.

[13] Andrew Forest Muir, "The Destiny of Buffalo Bayou," *Southwestern Historical Quarterly*, XLVII (October, 1943), 92–96; Earl Wesley Fornell, *The Galveston Era . . .*, pp. 29–30.

dream was revived in the summer of 1849 by Houston merchants who wanted to avoid "paying tribute to Galveston." The *Ogden*, hailed as the "first regular steam packet that has ever made the trip directly from New Orleans," arrived at the Houston landing on August 15, where it was greeted by cheers from crowds of people who lined the banks of the bayou and by the firing of a salute. "It is evident from the success that has attended this experiment that a line of steam packets could be established to run between New Orleans and Houston," commented the *Telegraph*. The editor proposed a short railroad to tap the Brazos area as a corollary to this proposed line. The new line also suggested an important new export trade for Texas by proposing to take cattle to New Orleans. The *Telegraph* estimated that each ship could take from two to three hundred head of cattle. Because cattle bringing from five to seven dollars a head in Houston brought from fifteen to twenty in New Orleans, the editor thought this trade would soon be as profitable as cotton. Although the *Ogden* departed on August 21 with about 150 head of cattle and made at least one other trip from New Orleans to Houston during the season, no regular line of packets came from the experiment.[14] Vessels small enough to cross the bars, it became evident, were too small for safe ocean travel.

The desire to make the channel navigable for larger vessels inspired several imaginative suggestions. Francis Moore, Jr., proposed that Cypress Creek, a small tributary of the San Jacinto River, be channeled into White Oak Bayou, thus doubling the size of Buffalo Bayou at Houston. Still others, upon examining maps and soil structures, decided that the mighty Brazos had once found its way to the sea by way of Buffalo Bayou. Why not dig a waterway, they asked, and bring the river back to its original channel?[15]

This last suggestion came at a time when people on the Brazos were especially resentful of Houston wharfage fees and brought howls of indignation. A group of Brazos merchants forthwith published what they called their Declaration of Independence from Houston. An irra-

---

[14] *Democratic Telegraph and Texas Register*, August 16, 23, 30; September 6, 1849; Dermot H. Hardy and Ingham S. Roberts, *Historical Review of South-East Texas . . .*, I, 217–262.

[15] *Democratic Telegraph and Texas Register*, February 8, 1849; October 15, 1852.

tional document charging Houston with everything from the failure of navigation on the Brazos to the "quartering of large bodies of Yankees among us," the Declaration ended with the charge that Houstonians were "threatening to turn the waters of the Brazos into the *diminutive rivulet, emphatically styled Buffalo Bayou.*" This slur on the bayou brought a hot rejoinder from Francis Moore, Jr., who printed the Declaration with caustic comments in his paper. The Bayou was not so a rivulet, said he: "It can float a seventy-four gun ship when the Brazos can be forded fifty miles below Washington."[16]

A more practical effort to make the bayou navigable to sea vessels was inaugurated by Sidney Sherman in the years immediately after annexation. Massachusetts-born Sherman had first seen the bayou with Sam Houston's army in April, 1836, and had distinguished himself at the Battle of San Jacinto. After the Revolution he established his home, Crescent Place, to the west of Morgan's Point. Becoming interested in the potential of the bayou, he had George Stealey make a survey of the stream in 1847. The survey convinced Sherman that if improvements were made at Red Fish and Clopper's bars, sea vessels could go as far as Harrisburg. Thus, in March, 1847, he acquired most of the assets of Andrew Briscoe's old Harrisburg Town Company and revived Briscoe's dream of making the town the metropolis of the bayou. Sherman estimated that the improvement of the bars would cost between twenty-five and thirty thousand dollars. He originally intended securing this money by the sale of Harrisburg town lots, but he wrote hopefully to an associate, John Grant Tod, about getting an "appropriation from Congress" to cover the expense.[17] Sherman eventually obtained backing from Boston financiers who were more interested in building a railroad than in improving the bayou.[18] Thus, the project of a railroad from Harrisburg to Richmond was revived, and energy and capital were diverted to this project to the neglect of the waterway.

16 *Ibid.*, February 8, 1849.

17 Sherman to Tod, October 2, 1847, quoted in Ben H. Proctor, "Sidney Sherman" (M.A. Thesis, The University of Texas, 1952), p. 119. Original in possession of W. H. Philpott, Jr., Dallas, in 1952.

18 See Andrew Forest Muir, "The Buffalo Bayou, Brazos & Colorado Railway Company, 1850–1861, and Its Antecedents" (M.A. Thesis, Rice Institute, 1942); Proctor, "Sidney Sherman."

When Sherman wrote of obtaining an appropriation from Congress for the improvement of the bars, he referred to the state legislative body rather than the national one. The use of federal funds for internal improvements became an issue of national politics early in the nineteenth century, and from the Jacksonian era until after the Civil War national policy held that rivers, canals, and roads within a single state were the responsibility of state rather than federal government. The State of Texas was as poor as the Republic in the first years of statehood, but, as the 1850's brought increased prosperity, the state assumed some responsibility for its streams. On February 7, 1853, the state legislature appropriated funds for the improvement of various waterways and allotted $4,000 each to Buffalo Bayou and the San Jacinto River.[19] The legislature gave more substantial assistance in a bill, popularly known as the rivers-and-harbors bill, passed on August 1, 1856. This bill, after being amended several times, appropriated $350,000 for the encouragement of navigation in Texas. The act stipulated, however, that no funds would be allotted to any project until local interests had first contributed one-fourth the amount to be granted by the state. No more than $50,000 of state funds could be applied to any one project, and the work was to be done under the supervision of a state engineer.[20]

The *Telegraph* announced the passage of the rivers-and-harbors bill on August 11, 1856, and suggested that, as the matter was "vitally important to the prosperity of our city," citizens hold a meeting that very night "to secure to our bayou some of the benefits arising from this act." By December 15 the city had subscribed $5,000 for bayou improvement, but the *Telegraph* expressed doubt that the legislature would allow the stream four times that amount. On April 7, 1857, the state engineer awarded a contract for the improvement of Clopper's Bar to David Bradbury for $22,725, and somewhat later a contract for $23,000 was awarded for the improvement of Red Fish Bar.[21]

After annexation the City of Houston continued to maintain the bayou above Harrisburg and pay the cost through wharfage. By the

19 H. P. N. Gammel, comp., *The Laws of Texas, 1822–1897*, III, 1305–1308.
20 *Ibid.*, IV, 427–431, 464–465.
21 *Texas Almanac*, 1858, p. 191; Galveston *Weekly News*, April 14, 1857.

early 1850's most of the overhanging limbs and snags that had plagued earlier navigation had been removed, but mud from city streets and cuts in the embankment were becoming a menace. Francis Moore, Jr., observed in 1852 that the stream was shoaling in places and was not as deep as when he first saw it fifteen years previously. He thought that it was wider, however, and that the points were worn and less sharp than they had been. Shortly after he made these observations, the city acquired a dredge boat. The first dredge was a makeshift affair that proved inadequate, but in mid-1856 Captain David Bradbury built a new one for the city that incorporated recent technological developments. The boat was designed to use on shoals within four miles of the town and to cut off some points so bigger boats could navigate the bayou. Launched on August 30, 1856, the new dredge was seventy feet long, thirty feet wide, and drew about four inches of water without engine and machinery. It proved successful and was hailed by the Galveston *Weekly News* as "the best dredge in our waters." After Bradbury obtained contracts for improving Clopper's Bar and the mouth of the Trinity River, he rented the dredge boat from the city to do the work.[22]

Navigation on the bayou during the 1850's was dominated by the Houston Navigation Company, a continuation of the Houston and Galveston Navigation Company. The original company was organized in 1851 by a group of Houston merchants and steamboat captains. Principal among them were merchants William Marsh Rice, William J. Hutchins, Paul Bremond, and Cornelius Ennis and Captains John H. Sterrett, James Montgomery, and Michael McCormick.[23] By the fall of 1856 the company had three steamboats—the *Neptune, San Antonio,* and *Jenkins*—regularly operating between Houston and Galveston, and the *Telegraph* reported that all had as much business as they could do. Early the following year Captain Sterrett brought the *Island City,* a new boat built in Ohio especially for the Buffalo Bayou trade, to Houston, and by 1858, after railroads had facilitated the movement of

[22] Houston *Tri-Weekly Telegraph,* July 14, September 1, October 20, 1856; January 9, April 13, 1857; *Weekly News,* April 14, 1857.

[23] Andrew Forest Muir, "The Railroads Come to Houston, 1857–1861," *Southwestern Historical Quarterly,* LXIV (July, 1960), 42–63.

goods from the interior to Houston, the company had seven boats on the channel, having added the *Bayou City, Neptune No. 2,* and *Diana.*[24] A company steamer left each of the cities at three o'clock every afternoon except Sunday and made the trip in eight hours. Fares for cabin passage dropped to two dollars in the middle 1840's but were raised to three dollars in 1849 and continued at that rate throughout the 1850's. Tariff for a bale of cotton was fifty cents. Rates were apparently considered reasonable, for, while there were vociferous complaints about Houston wharfage fees, there were none about freight rates—this in spite of the fact that the company held a virtual monopoly on Bayou shipping.[25]

The bulk of the cargo moving downstream was cotton on its way to world markets while the bulk of the upstream cargo was manufactured goods. One of the most unusual cargoes on the bayou during this period was a boatload of camels bound for Francis R. Lubbock's ranch on Sims Bayou. In the fall of 1858 an English lady brought forty of the animals to Galveston, probably as a front for a slave-smuggling operation. Not finding a buyer immediately, she arranged for Lubbock to care for the camels. He chartered a steamer, brought them up the bayou, and kept them on his ranch for about a year. The camels were a great curiosity for Texans, who flocked from a distance to see the animals gambol like sheep in the pasture or swim in Buffalo Bayou. Occasionally the foreign drivers rode the camels into Houston, where they created a sensation.[26]

By far the most active boatman on the bayou throughout the Republican and early statehood periods was Captain John H. Sterrett, agent for the Houston Navigation Company and commodore of its fleet. Captain Sterrett, described by Mrs. William Fairfax Gray as "very polite & gentlemanly," brought the Gray family to Houston on the *Rufus Putnam* in 1838 and in the nineteen years following made an estimated

[24] *Tri-Weekly Telegraph,* October 20, November 7, 1856; January 12, 16, 1857; November 4, 1860.

[25] *Ibid.,* November 12, 1856; Muir, "Railroads Come to Houston," pp. 42–63; Jacob de Cordova, *Texas . . .,* p. 193.

[26] Francis Richard Lubbock, *Six Decades in Texas; or, Memoirs of Francis Richard Lubbock,* pp. 239–241.

four thousand trips between Houston and Galveston. At various times he was the master of the *Lady Byron, Albert Gallatin, Neptune, Island City,* and *Reliance.* The *Reliance,* under his command in 1849, was hailed as probably the only temperance steamer in the state of Texas, that is, it had no bar.[27]

In the early 1850's a rivalry reminiscent of Mississippi River steamboating developed between Captain Sterrett, then captain of the *Neptune,* and Captain Webb of the *Farmer.* The rivalry became so intense that in racing on a trip to Galveston in January, 1853, the two boats actually came in contact several times. On that occasion neither vessel was damaged and no passengers were hurt, but two months later, on March 23, another race ended in one of the greatest disasters that ever happened on the channel. The boiler of the *Farmer* exploded as the ship was slightly to the west of Pelican Island. As the number of passengers aboard was not known and as many of them were transients, the exact number of deaths was never determined, but the Galveston *Tri-Weekly News* estimated the total at thirty-six, including the captain and twelve other crew members. General Sidney Sherman, who was aboard, narrowly escaped with his life. Although Captain Sterrett acquitted himself nobly at the scene of the accident by rescuing the survivors, both he and Captain Webb were roundly criticized by the local newspapers for "criminal recklessness." The tragedy had a sobering effect on navigation on the channel. Thereafter the Houston Navigation Company left racing to Mississippi steamboats while it sought and gained a reputation for safety.[28]

Although the prosperity of the mid-fifties brought new boats and a businesslike bustle to the bayou, visitors still found their journey a memorable one. The Honourable Amelia Matilda Murray, a lady-in-waiting to Queen Victoria, was as fascinated by the voyage as her fellow countrywoman, Mrs. Houstoun, had been a decade earlier. The journey was "a kind of amphibious proceeding," said Miss Murray, belonging to neither the sea nor the earth:

[27] *Telegraph and Texas Register,* November 29, 1849; De Cordova, *Texas,* p. 235; Marguerite Johnston, *A Happy Worldly Abode . . .,* p. 18.

[28] *Telegraph and Texas Register,* January 21, 1853; *Tri-Weekly News,* March 29, April 5, 1853.

Negroes holding braziers of blazing pine-wood, stood on either side of the
vessel, illuminating our passage, the foliage and even the beautiful flowers
so near that we could almost gather them as we floated by; a small bell was
ringing every instant, to direct our engineers; one moment the larboard
paddle, then the starboard, was stopped or set in motion, or the wheels
were altogether standing still, while we swung around the narrow corners
of this tortuous channel; the silence of the bordering forests broken alone
by the sobs of our high-pressure engine. . . . Now and then a night bird, or
frog croaking with a voice like that of a watchman's rattle, accompanied
the bells and the escape valve.[29]

Although the struggle between Galveston and Houston over water
routes was spirited, the battle royal between them during the 1850's
centered around land routes. As increased population and prosperity
ushered in the railway era, a mighty political and economic struggle
developed over how the railroads would be routed and financed. Galveston interests—most vocally represented by Willard Richardson, editor of the Galveston *News*—proposed a network of railroads leading
"fan-like" to Galveston and bringing the produce of the state to her
wharves for shipment.

In opposition to the Galveston Plan was the Corporate Plan, supported by railroad capitalists in the United States and by Houston merchants. Under this plan Texas railroads would become a part of the
transcontinental system designed by planners in the United States to
run east and west across the nation. If this plan were adopted, Houston
stood to become the railroad center of Texas, and the trade of the state
would be routed not to the sea but through the rail centers of St. Louis
and Chicago. Thus, Galveston would be relegated to a minor position
as far as rail transportation was concerned.

Proponents of the Galveston Plan realized that they could not obtain
financing from the usual sources in the East if their roads did not tie in
with the transcontinental system. Hence they advocated that the railroads be built not by private capital but by the state, and their plan

---

[29] Amelia Matilda Murray, *Letters from the United States, Cuba and Canada*,
p. 292.

became popularly known as the State Plan. Lorenzo Sherwood and John W. Dancy led a legislative battle for this plan in the summer of 1856 and for a while they seemed likely to succeed.

As the battle reached a critical stage, the attention of the entire state focused on it. Edward Hopkins Cushing, who succeeded Francis Moore, Jr., as editor-owner of the Houston *Telegraph,* vigorously opposed the Galveston-oriented plan, charging that the island city was "making railroads on paper by the thousands of miles, all terminating at her wharves, but she calls on other people to build them." A meeting called at Houston in April, 1856, branded the State Plan as "ruinous," and later a group of Houston merchants—including Francis Richard Lubbock, Thomas William House, and William Marsh Rice —toured the state fighting it. The issue was decided in their favor on August 13 when the legislature passed a bill favoring the Corporate Plan and granting generous assistance in the form of loans and land grants to private builders.[30] The decision gave Houston a clear-cut victory over Galveston in the battle for interior routes and, in large measure, determined the future of the two cities.

Even before the issue was settled, however, Buffalo Bayou had become the focus of railroad activity in Texas. Sidney Sherman, at the instigation of his Boston backers, obtained a charter for the Buffalo Bayou, Brazos and Colorado Railway Company on February 11, 1850. The company began construction on the road from Harrisburg to Richmond the following year, and in the fall of 1852 brought the first locomotive, the *General Sherman,* to Texas. The locomotive was second-hand to begin with and was damaged by a hurricane at Galveston before it could be shipped up the bayou, but, even so, it ushered in a new era of transportation. By the summer of 1853 twenty miles of track had been laid to Stafford's Point, and in September the company announced biweekly rail service between that place and Harrisburg.

If, as critics charged, Houston had been cool toward railroads in the early 1850's because of a vested interest in wagon freighting, this coolness was dispelled by the whistle of Texas' first locomotive. Shortly

[30] *Tri-Weekly Telegraph,* April 11, 21, May 9, 1856; Fornell, *Galveston Era,* pp. 157–179.

after the arrival of the *General Sherman* in Galveston, Paul Bremond and other Houstonians interested in the plank-road company dropped that project in favor of a railroad to the north. Bremond began construction on the road in 1855, and in 1856 the Houston and Texas Central began operation on the twenty-five miles between Houston and Cypress. By 1860 the line reached northward to Hockley, Hempstead, and Millican.

In the same year that the Houston and Texas Central began operations, Houstonians decided to take advantage of a provision of the Buffalo Bayou, Brazos and Colorado's charter permitting them to build a branch to join it. Almost simultaneously planters of the wealthy sugar-producing counties of the lower Brazos also saw the advantage of joining the Harrisburg line. They began building a railroad northward from Columbia that connected with the Houston tap. The two systems eventually combined under one ownership and became known as the Houston Tap and Brazoria Railroad, or more familiarly as the Sugar Railroad.

Construction began on yet another railroad to Houston in 1856. Promoted by Galveston and Houston merchants, the Galveston, Houston and Henderson Railroad Company began building at Virginia Point, on the mainland across from Galveston. By the fall of 1859 the company had initiated triweekly service from that point to the outskirts of Houston. Early the next year a railroad bridge, financed by the city of Galveston, was completed, giving the island a direct connection with the mainland.

Another railroad project, the Texas and New Orleans, began construction at various points between Houston and New Orleans in 1857. This line was opposed in the Texas legislature by Galveston interests who correctly saw it as a threat to their hold on the New Orleans trade. Begun in spite of their objections, the railroad was in operation only in parts when the Civil War interrupted construction.

By the eve of the Civil War, Houston was established as the railroad center of Texas. Five railroads radiated from the town, and, of an estimated 450 miles of track in Texas, more than 350 led to Houston. The rails brought an era of unprecedented prosperity to the town in the late 1850's, prosperity that was best measured then and until well into the twentieth century by the number of cotton bales received. For 1854 the number was 39,923; by 1858 it was 63,453; and by 1860 it had jumped to 115,010.[31] The prosperity of Houston commerce is also reflected by the fortunes of her merchant princes as reported in the 1860 census. The wealthiest, William Marsh Rice, was worth $750,000; William J. Hutchins, $700,000; Thomas William House, $500,000; and Cornelius Ennis and Paul Bremond, $400,000 each.[32]

Frederick Law Olmsted saw evidences of the growing prosperity of the town when he visited in the mid-1850's. "It shows many agreeable signs of the wealth accumulated in its homelike, retired residences, its large and good hotel, its well-supplied shops, and its shaded streets," he wrote. "The principal thoroughfare, opening from the steamboat landing, is the busiest we saw in Texas. Near the bayou are extensive cottonsheds, and huge exposed piles of bales." Although Harrisburg had shown promising signs of rivaling Houston in the early 1850's, these were gone by the time of Olmsted's visit. Harrisburg was "a settlement of half-a-dozen houses," he wrote, and although its navigation was superior, Houston had "ten or fifteen years, and odd millions of dollars, the start."[33]

For old-time Texans who could remember when Houston was merely a promoter's dream, the growth of the town was nothing less than astonishing. One old Texan philosophized after a visit that in so far as future greatness was concerned, situation was not as important to a town as an enterprising population. "There was a time when it was thought that San Felipe, Velasco, and San Luis would become large towns," he said. "And why did they not?"

They were well situated—their owners lacked enterprise. Compare the two towns of Columbus and Houston;—the one situated at the head of tidewater on the largest river in the State, in the center of the richest planting section in the world—the other on a shallow Bayou, naturally incapable of navigation to any extent, surrounded by post oak and pine barrens and boggy prairies,—one has had all the advantage of situation, the other of

[31] Hardy and Roberts, *South-East Texas*, I, 243.
[32] Muir, "Railroads Come to Houston," p. 54.
[33] Frederick Law Olmsted, *A Journey Through Texas; or, a Saddle-Trip on the Southwestern Frontier*, p. 361.

an energetic people. Notwithstanding Houston has become the greatest
business emporium of the State; while Columbia, Brazoria and Velasco . . .
are now back where they were twenty years ago.[34]

Not content with new prosperity and with having the rail battle settled in their favor, Houstonians returned with fresh vigor to the battle
with Galveston over water routes in the late 1850's. The railroads to
the interior brought increased traffic on Buffalo Bayou, but the completion of the road to Galveston loomed as a threat to bayou trade. Not
only did the rail journey take less than half the time, but it cost less.
For example, the total cost of bringing a barrel of flour from New Orleans to Galveston, thence by rail to Houston, was ninety-eight cents,
while the cost by Buffalo Bayou after adding ten cents per barrel wharfage was $1.05.[35]

These figures caused some observers to suggest that the Buffalo
Bayou trade was becoming obsolete, but this Edward H. Cushing denied. Cushing had vigorously supported railroad building, but after the
lines were completed he saw danger in permitting them to gain a monopoly over local transportation. Outside capitalists owned a controlling interest in the railroads, he warned. If Houston abandoned the
bayou then the town would be left at the mercy of the outsiders. To
save bayou trade he urged the repeal of the wharfage fees, long the
bane of the interior. Of over $8,500 collected in the first three months
of 1860, he pointed out, only about $1,100 was spent on bayou im-
provement. Thus, Houston could no longer defend the fees as necessary to improve the bayou. Nor with railroads leading to the interior
could the town claim that the fees were necessary to build roads. The
wharfage was "highway robbery," said Cushing, and a direct threat to
Houston's water commerce. Influential merchants backed Cushing in
the fight, and the wharfage was repealed in a special election in May,
1860.[36]

Its repeal cleared the way for the struggle over water routes. Where
Galveston in the early 1850's had attributed high costs of transportation to the Houston wharfage and posed as the champion of the in-

[34] *Tri-Weekly Telegraph*, April 13, 1857.
[35] Hardy and Roberts, *South-East Texas*, p. 243.
[36] *Ibid.*, p. 243; *Tri-Weekly Telegraph*, April 3, 17, May 22, June 19, 1860.

terior, the island's own waterfront policies had become as onerous to the hinterland as Houston's by late in the decade. In 1854 a group of wharf owners, headed by Michel B. Menard and Samuel May Williams, organized the Galveston Wharf & Cotton Press Company with capital stock of about a million dollars. Familiarly known as the Galveston Wharf Company or by its enemies as the Octopus of the Gulf, this company was semipublic in nature, one third of the stock being held by the city and the other two-thirds by private interests. Because it was semipublic, the company was relieved of the usual burden of state taxes; and because of the city's one-third interest, the company controlled undeveloped waterfrontage owned by the city. By 1859 the company counted as its stockholders the most influential men of Galveston—among them, Ebenezer B. Nichols, Henry Rosenberg, Robert Mills, and John Sealy—and held a monopolistic control of the port. Of ten wharves at Galveston, the wharf company owned seven, and, because of its privileged position, it exercised control over the other three—one of them owned by Thomas M. League and another owned in part by Thomas W. House. Nor did the company hesitate to use its monopoly to exact what the hinterland called "tribute" of the goods that passed through Galveston. In 1859, while admitting that most of the profits were reinvested in wharf improvements, the company paid $70,000 in dividends.[37]

The shortsighted policies of the Galveston Wharf Company goaded Houston interests into seeking new means of bypassing the island. As ocean vessels were becoming larger, there was no longer talk of bringing them direct to Houston, but a more practical suggestion was offered. Why not avoid Galveston altogether by unloading vessels in the channel and bringing merchandise up Buffalo Bayou by barges? And why not compress cotton at Houston, put it on barges for the journey downstream, and load it on ocean vessels without touching the island? When first made, these suggestions were greeted with amused contempt in Galveston. "To concede that Houston can do her own shipping from the mouth of Buffalo Bayou is a little hard for us to swal-

[37] Galveston City Directory, 1859–60, pp. 44–45; Fornell, Galveston Era, pp. 15–17.

low," commented a Galveston editor.[38] But when barges actually began unloading in mid-channel, the Galveston Wharf Company retaliated quickly by levying an additional charge on such vessels when they docked at Galveston to take on a return cargo. This, declared the Houston editor, was "an attempt to force all the trade of Houston and the interior to pass over the wharves at Galveston and thus pay tribute whether willing or not." Houston interests, with their wharfage repealed, squared away for battle when hostilities of a different nature developed. In November, 1860, Abraham Lincoln was elected President of the United States; the following month South Carolina seceded from the Union; and shortly thereafter Texas became one of the Confederate States of America. Thus, Galveston and Houston postponed their economic battle and entered the dark decade of the Civil War and Reconstruction.

[38] *Tri-Weekly Telegraph*, November 14, 19, 24, 1856; June 26, 1860.

V. COMMODORE MORGAN AND
THE OCTOPUS OF THE GULF

T<small>EXAS, BEING ON THE PERIPHERY OF THE</small>
South, did not suffer devastation from invading armies, but she shared
in the general economic ruin that the Civil War brought to the Confederate States. For both Galveston and Houston the war ended a period of unprecedented prosperity. A Federal blockade of Confederate
ports was extended to the Texas Gulf Coast in the summer of 1861,
eventually limiting navigation there to enemy ships and blockade runners. Commerce on Buffalo Bayou during the war years consisted primarily of cotton shipped to Galveston, there to be slipped through the
blockade to market, and of merchandise brought back by the blockade
runners. As a rule, vessels eluding the Federal fleet made for Mexican
ports or the West Indies, whence their cargoes were sent to England or
—ironically in view of the hostilities—to Northern textile mills. As
cotton brought as much as a dollar a pound upon delivery and as merchandise brought back to Texas sold at premium prices, the trade was
profitable in proportion to the risk involved.

Foremost among those engaged in the trade was Thomas William
House, whose mercantile interests at Galveston and Houston dated

back to the early days of the Republic and whose son, Edward Mandell, would be the adviser of President Woodrow Wilson during a later war. According to tradition, one of House's ocean vessels ran the blockade at Galveston and came directly up the bayou to Houston during a flood in the spring of 1863. The vessel unloaded a cargo of arms and ammunition at the foot of Fannin Street, so the story goes, and then took on a cargo of cotton and, returning to Galveston, again ran the blockade.[1]

Even this precarious commerce on the bayou was interrupted in late 1862 when the Federals took Galveston. Confederate General John Bankhead Magruder, with military headquarters at Houston, immediately resolved to retake the island, a decision that gave the bayou its only glimpse of military action during the Civil War. In a secluded spot on the bayou a few miles below Houston the Confederates converted the *Neptune* and *Bayou City,* both veterans of the bayou trade, into gunboats and protected their hulls with compressed cotton bales. As the old year gave way to the new these makeshift warships along with several tenders made their way downstream while a supporting land force headed for the railway bridge at Virginia Point. Unfortunately, General Magruder had not considered the vagaries of the tides in planning the attack, so his fleet faced an unforeseen problem when it reached Galveston Bay. If the ships waited until the appointed hour to cross Red Fish Bar, they ran the risk of going aground in low tide; but if they crossed while the tide was high, their presence would warn the enemy of the attack. Rather than endanger the surprise, the fleet held back, stuck in low tide on the bar, and arrived late for the battle. Even so, the improvised vessels captured the *Harriet Lane,* and helped expel the Federals from the island on January 1, 1863.[2] The victory took its toll on the men who had been active in developing the bayou. Sidney Sherman lost a son in the battle, while Captain John H.

[1] Benajah Harvey Carroll, Jr., *Standard History of Houston,* p. 251. Some of House's activties during the war may be traced in his papers in the Archives of The University of Texas, Austin.

[2] Thomas North, *Five Years in Texas . . .,* pp. 108–110; Charles C. Cumberland, "The Confederate Loss and Recapture of Galveston, 1862–1863," *Southwestern Historical Quarterly,* LI (October, 1947), 109–130.

Sterrett received a wound in the hip that caused him to limp badly for the remainder of his life.[3]

A Confederate shipyard was established at the mouth of Goose Creek and an ordnance depot at Houston, but except for the Battle of Galveston, the bay area saw little glory to relieve the drabness of war. Indeed, Texas as a whole saw so little of the war that one unsympathetic observer commented at its end that "Texas was never whipped in spirit, only nominally whipped," and that Texas was not really one of the Confederate states, but "like Old Dog Tray" had simply been found in bad company.[4]

Even so, the Confederate soldiers who swarmed up Buffalo Bayou en route home after the collapse of the Confederacy were bitter in defeat and even more bitter in their hatred of cotton speculators who had profited by the war. As Confederate stores and arms were destined to be turned over to the Federals, the returning soldiers helped themselves to such goods wherever they found them. Just before both soldiers and civilians began sacking the ordnance depot at Houston, the officers in charge ordered hundreds of bomb shells removed. These were dumped into Buffalo Bayou near Travis Street. Shortly after the war a man was killed while retrieving one of these shells, and as late as the turn of the century these relics of the war were still being dredged from the bottom of the bayou.[5]

Under the unsettled conditions that accompanied the breakup of the Confederacy, the Twin Sisters, the little cannon of San Jacinto, disappeared, giving Buffalo Bayou its most intriguing legend. The cannon were turned over to the United States government after the annexation of Texas and removed to Baton Rouge, Louisiana. When the Civil War began, Louisiana took over the United States arsenal there and returned the cannon, then in unusable condition, to Texas, where the last official record places them near Austin on November 30, 1863. Many stories have circulated as to the ultimate fate of the Twin Sisters, but the most persistent says that they were buried somewhere near

[3] O. F. Allen, *The City of Houston . . .*, p. 29.
[4] North, *Five Years in Texas*, p. 102.
[5] Allen, *City of Houston*, pp. 15, 50.

Harrisburg at the close of the Civil War. According to Dr. H. M.
Graves, when he and several other Confederate soldiers arrived at Harrisburg in August, 1865, they saw among piles of junk artillery awaiting delivery to the Federals two small cannon identified by brass plates
as the Twin Sisters. Determined to save these relics of the Republic of
Texas from the ignominy of surrender, Graves and his party removed
them during the night to a point about half a mile from the bayou,
where they were dismantled and buried. As Graves could not find the
burial place when he returned years later, he never substantiated his
story by producing the cannon. The account of a Union soldier places
them at Houston in July, 1865, however, and the legend persists that
the little cannon found a last resting place beside the stream that saw
their greatest glory. As late as the middle of the twentieth century one
man who believed them there offered a five-hundred-dollar reward for
their recovery and old-timers still watched expectantly when any exca-
vations were made in the area.[6]

Even though Texas escaped the more obvious battle scars, a way of
life disappeared along with the Twin Sisters in 1865, and the defeated
soldiers returned to a land whose economy had been set back to the
days of the Republic. As the military headquarters of Texas, Houston
gave the appearance of a bustling town throughout the war, but the
transportation system on which its commerce was based suffered serious deterioration. Some of the railroads that had brought it prosperity
in the late fifties were abandoned and all others were in disrepair. "It
was flattery to speak of them as 'streaks of rust'," recalled one observer
years later. "The roadbed and right of way were about all that was left
of them. The owners of the roads were in about as bad shape financial-
ly, as were the roads physically."[7] Also in sad disrepair was Buffalo
Bayou, Houston's lifeline to the sea, whose hard-won improvements
of previous years all but disappeared during four years of neglect.

[6] Ernest W. Winkler, "The 'Twin Sisters' Cannon, 1836–1865," *Southwestern
Historical Quarterly*, XXI (July, 1917), 61–68; "Texas Collection," *ibid.*, LV
(April, 1952), 503–504.

[7] S. O. Young, *A Thumb-Nail History of the City of Houston, Texas* . . ., pp.
70–71.

Shoals formed near the city, snags accumulated, and the bars returned to their natural state.

In contrast to Houston, Galveston—because of its exposed position —had been virtually abandoned by its civilian population during the war, but its economy bounced back to normal almost immediately upon the termination of hostilities. Indeed, by delaying the completion of rail connections to St. Louis, New Orleans, and other points north and east, the war prolonged Galveston's position as the principal gateway to Texas. Among economic facts of life not changed by the war was the hold of the Galveston Wharf Company on the island's waterfront, a circumstance that created fortunes there and aroused resentment in the interior. While the rest of the state slowly recovered from the effects of war and reconstruction, Galveston—and more specifically the stockholders of the wharf company—reaped a golden harvest on cargo passing through the harbor. Galveston's population—7,307 compared to Houston's 4,845 in 1860—was 13,818 to Houston's 9,382 by 1870 and 22,248 to Houston's 16,513 a decade later. Within a quarter of a century after the close of the Civil War the island had won the state its first reputation for millionaires. "This is the richest city of its size on the continent," declared a visiting journalist, who saw there the finest buildings and costliest private residences in Texas and who thought millionaires were thicker there than anywhere else he had ever been.[8]

But even Galveston had its transportation problems in the postwar period. Although a number of railroads had been chartered to build to the island, only one—the Galveston, Houston and Henderson—had been constructed, and it stopped at Houston. This road connected with two others—the Houston Tap and Brazoria and the Buffalo Bayou, Brazos and Colorado—but it was of a different gage. Thus, whether Galveston merchants shipped goods to the interior by rail or water, the cargo was rehandled at Houston with a consequent addition to the freight charges. The Galveston road was connected to the Houston and Texas Central, a road of the same gage, in 1865, but still islanders felt aggrieved because their two major highways to the interior led through

[8] Walter B. Stevens, *Through Texas*, pp. 96–97.

Houston. Their irritation became so acute in 1873 that a group of merchants headed by John Sealy planned a railroad for the openly avowed purpose of reaching the hinterland without passing through Houston or even touching Harris County. Galveston County subscribed half a million dollars in bonds toward the road's construction, and Galveston citizens invested heavily in its stock. Chartered as the Gulf, Colorado and Santa Fe Railway on May 28, 1873, the road was begun two years later and reached Fort Worth in 1881.[9]

Because of the towns' efforts to bypass each other in reaching markets, the economic rivalry between Houston and Galveston was resumed in the mid-1860's as though a bloody war had not interrupted it. Houston was reinforced by new allies in this period, however, allies who saw in the Galveston Wharf Company, or the Octopus of the Gulf as they called it, a convenient scapegoat for all the economic ills of the state. Discontented farmers blamed the company for the small profits left to them for their year's work and charged that the company took advantage of its position to collect unreasonable rates. The Grange eventually took up the battle for the farmers, pointing out that, while draymen would transfer cotton from railroad to ship for fifteen cents a bale, the wharf company collected forty cents. Thus, the farmer was robbed of twenty-five cents on every bale of cotton, said the official Grange organ.[10] Consumers in the interior attributed the high cost of imports to the policies of the company, while citizens of Galveston who did not own company stock joined in the complaints in the late 1860's, charging that the city had granted too many concessions on its waterfront to the company.

The company mollified Galvestonians in 1869 by giving the city a larger share of stock, but no concessions were made in response to the

---

9 S. G. Reed, *A History of Texas Railroads*, p. 78; "Construction of the Original Gulf, Colorado and Santa Fe Railway," *Houston Port Book* (November, 1946), pp. 39–40. This road eventually became a part of the Santa Fe system. Despite its original purpose, it served Houston over trackage leased from the International and Great Northern from 1880 and built its own line from Alvin in 1883. Santa Fe passenger trains now go out of Houston to Rosenberg on Southern Pacific tracks, leased at considerable cost.

10 John S. Spratt, *The Road to Spindletop: Economic Change in Texas, 1875–1901*, p. 161.

chorus of complaints from Houston and the hinterland. Secure in the control of the best harbor in the state, the wharf company exacted all the profit its monopoly permitted, thus playing a leading role in driving Houston to seek deep water. "It is strange, but true," says one commentator, "that the first great assistance Houston had in bringing the question of bayou improvement before the public came from Galveston, its bitterest commercial rival."[11]

Sharing blame with the Galveston Wharf Company for high transportation costs in the late 1860's was Commodore Charles Morgan, who had pioneered Gulf Coast trade in Texas and who was granted preferential treatment by the wharf company until 1874. According to tradition, Morgan had sent his first steamship to Texas the year before the Texas Revolution. Although there is only nebulous evidence to substantiate this early voyage, Morgan did inaugurate the first scheduled steam-packet service to the Republic by sending his *Columbia* to Galveston in November, 1837.[12] During the next few years the *Cuba* and *New York* were added to the trade, and before annexation other Morgan ships—among them the *Savannah, Kingston, Republic,* and *Galveston*—had visited the Texas coast.

During the Republican period the Houston newspapers welcomed Morgan ships and commended the line for its regular service, but by 1868 Morgan's hold on Gulf shipping was condemned as a monopoly. Railroads would eventually supersede steamers, said the Houston *Telegraph,* but until that time the Morgan line was Texas' only means of communicating with the outside world, and as such it held "an outrageous monopoly" on commerce. If the wharf company was an octopus, the Morgan line was an "anaconda coiled about the neck of the State." To illustrate his point, the editor cited an instance of unreasonable charges. The freight on a cargo from Philadelphia to New Or-

---

[11] Carroll, *History of Houston,* p. 246.

[12] The most detailed history of Morgan's career is James P. Baughman, "The Maritime and Railroad Interests of Charles Morgan, 1837–1885: A History of the 'Morgan Line'" (Ph.D. Thesis, Tulane University, 1962). The earliest reference Baughman found to the 1835 voyage to Texas is Lewis E. Stanton, *An Account of the Dedication of Morgan School Building . . .* (New York, 1873), p. 10. In an extensive search of contemporaneous sources, he found no mention of the voyage. See Baughman, "Charles Morgan," p. 16.

leans, a distance of about two thousand miles, was $255.75; but freight on the same cargo from New Orleans to Port Lavaca, Texas, a distance of about five hundred miles, was $504.45.[13]

In addition to freight charges, another factor, quarantine, figured prominently in economic rivalries on the Gulf Coast in this period. Every summer a few sporadic cases of yellow fever appeared on the Southern coast, and in some years, such as 1838 and 1867, terrible epidemics decimated the population. As the cause of the dreaded fever was unknown, its appearance struck panic among the citizens, and, as they knew nothing else to do about it, they created boards of health in the towns whose first duty was to declare a quarantine against any neighboring city suspected of harboring the disease. While this was a valid action under the circumstances, the boards were often accused of declaring a quarantine for economic rather than health reasons. Yellow fever customarily appeared during the season when produce was moving to market and when farmers had money to spend. Thus, by halting or diverting the flow of commerce, the quarantine had economic implications. Although yellow fever was certainly no jesting matter, the use of the quarantine became a standing joke in some circles. All that was needed for Galveston's board of health to declare a quarantine against New Orleans, observed one wag, was to hear that a man had arrived at the Crescent City who within twenty-one days had drunk a cup of coffee, the bean of which had come from Rio de Janeiro, where yellow fever had been epidemic the previous year. "People of Galveston regret the necessity that compels them to use these stringent measures," said he, tongue in cheek, "but the health of the state must be cared for, even though it should prevent the interior merchants from receiving goods from New Orleans, and cause them to patronize the Galveston market." By the same token, all that was needed for the Houston board to declare a quarantine against Galveston was to hear that a passenger was aboard a schooner bound for the island who ten days earlier had sat at the same table with the man who drank the germ-impregnated coffee. "The Houstonians dislike very much to be compelled to appear

[13] Houston *Daily Telegraph*, April 4, 1868.

COMMODORE MORGAN AND THE OCTOPUS OF THE GULF   87

so particular," continued the jokester, "but the germ must be kept away from the people of the interior, even if, in doing so, the people of the interior be kept away from Galveston, and therefore be compelled to buy their goods in Houston."[14]

While Galveston businessmen were organizing a railroad to bypass Houston, Houston businessmen were renewing their efforts to bypass the island. In the years immediately following the war Houstonians made both short- and long-term plans to reach the sea. For immediate relief, the city council encouraged the organization of the Houston Direct Navigation Company for the purpose of putting barges on the bayou to load and unload ocean vessels in mid-channel. Chartered on October 9, 1866, this company dominated navigation in the following decades as the old Houston Navigation Company, a casualty of the war, had dominated it during the fifties. Captain John H. Sterrett, who had pioneered the bayou trade in the late 1830's and who had been general agent of the old company, was one of the incorporators and the general agent of the new. Other incorporators were William Marsh Rice, also a veteran of the old company, Charles Septimus Longcope, R. J. Willis, Thomas M. Bagby, Joseph Robert Morris, S. L. Hohenthal, E. H. Schmidt, L. L. Allen, Alexander Sessums, and L. J. Latham. By its charter the company was given the right to improve navigation of Buffalo Bayou subject to supervision by the state engineer. The charter also specified that within six months the company would "have on the waters of Buffalo Bayou and Galveston Bay and Harbor, a sufficient number of steamers, barges and propellers, to meet the demands of commerce." The incorporators were specifically denied exclusive rights to navigate and improve the bayou.[16]

The Houston Direct Navigation Company quickly developed a thriving business, due primarily to the shortcomings of the Galveston harbor. In addition to the twelve-foot bar that blocked the way between Galveston Bay and the Gulf of Mexico, a so-called inner bar formed between Bolivar channel and Galveston harbor proper about 1866–

---

[14] Alexander E. Sweet and J. Armoy Knox, *On a Mexican Mustang Through Texas from the Gulf to the Rio Grande*, pp. 25–27.

[16] H. P. N. Gammel, comp., *The Laws of Texas, 1822–1897*, V, 1334–1337.

1867. Attributed to obstructions placed in the harbor during the Civil War, this bar shoaled to about nine and one-half feet despite the city's efforts to remove it. Because of these bars, large ocean vessels calling at Galveston adopted the practice of unloading in mid-channel and lightering their cargoes over the bars. This practice worked to the advantage of Houston, for, once the cargo was transferred to barge or small craft, it could be carried to Houston almost as easily as to Galveston, and there were advantages to carrying it to Houston if it were destined for the interior. Then the cargo was fifty miles farther on its way, it could be transferred directly to the railroad for shipment, and it avoided Galveston wharfage fees. By the spring of 1868 the Houston Direct Navigation Company had a shipping agreement with the New York steamship company of C. H. Mallory and was advertising "through bills of lading from Houston to New York and from New York to Houston without touching Galveston, at a saving of 20% to 40% to the shipper."[16]

In that year the profits of the company were so substantial that Captain Sterrett had a new luxury boat built in Louisville for the bayou. Named the *T. M. Bagby,* the boat was 175 feet in length and 50 in beam. Both it and its sister ship, the *Diana,* were described as "floating palaces" and widely acclaimed as being as fine as any on the Mississippi River. Other famous bayou steamers of the late sixties and early seventies were the *Lizzie,* named by Captain Dave Connor for his daughter, and the *Charles Fowler,* the only boat on the bayou to boast a calliope. Although the Galveston-Houston railroad took much passenger traffic from the channel, the steamboat trip between Galveston and Houston became popular with excursioners and honeymooners. Indeed, on some occasions entire wedding parties took the cruise. In the twentieth century, when life moved at a faster pace, old-timers recalled these steamboat days with nostalgia.[17] "A trip to Galveston on one [of the riverboats] was a delightful experience," E. N. Gray wrote in his memoirs. "You started late in the afternoon, had a fine supper, listened to the band; danced or played cards, had a good sleep, breakfast next morn-

[16] *Daily Telegraph,* March 28, 1868.
[17] Houston *Daily Post,* April 8, 1908.

ing, and landed at Galveston in ample time to attend to any business you might have and take the return boat late in the evening."[18]

John Shearn, president of the Houston Direct Navigation Company in 1869, estimated that in that year 11,554 passengers traveled on the bayou. Reckoning freight carried on the stream in barrels of five cubic feet to the barrel, he estimated that 546,608 barrels had been transported upstream and 268,858 down for a total of 815,466 for the year. Shearn predicted that in the following year ninety tons of railroad iron and materials would be brought up the bayou for the construction of the International and Great Northern Railroad in interior Texas.[19]

By 1872 the Houston Direct Navigation Company had four passenger steamers, eighteen barges, and three tugs on the channel and was grossing $165,000 a month. By the next year the fleet had increased to six boats, forty barges, and five tugs with a carrying capacity equal to twenty thousand bales of cotton. It was estimated in 1873 that the company carried three-fourths of the freights and products of the interior and that it saved producers and consumers of Texas one million dollars a year in Galveston handling charges. Between the years 1869 and 1881 the company carried 1,985,806 bales of cotton down the bayou.[20]

Successful though this company was, its operations were regarded as mere stopgap measures until the channel could be deepened and ocean vessels brought up the bayou to connect with the railroads. It was estimated that when this connection could be made the saving in transportation costs would amount to three million dollars annually for the people of Houston and the hinterland.

To hasten this happy day, the city council had approved on October 19, 1865, an ordinance authorizing the mayor to accept voluntary loans from citizens for the improvement of Buffalo Bayou, the loans to be

[18] E. N. Gray, *Memories of Old Houston*, n.p.

[19] "Examination of Buffalo Bayou, Tex.," *Report of the Secretary of War, Chief of Engineers' Report*, 42 Cong., 2 Sess., Vol. II (Serial 1504), pp. 533–537.

[20] *Texas Almanac*, 1872, p. 147; *Houston City Directory*, 1873; "Statement Showing the Importance of Improving the Navigation of Buffalo Bayou . . .," *House Misc. Doc.*, 47 Cong., 1 Sess., No. 32 (Serial 2046).

secured by bonds bearing 10 per cent interest and to be applied to future taxes. In the spring of 1867 the council took the further step of
commissioning Hugh Rice, a civil engineer and Houston broker, to
make a survey of the proposed channel from the foot of Main to Bolivar Roads. After Rice completed the survey in August, the councilmen ordered a thousand copies printed, and these were widely distributed and discussed. That fall the councilmen unanimously adopted a
resolution calling for public subscriptions in the amount of $75,000
for the purpose of opening Red Fish and Clopper's bars, the subscrib-
ers again to receive the city's certificates of indebtedness and the amount
to be applied to future taxes. On October 31, 1867, Mayor Alexander
McGown appointed a committee of three councilmen and six citizens
to solicit the necessary subscriptions. At the same time the council advertised for sealed bids for dredging the bars.[21]

Reconstruction politics interrupted this effort at channel improvement. Early in December, General Joseph Jones Reynolds, commander
of the military district, removed many of the city councilmen and replaced them with his own appointees, and the following August he
removed Mayor McGown and put Joseph Robert Morris in office.[22]
Thus the city became preoccupied with Reconstruction to the neglect
of the channel. Still citizens spoke hopefully of the project. "Galveston
is 'the' seaport of Texas," commented the *Telegraph* in the fall of
1868, "but we intend to bring more of the sea up here than we have
got now, and then we expect to be the very best seaport in Texas." For
Galvestonians who ridiculed this idea, the editor had a squelcher: "The
ship channel . . . has been derided by some too shortsighted to drink
in the glory of its achievement, but many of this class will live to see it
an accomplished fact, and also to see the largest class of seagoing vessels lying in perfect safety at our wharves."[23]

Among the most dedicated to the idea of a ship channel was John

---

[21] Minutes of the City Council, City of Houston, Book B, 1865–1869, pp. 276,
275, 311, 312, 329–330. Councilmen appointed to the committee were H. F. Hurd,
C. J. Grainger, and J. E. Schrimpf. The citizens were E. H. Cushing, F. W. Heitman,
James T. D. Wilson, Thomas W. House, and H. S. Fox.

[22] *Ibid.*, pp. 339, 409.

[23] *Daily Telegraph*, September 1, 1868.

Thomas Brady, who launched his own project to develop the bayou in the postwar years. As a representative of Harris County in the tenth and eleventh legislatures and chairman of the legislature's committee on internal improvements, Brady became interested in the potential of the bayou. Observing the obvious fact that navigation became more difficult above Harrisburg, he caught the vision that had inspired Andrew Briscoe and Sidney Sherman in an earlier day. Why not develop a point near Harrisburg as the terminal for ocean vessels? In a significant variation of the schemes of Briscoe and Sherman, Brady planned a railroad from a point near Bray's Bayou to connect with the roads at Houston. Then, he reasoned, vessels could transfer their cargoes to rail without navigating the difficult stretch of the waterway.[24]

Brady drew the paper city of New Houston above Harrisburg at the point he chose as the junction of rail and water transportation and organized the New Houston City Company to sell lots there. Then he organized the Texas Transportation Company to build the railroad to connect New Houston with the roads that converged at old Houston. The company was incorporated on September 25, 1866, by Thomas William House, Alexander Sessums, J. T. Tinsley, S. P. Hamblen, J. S. Sellers, C. H. Jordan, N. P. Turner, and H. N. Duble.[25] Brady was the first president and Hamblen the first secretary of the company. A contract for the construction of the road was signed in early 1867 and the road was nearing completion by that fall.[26]

As the success of the railroad depended on bringing ocean vessels to connect with it, the incorporators of the Texas Transportation Company made plans to dredge the bayou. By using Hugh Rice's survey and the figures of city engineer William H. Griffin, Hamblen estimated the cost of dredging the channel to thirteen feet at Constitution Bend as follows:[27]

[24] Memorandum, dated New York, November 7, 1867, in Brady Family Papers. I am indebted to Judge Wilmer B. Hunt, grandson of John Thomas Brady, for making this and other family documents relating to this enterprise available.

[25] Gammel, *Laws of Texas*, V, 1259–1261.

[26] Memorandum of an agreement for construction of railroad bed, January, 1867, Brady Family Papers.

[27] Hamblen to J. T. Brady, September 2, 1867, in R. M. Farrar, *The Story of Buffalo Bayou and the Houston Ship Channel*, n.p. Original in Brady Family Papers.

Cost of Dredge Boat & Flats	$125,000
Cost of 27 months at $4,000.00 per mo.	108,000
Cost of wear and tear	31,250
	$264,250
Less sale, or value of dredge boats after work is completed	93,750
	$170,500

He estimated that it would cost another $8,000 to excavate Red Fish and Clopper's bars to eight feet, and he suggested forming a ship-channel company under the charter of the Texas Transportation Company to do the work. Although Hamblen attempted to raise funds for opening the bars in the fall of 1867, his company foundered on financial difficulties and did little beyond plan improvements for the channel.

Two years later, however, private and public interests joined together for the purpose of making major improvements on the channel. The Constitutional Convention of 1869 authorized the incorporation of the Buffalo Bayou Ship Channel Company by A. S. Richardson, William J. Hutchins, T. H. Mundine, John Shearn, Thomas William House, R. O. Love, William Marsh Rice, Abram Groesbeeck, Joseph Robert Morris, H. R. Allen, and S. Harper.[28] The City of Houston subscribed to three hundred shares, $30,000, of the capital stock of this company, and lent its credit to the company by issuing City of Houston Ship Channel Bonds in the amount of $100,000, which bonds were exchanged for the company's bonds in the same amount. The city also transferred to the company the right to collect tonnage fees, a right the city had held since the 1840's but not exercised since before the Civil War. According to an agreement between the city and company, the company could impose a toll on vessels of ten cents each way per ton measurement after Red Fish and Clopper's bars had been made navigable to ships drawing six feet of water. When the navigable depth was increased to eight feet, an additional fee could be levied; and when

[28] Gammel, *Laws of Texas*, VI, 557–560.

the channel was navigable from the Gulf of Mexico to Houston for ships drawing nine feet of water, the company could impose a toll not to exceed thirty cents each way per ton measurement.[29] In return for these concessions, the company promised that within three years it would open a nine-foot channel from Bolivar Roads to the foot of Main Street.

The company planned as its major project a canal across Morgan's Point in order to avoid Clopper's Bar. By the fall of 1869 the company had acquired right of way for the canal, but work on the project was delayed by a question of whether the convention had the power to authorize the formation of the company.[30] This question was resolved on July 28, 1870, when the state formally granted a new charter. Added to the list of incorporators at that time were the names of Eugene Pillot, H. E. Perkins, Timothy H. Scanlan, James G. Tracy, Eber Worthington Cave, J. W. McDonald, and Peter Gabel. Because of the delay caused by the uncertainty of the charter, the city extended the time for the completion of the channel to January 1, 1876.[31]

Many of the stockholders in the Buffalo Bayou Ship Channel Company also held stock in the Houston Direct Navigation Company. Within a short time the same men headed both companies, and, as a result, the companies have often been confused. As those most active in the Confederate cause were impoverished and stripped of influence during the Reconstruction years, most of the men prominent in both companies were men who could take the iron-clad oath. That is, if they had been Confederates at all, they had been lukewarm ones. Some of the men were closely linked with the Reconstruction government of Houston. Joseph Robert Morris, for example, had been appointed mayor by Joseph Jones Reynolds, and later Timothy H. Scanlan was appointed mayor by the unpopular Reconstruction governor, Edmund Jackson Davis. As a group, however, these men were more interested in business than politics, and most of them classed themselves as Conservatives politically, meaning they preferred to forget the Civil War alto-

---

[29] *Ibid.*, pp. 557–560; Minutes of City Council, City of Houston, Book B, 1865–1869, pp. 465–469; Baughman, "Charles Morgan," p. 226.

[30] Deed Records of Harris County, Texas, Vol. 8, pp. 216–217.

[31] Gammel, *Laws of Texas*, VI, 557–560.

gether. The position of Eber Worthington Cave, one of the most dedicated champions of the ship channel in the late nineteenth century, was fairly typical. As secretary of state of Texas in 1861 when Sam Houston was governor, Cave had joined Houston in opposing secession and had resigned after Houston was ousted from office. But after secession was an accomplished fact, Cave lent his support to the war by organizing companies for the battle front and participating in the Battle of Galveston.

In addition to investing in the Buffalo Bayou Ship Channel Company and encouraging other channel improvements, the city promoted navigation by petitioning the national government to make Houston a port of entry. First presented in 1867, the request was granted on July 14, 1870, when Congress designated the city a port of delivery and provided that a surveyor of customs should reside there.[32]

The year 1870 marked a new era in the improvement of harbors and rivers. The Civil War having answered affirmatively the question of whether the national government should invest in internal improvements, the state legislature by a joint resolution on May 24, 1870, requested that the United States improve the bars along the Texas coast. As a result, First Lieutenant H. M. Adams of the United States Army Engineers, assisted by William D. Duke, made the first federal survey of Houston's proposed ship channel between December 16, 1870, and January 6, 1871. Lieutenant Adams reported that Buffalo Bayou was at least four feet deep and seventy feet wide as far as Houston, but he thought improving the stream from that place to Harrisburg would be an expensive task. In addition to the sharp bends and tortuous course, navigation on this stretch was threatened by soil erosion. Old residents told him that some twenty years earlier the bayou had been much deeper and that it had gradually filled up due to the clearing and cultivation of the banks. "The gullies leading into the stream are numerous, and every rain brings in large amounts of sand and soil," Adams wrote. "Where there was 15 or 20 feet of water twenty years ago, only three

---

[32] Minutes of City Council, City of Houston, Book B, 1865–1869, p. 338; Dermot H. Hardy and Ingram S. Roberts, *Historical Review of South-East Texas . . .*, I, 250.

or four feet is now found." To widen the stream in this area would increase the dangers of erosion, because the banks for five and a half miles below Houston were high, measuring generally about fifteen or twenty feet above the water but in some places rising to forty-five. If these banks were cut away, many trees and stumps would have to be removed, and the side slopes would then have to be protected to prevent soil from washing in and filling the channel. Lieutenant Adams estimated the cost of making the channel one hundred feet wide and six feet deep between Houston and Harrisburg at $319,212. The removal of stumps and trees accounted for $7,000 of this amount; the widening of the stream for $287,073; and the protection of the channel by sheeting piles for $24,139.

Adams thought the improvement of the stream between Harrisburg and Galveston would be much less expensive. There the only obstructions to navigation by vessels drawing eight feet were Red Fish and Clopper's bars, and these could be improved by dredging. He estimated that Red Fish could be made one hundred feet wide and six feet deep for $10,560.50 and Clopper's for $52,244.50.

Lieutenant Adams appreciated the advantages of the proposed ship channel. Larger vessels coming to Houston would bring competition to the single railroad connection between that place and Galveston, diminish the cost of all supplies to interior Texas, facilitate the export of produce, and aid in the construction of the railroads then being pushed forward from Houston. Because of these advantages, he supported the building of a channel one hundred feet wide and six feet deep, a size he thought adequate to serve the trade.

Lieutenant Adams had misgivings about the right of the Buffalo Bayou Ship Channel Company to collect tolls on vessels using the channel. He recommended that before public money was spent on the project, the government reimburse the company for its improvements and the company in turn relinquish its right to tolls. At the time of Adams' survey, the company had two dredges on the channel and work was in progress on the canal across Morgan's Point. "They are making the revenue more secure by cutting a channel across Morgan's Point so as to avoid Clopper's Bar," he wrote, "and at the same time oblige deep draught vessels to pass through the canal owned by the company."[33]

In response to the engineers' recommendations Congress made the first federal appropriation for work on the channel on June 10, 1872. The amount was only $10,000, far less than Houstonians hoped for, but it was looked upon as an omen for the future. This amount was applied to the improvement of Red Fish Bar. With the Buffalo Bayou Ship Channel Company cutting across Morgan's Point to avoid Clopper's Bar, Houstonians saw two major obstacles to navigation being removed, and hopes ran high that large vessels would soon be coming to the vicinity of Houston. "Houston merchants calculate when they complete the *ship* channel, so that ocean steamers can come up to Houston as easy as they can enter Galveston Bay . . . to compete with Galveston as to future growth and commercial importance," wrote one observer.[34] But even after work began on the channel, Galvestonians refused to take the project seriously and made merry over the fact that Congress had declared Houston a port. "I had heard that the Legislature made laws, but I never knew it made seaports," was a typical comment on the island.[35]

By 1873 the islanders' merriment seemed justified. The panic of that year threw the Buffalo Bayou Ship Channel Company into dire financial straits and brought work on the channel to a halt. In an effort to obtain federal aid to continue the work, Mayor Timothy H. Scanlan presented a petition to Congress on December 6, pointing out the importance of the project to the commerce of interior Texas. The citizens had expended $200,000 on the channel, he said, while the United States had contributed only $10,000.[36]

At this point another organization came into being that exerted profound influence on the commerce of Houston as well as the future of the channel. A group of cotton factors and businessmen met in the parlors of the Hutchins House in May, 1874, and organized the Hous-

[33] "Examination of Buffalo Bayou, Tex." *Report of the Secretary of War, Chief of Engineers' Report*, 42 Cong., 2 Sess., Vol. II, pp. 533–537.

[34] J. M. Morphis, *History of Texas*, p. 502.

[35] Sweet and Knox, *On a Mexican Mustang*, p. 51.

[36] Reed, *History of Texas Railroads*, p. 239.

ton Board of Trade. Designed to regulate and systematize the cotton business, the organization changed its name to the Houston Board of Trade and Cotton Exchange on June 12, 1874, and became familiarly known as the Cotton Exchange. Cotton was then and into the twentieth century the major export from Houston, and the bulkiness of the product plus the fact that much of it went to foreign markets made cheap transportation—and especially cheap water transportation—highly desirable. Thus, almost from the day of its organization the Cotton Exchange maintained a standing committee for the ship channel, and its members became foremost among the boosters of the project. Indeed, Charles Septimus Longcope, first president of the Houston Direct Navigation Company, was also first president of the Cotton Exchange.[37]

Despite the efforts of the newly founded Cotton Exchange and the pleas of Mayor Scanlan, the Panic of 1873 interrupted work on the ship channel. But what Houston's friends could not do, her bitterest commercial rival could. The Galveston interests that had already driven the inland city to seek deep water, again came to the rescue and provided the impetus that brought the first regularly scheduled line of ocean vessels to Houston. The Galveston Wharf Company had granted Commodore Charles Morgan free use of its facilities in 1867 and again in 1871, but this concession was terminated in 1874. Not only that, but the company increased its wharfage rates in that year so that in some instances the tariff for one night's storage in Galveston was within a few cents of the freight rate from New Orleans. According to tradition, company officials laughed in Morgan's face when he protested.[38]

The wharf company's action came at a time when Morgan was already annoyed with waterfront policies at Galveston. Every year since 1870 the island's board of health had declared a quarantine against Louisiana ports at the height of the business season. This meant that Morgan's ships lay in quarantine twenty-five days each time they called at Galveston, and, although he doubled his rates during the quarantine,

[37] Max H. Jacobs and H. Dick Golding, *Houston and Cotton*, p. 21.
[38] Baughman, "Charles Morgan," p. 225; Galveston *Daily News*, January 20, 1875.

the practice still cut sharply into his receipts. Morgan believed the quarantines were declared so Galveston merchants could clear their shelves of old merchandise before receiving new, and he suspected that the Mallory Line of steamers, which had direct connections between Galveston and New York, promoted the quarantines in order to beat Lousiana competitors to Texas markets. To add to his chagrin, from the summer of 1870 Galveston assessed a fee on all vessels stopping at its quarantine station, a fee Morgan believed an illegal tax on interstate commerce.[39]

Commodore Morgan was not a man to accept such conditions with resignation. A Connecticut farm boy who had fought his way to the top of a highly competitive business, his past experience made him more than a match for what Houstonians sometimes called the "miniature Venice of the Gulf." In a tilt with Commodore Cornelius Vanderbilt, he had driven Vanderbilt from the field, licking his wounds and commenting (according to legend), "I will not sue because that will take too long. I will ruin you." But Vanderbilt did not ruin Morgan; instead, as Morgan's Civil War career suggests, he thrived. During the war Morgan reaped a fortune by building boats for the federal government—but at the same time his *Frances* was running the blockade between Havana and Confederate ports. His business acumen is perhaps best illustrated by another Civil War transaction. He chartered three vessels to the Federals for a gross profit of $701,000 before selling them outright to the government for $495,000 in August, 1865. One year later he repurchased the vessels for $225,000.[40]

More pertinent to Morgan's battle with Galveston was his reaction to maritime conditions in New Orleans in the early 1870's. Dissatisfied with high pilotage rates on the lower Mississippi, high municipal taxes, and high wharfage at New Orleans, Morgan shifted the headquarters of his steamship line to Brashear City, later renamed Morgan City, and began dredging a seaway from the Atchafalaya River to the Gulf in 1871. This channel was opened on May 4, 1872. Thus, when

---

[39] Baughman, "Charles Morgan," pp. 223–224.
[40] *Ibid.*, p. 151.

the Galveston Wharf Company affronted the Commodore in 1874, he had idle dredging equipment on his hands and a wealth of experience in using it.[41]

Moreover, Morgan was looking to the future in 1874. The previous year two railway systems had linked Texas with points outside the state. Morgan correctly saw these as a potential threat to his Gulf trade, and, seeing the futility of fighting progress, he proposed to meet the competition by the simple expedient of acquiring railroads of his own to connect with his steamers. He had bought the New Orleans, Opelousas and Great Western Railroad at auction on May 25, 1869, and coordinated its operations with those of his steamship line on Brashear Bay. By the early 1870's he was planning rail connections between Houston and New Orleans and casting a speculative eye at other railroads—more especially the Houston and Texas Central—that led to Houston.[42]

Because of this combination of circumstances, Morgan was receptive when Eber Worthington Cave, then president of the hard-pressed Buffalo Bayou Ship Channel Company, approached him about taking over the company's operation and developing a waterway to Houston. On July 1, 1874, Morgan signed a contract, agreeing to construct a nine-foot channel at least 120 feet wide from Galveston Bay to the environs of Houston. In return he would receive $806,500 in the unissued capital stock of the ship-channel company. Morgan immediately put his dredges to work under the supervision of Captain John J. Atkinson.[43] "Morgan's great work here goes bravely on, and will soon be finished," wrote Norwood Stansbury, who worked on the project during the summer of 1875.

Eight dredges, two derricks, a half dozen tugs and any number of scows, barges, etc., are engaged night and day in cleaning out the channel to Buffalo Bayou. The bay at night for miles is one blaze of light, and the air is burthened with the din of machinery. Hundreds of men find employment

[41] *Ibid.*, pp. 207–209.
[42] Reed, *History of Texas Railroads*, pp. 239–240.
[43] Baughman, "Charles Morgan," p. 227.

during these hard times at liberal wages, and the cash at the end of the month is as sure as the rising of the morning sun.[44]

The prospect of Morgan vessels on the channel made the six-foot depth recommended by the army engineers in 1871 seem inadequate. Thus, Morgan joined Houstonians in asking that a depth of twelve feet be recommended. Such a depth would enable any ship that could cross the Galveston bar to proceed to Houston and throw open a large section of the country to the sea, Charles J. Whitney, Morgan's son-in-law and agent at New Orleans, pointed out. The engineers complied with this request in 1874. In that year Congress appropriated another $10,000 for the improvement of Red Fish Bar. On March 3 of the following year two additional appropriations were made. The amount of $10,200 was appropriated for the deepening of the bar, and an appropriation of $25,000 was allotted for the improvement of the channel between the mouth of the San Jacinto River and Bolivar channel.[45]

Shortly after Morgan acquired the Buffalo Bayou Ship Channel Company, he also acquired a controlling interest in the Houston Direct Navigation Company and the Texas Transportation Company. The chief asset of the latter company was its charter permitting the construction of a railroad from near Bray's Bayou to connect with trunk lines in Houston. Under this charter, Morgan selected a point opposite the junction of Buffalo and Sims bayous as the terminus of his ships and began construction of a railroad to connect that point with the railroads at Houston. A newspaper reporter who visited the site in the spring of 1876 found a flurry of activity. Several hundred men were at work on the railroad; others were building eleven hundred feet of wharves; and a dredge was scooping out a turning basin 250 feet across and 16 feet deep for Morgan vessels. Because Eber Worthington Cave had done so much to interest Morgan in the project, local resi-

[44] Norwood Stansbury, "Letters from the Texas Coast, 1875," James P. Baughman, ed., *Southwestern Historical Quarterly*, LXIX (April, 1966), 511.

[45] "Improvement of Ship Channel in Galveston Bay, Tex.," *Report of the Secretary of War, Report of the Chief of Engineers*, 48 Cong., 1 Sess., Vol. II, Part 2 (Serial 2184), pp. 1076, 1083.

dents called the terminal point Cave City, but Morgan named it Clinton after the Connecticut town where he was born.[46]

By April 22, 1876, the ship channel had been improved so that a Morgan ship drawing nine and one-half feet of water could come through Bolivar channel, through the cut at Morgan's Point and upstream to Sims Bayou. The ship, also named *Clinton* after Morgan's birthplace, carried seven hundred tons of cargo, of which five hundred were steel rails for the transfer railroad. The railroad was completed to Houston on September 12, and ten days later the *Clinton* arrived at the terminus with the first load of freight destined for the interior of Texas by the new route. A tropical storm broke over the channel just before the *Clinton* made its voyage, causing apprehension that the channel would be damaged. These apprehensions proved groundless, however, and the arrival of the *Clinton* was hailed by the Houston *Daily Telegraph* as a historic event. "An Ocean Steamer Comes Through the Ship Channel Loaded Down with Freight, Galveston's Cuttle Fish—Its Wharf Company Flanked and Checkmated!" read the banner lines. "This is a practical result beyond quibble and doubt of the success of the Ship Channel and proves its reality to the understanding of all," exulted the editor. "The merchants are free of the extortions of Galveston's *bete noir*, its hideous wharf monopoly."[47]

[46] *Daily News*, April 21, 23, 1876.
[47] *Daily Telegraph*, September 23, 1876; *Daily News*, September 12, 1876.

VI. THE DRIVE FOR DEEP WATER

⌇⌇⌇⌇⌇⌇⌇⌇⌇⌇⌇⌇⌇⌇⌇⌇⌇⌇⌇⌇⌇⌇⌇⌇⌇⌇⌇⌇⌇⌇⌇⌇⌇

T HE YEARS AFTER CHARLES MORGAN SENT HIS
first vessel to the terminal at Clinton were busy ones for the channel.
In the year 1876 after the opening of the channel in September, Morgan ships made 47 round trips to Clinton from Louisiana ports, carrying 49,349 tons of cargo. In the following year his ships made 206
round trips carrying 216,300 tons; for 1878 the figure was 226 with
237,300; and for 1880, 239 with an average tonnage of 1,200. At the
peak of its service to Houston the Morgan line had a fleet of about ten
steamships, two steamboats, thirty-two schooners, seven steam tugs,
and eighteen barges in service on the channel.[1]

Although many local people had predicted that after Morgan acquired control of the Houston Direct Navigation Company he would
reduce its operations, the company continued to carry heavy cargoes of
low-grade freight between Houston and ships outside the Galveston
Bar or in port at Galveston. Indeed, the company continued operations
on the channel for more than forty years after the Morgan line had

---

[1] "Statement Showing the Importance of Improving the Navigation of Buffalo
Bayou . . .," *House Misc. Doc.*, 47 Cong., 1 Sess., No. 32 (Serial 2046).

abandoned it. In the year 1880 the company transported 151,349 bales of cotton on the channel and in the following year 251,147 bales. George W. Kidd, secretary of the Houston Cotton Exchange, estimated the total tonnage transported by the company in 1880 and 1881 as follows:[2]

	1880	1881
Cotton	37,837 tons	63,377 tons
Lumber	30,000	55,000
Coal	10,000	15,000
Iron rails	60,000	30,000
Miscellaneous	41,000	24,500
Total	178,837	187,877

The increase in traffic on the channel was accompanied by corresponding improvements in facilities and methods of handling at Houston. With the encouragement of the Houston Cotton Exchange, several new cotton compresses were organized. Morgan established a compress at Clinton; the Bayou Warehouse & Compress Company built a large plant; and the Houston Cotton Compress Company, founded shortly before the Civil War, improved its facilities. By the early 1880's five large compresses were in operation in the area, all of them conveniently located between the bayou and railroad connections so that cotton could be received from the interior, compressed, sent down a chute to barges on the bayou and thence to ocean vessels.

After railroads to the north connected Houston with grain-producing areas, some enterprising Houstonians saw the potential of their town as a grain market. Thus, in 1877 the Houston grain elevator, with a capacity of 150,000 bushels, was built. The manner in which this facility handled grain aroused wide-spread admiration. "While a railroad track connecting with the entire railroad net of Texas enters the elevator on one side, discharging right into the receiving vats, there are two chutes from the third story conducting grain to the barges on the bayou close by, thus obviating all drayage and incidental expenses," said the *Hous-*

[2] *Ibid.*

ton City Directory of 1877. "The same barges carry the grain along side the deep-sea going vessels, which cannot enter the port proper of Galveston, saving also in this instance the additional expense of lighterage, wharfage, drayage, etc., that Galveston forwarding agents charge."[3]

In the first busy years of the Morgan era the channel seemed inadequate for the traffic it carried, and the federal government took an increased interest in it. Although the first federal survey had recognized the potential of the channel and a later survey recommended deepening it to twelve feet, Congress had appropriated little money for the project before Morgan began work, and government engineers had not determined the route across Galveston Bay. In the summer of 1876 Congress asked the engineers to recommend a route, and the following spring in response to this request J. A. Hayward surveyed the upper bay and H. C. Ripley the lower. The routing of the channel aroused considerable controversy. Some observers thought it should be taken through Morgan's Canal, while others, leary of the tolls collected there, thought it should go by way of San Jacinto Bay and Clopper's Bar. Opinion also varied about the route from Red Fish Bar to the Gulf. Some advocated taking it west of Pelican Island and into Galveston Channel, while others advocated a route straight to Bolivar Roads. Many Galvestonians opposed the Bolivar route, expressing fears that such a cut would endanger the permanence of Galveston Channel. After the survey of 1877 Hayward recommended that the route in the upper bay go through Morgan's Canal. He expressed misgivings about this route because of the tolls, but found that it was more economical by $200,000 than the one through Clopper's Bar. Ripley recommended that the channel across the lower bay go straight from Red Fish to Bolivar Roads. Rather than endanger the Galveston Channel, he believed, the cut would improve it by helping prevent the inner bar.[4]

After the route was determined, Congress made more generous ap-

[3] Dermot H. Hardy and Ingham S. Roberts, *Historical Review of South-East Texas . . .*, I, 302–304.

[4] "Survey for a Ship Channel through Galveston Bay, Tex.," *Report of the War Department, Report of the Chief of Engineers*, 45 Cong., 2 Sess., Vol. II, Part 1 (Serial 1795), p. 458.

propriations than formerly for the channel. In 1876, $75,000 was al-
lotted; in 1878, $80,000; in 1880, $50,000; in 1881, $50,000; and in
1882, $94,500.[5]

But even while these sums were being expended, circumstances were
bringing the Morgan interlude on the channel to an end. Charles Morgan had originally conceived of his Clinton operation as a temporary
link between his railroads in Louisiana and rail connections in Texas.
As soon as a railroad was completed between the two points, he intended reducing the channel operation. Charles Morgan died in 1878,
but his heirs held to his long-range policy, and, after the opening of
the Morgan railroad between Houston and New Orleans in 1880, traffic was diverted from the channel to that route. This change was noted
by Major S. M. Mansfield of the army engineers when he reported on
the ship-channel project in 1883. "Conditions have changed materially
since 1876 when this project was adopted," he wrote. "The completion
of the railroad through from Houston to New Orleans and changes in
the railroad system of Texas are about to result in the abandonment of
Clinton as a transfer point."[6] As Major Mansfield had predicted, Morgan steamers discontinued regular sailings from Clinton to Louisiana in
the early summer of 1883, and in August of that year Captain Charles
Fowler, Morgan's agent in Galveston, announced that thenceforth he
would send all traffic from the island by rail and that Morgan steamships formerly in the trade would be deployed to other Texas ports.[7]

In addition to the new rail connections, another factor contributed
to the decline of the channel's traffic in the mid-eighties. When the
twelve-foot project for the Galveston Bay Ship Channel had been
adopted in 1876, Houstonians had anticipated that upon its completion
their city would be on par with Galveston insofar as ocean transportation was concerned. That is, any vessel that could cross the outer bar
at Galveston could proceed to Houston. But by 1880 this too had
changed. The rapid development of the Western states after the Civil

<hr />

[5] "Improvement of Ship Channel in Galveston Bay, Tex.," *Report of the Secretary
of War, Report of the Chief of Engineers,* 48 Cong., 1 Sess., Vol. II, Part 2 (Serial
2184), p. 1081.

[6] *Ibid.,* p. 1080.

[7] Houston *Daily Post,* August 10, 16, 1883.

War brought demands by them for cheaper transportation and an easier access to the sea. In response to these demands, army engineers selected Galveston as the Gulf port for the American West in 1880 and began work on the bar. By 1883 Major Mansfield reported that the depth of water on the bar had been increased by an average of two feet or more and ships that had previously lightered their cargoes over the bar had begun loading in the harbor.[8]

Some Galvestonians disputed Major Mansfield's figures, and, impatient at the slow progress made on the bar, organized a deep-water committee on the island in 1883. This committee launched the deep-water movement that united the Trans-Mississippi West in a demand for better water transportation. Committees were formed in various states, and conventions were held throughout the 1880's, the first being held at Fort Worth and others at Denver, Topeka, and other cities. In each of these conventions the Westerners petitioned the government to increase its efforts on the Galveston harbor. Work at Galveston proceeded slowly, but each additional inch of water over the outer bar made the twelve-foot channel to Houston more obsolete. Nevertheless, farsighted Houstonians joined wholeheartedly in the deep-water movement, seeing with enlightened selfishness that the bar at Galveston was the first obstacle to be removed before their town would see the largest ocean vessels.[9]

In addition to calling attention to the new railroads and Galveston harbor improvements, Major Mansfield administered yet another blow to Houstonians' hopes for a ship channel in his report of 1883. He noted that the channel already dredged was filling badly and that it could be maintained only by expensive revetments or continual dredging. Moreover, he reported, no use had ever been made of the cut through the lower bay; indeed, Morgan steamers were the only deep-draft vessels plying the route and they did not use the cut because it was not sufficiently marked. Besides, they were limited in size by the depth of water at their other ports of call, so the bay furnished sufficient water for them in its natural state. Major Mansfield concluded

[8] "Improvement of Ship Channel," *Report of the Secretary of War*, 48 Cong., 1 Sess., Vol. II, Part 2 (Serial 2184), p. 1059.

[9] Hardy and Roberts, *South-East Texas*, I, 318.

that the channel was not worth the necessary expenditures: "The only interest to be subserved is the local commerce between Houston and Galveston," he wrote, "and there is water enough in our judgement (8.9 feet) to accommodate this commerce as at present served by the Houston Direct Navigation Company tugs and barges."[10] This report resulted in a suspension of government funds for the ship channel. No appropriations were made for any river or harbor project in 1883. Not until 1888 was another appropriation made for the Galveston Bay Ship Channel.

Those most concerned about the channel were well aware of the detrimental effect of railroads and deep water at Galveston. As Morgan interests began the reduction of operations at Clinton, the Houston Cotton Exchange led a movement to continue federal improvements. In 1880 a statement to Congress prepared by George W. Kidd stressed the importance of Houston as a distribution point. At that time nine railroads converged on the city. These had more than 2,200 miles of rail in operation and 1,800 more under construction. Moreover, with the completion of the transcontinental line under construction by Collis P. Huntington, Houston would be the first tidewater point on that line between San Francisco and the Atlantic. "Buffalo Bayou, notwithstanding the narrow crooks and sharp bends as it approaches Houston, transports by far more commerce than any other tide-water from the coast of Texas . . .," concluded Kidd. "This bayou even in its present unimproved condition is very important to the commerce of the country and the benefits will be much greater when widened and straightened and with a depth of twelve feet from Clinton to Houston."[11]

S. A. McAshan, president of the Houston Cotton Exchange, prepared a similar statement to be presented to Congress in 1883, but the efforts of Houstonians to save the ship channel at this time were unsuccessful. Because of their efforts, however, the Congress adopted a Buffalo Bayou project separate from the ship-channel project in 1881. This one provided for the improvement of the bayou between Clinton

---

[10] "Improvement of Ship Channel," *Report of the Secretary of War*, 48 Cong., 1 Sess., Vol. II, Part 2 (Serial 2184), pp. 1085–1086, 1080, 1077.

[11] "Statement Showing the Importance of Improving the Navigation of Buffalo Bayou," *House Misc. Doc.*, 47 Cong., 1 Sess., No. 32 (Serial 2046).

and Houston, and appropriations were made for it even after they were
discontinued on the ship-channel project. Work continued on this
stretch of the bayou throughout the 1880's, but the adverse report of
Major Mansfield in 1883 marked the end of the glamorous days of
riverboats on the Houston Ship Channel. As the decade wore on, traffic was limited more and more to low-grade freight while the passenger
boats passed into oblivion.

Even when the Morgan era was at its peak, local interests had not
been satisfied with operations on the channel. By long tradition, Houstonians considered the foot of Main Street as the proper terminal of the
Houston Ship Channel. Thus, while Charles Morgan thought of Clinton as a temporary terminal until he could complete railroad connections between Louisiana and Texas, Houstonians thought of it as temporary until the channel could be extended to Main Street. Even the
traffic at Clinton did not meet the high expectations of local interests.
Although one vessel had sailed directly from Clinton to Philadelphia
in 1878, the channel did not accommodate the larger class of ships.
Morgan vessels plying the trade were designed for the Louisiana-Texas
coast, and, customarily, cargo between Houston and the Atlantic Coast
or other distant points was transshipped at Louisiana ports.

In addition to these disappointments, the policies of Morgan and his
heirs aroused resentment. Charles Morgan was hailed as a hero in
Houston at the time he was outflanking the Galveston Wharf Company to develop the ship channel, but his hold over local transportation
soon created anxiety in Houston. His interests in the Bayou trade—the
Morgan Line, Houston Direct Navigation Company, Buffalo Bayou
Ship Channel Company, and Texas Transportation Company—gave
him an iron hold on the channel. In addition, he acquired a controlling
interest in the Houston and Texas Central Railroad in 1877, and in
the 1880's his heirs consolidated their transportation empire with that
of Collis P. Huntington in the Southern Pacific Company.

A particularly thorny subject along the channel was the right of
Morgan interests to charge a fee for passage through Morgan's Canal.
Even when this right was still in the hands of local men in 1870, Lieu-
tenant Adams had recommended that the government acquire it before

beginning work on the channel. This was not done then, and, as the government expended more and more money on the project, the subject became progressively more sensitive. John H. Reagan, senator from Texas and late Postmaster General of the Confederacy, voted against a channel appropriation in 1876 because he thought it abetted Morgan's monopoly. Morgan was enjoying his moment as a local hero at that time, and the vote stirred up a hornet's nest of criticism of Reagan in Houston. The Senator was accused of being partial to the Galveston Wharf Company and antagonistic to the ship channel. But within a few short months Houstonians were willing to accept Reagan's explanation that he was most emphatically *not* opposed to the ship channel. Rather he was opposed to a monopoly of it by a private corporation.[12] As Morgan had spent a large sum on the canal, he stood on his right to collect tolls there, but since deep-draft vessels could not reach his canal without first passing through Red Fish Bar, where government money had made the improvements, citizens argued that public money had been spent to assure Morgan of his tolls. These tolls became anathema to local interests and were widely condemned as exorbitant. The Galveston *Daily News,* for example, reported a few months after the opening of the channel that the schooner *George Sealy* paid a total of $105.26 to pass in and out of Morgan's Canal, this in addition to towing fees.[13] As if to add insult to injury, a heavy chain was stretched across the canal to assure that no vessel passed without paying. This chain soon became infamous as a symbol of Morgan's hold on the channel.

In response to local agitation, Morgan interests proposed turning over their improvements to the United States government in the late seventies. Congress accepted this proposal on March 3, 1879, but a formal contract was not drawn until January 22, 1881, and then it was agreed that the improvements would not be transferred until the government had completed its channel to Morgan's Cut. Because the suspension of appropriations for the ship-channel project delayed work in the mid-1880's, the channel was not completed to connect with the

[12] Reagan to A. C. Gray, December 1, 1877, Vandale Collection; Houston *Daily Telegraph,* May 2, 1876; Houston *Daily Post,* April 26, 1908.

[13] Galveston *Daily News,* February 16, 1877.

cut until July, 1889. Thus, throughout the eighties the chain continued
to block the channel. Even with the channel completed, the transfer
of the improvements was delayed. The Rivers and Harbors Act of September 19, 1890, provided for a commission of army engineers to estimate the value of Morgan's improvements. The commission reported
on December 4 of that year, but by the spring of 1892 the transfer
still had not been completed nor the chain removed. At that time a
strong-minded Scotsman, Andrew Dow, who had tugs and barges on
the channel, announced his intention to cut the chain. Citizens supported him by holding an indignation meeting, and someone wired John
Henry Kirby, a local lumberman who was then in the East on business.
Kirby went to Washington to consult with Representative Charles
Stewart and the War Department with the result that the transfer was
at last completed, and the United States paid $92,316.85 for Morgan's
Canal and improvements.[14] "Ship Channel matter settled. War Department will at once have chain removed and channel kept free," Representative Stewart wired the Houston *Daily Post* on May 2. The *Post*
greeted the news with the lines: "Down It Comes, That Old Rusty
Chain Now Stretched Across Buffalo Bayou." The news story hailed
the event as a milestone, and at the same time called attention to a problem that plagued the bayou long before and long after it knew Morgan's chain: "This would seem to settle the matter definitely, and now
the bounding bayou is free. That is, it is free from the famous chain,
but not yet free from the shortsighted people of Houston who are in
the habit of dumping into it dirt, trash and various kinds of matter calculated to fill up the stream."[15]

By the time Morgan's chain came down, the great riverboat days of
the bayou were a thing of the past. The captains who had pioneered
the trade had died or grown old; the famous *T. M. Bagby* had been
sold to either the Red River or Alabama River trade (no one could remember exactly which); and other once-proud steamboats had been
converted into barges. Houstonians were already remembering those

[14] Harris County Deed Records, Vol. 58, p. 630; Thomas H. Ball, *The Port of
Houston: How It Came to Pass*, p. 3.

[15] *Daily Post*, May 3, 4, 1892.

bygone days on the bayou with nostalgia, but the vast majority of them thought of the stream only as an avenue for freight barges.[16]

Still a dedicated minority clung to the idea of ocean vessels on the channel. John Thomas Brady, who had dreamed of a railroad from the head of navigation to Houston in the sixties, who had chartered the Texas Transportation Company for the purpose of building such a road, and who had seen Charles Morgan make a success of both the dream and the company, still believed his dream valid. Morgan had built the Texas Transportation Company's railroad along the north side of the bayou. Brady owned a large tract on the south side near Harrisburg and on April 2, 1889, he chartered the Houston Belt and Magnolia Park Railway Company for the purpose of building a southside road from between Bray's Bayou and Long Reach to Houston. The railroad, about fifteen miles long, was to connect with all railroads in the city and to be "located so that it or any part of it may be used as a belt or connecting line." Brady constructed this road, but again his timing was faulty. Excursioners used the road to go to Magnolia Amusement Park, which Brady had built on his Harrisburg property, but no ocean liners brought cargo to be transported to Houston. This company like the earlier one ran into financial problems, but Brady did not live to see them. In June, 1890, while inspecting the channel he suffered a stroke from which he soon died. His southside railroad went into the hands of receivers on November 3, 1891, and sold at public auction for $9,100 in 1896. Brady lost heavily on both his ventures at building railroads to connect bayou ships with Houston, but both were destined for ultimate success. The Texas Transportation Company became a part of the Southern Pacific system and the Houston Belt and Magnolia Park Railway a part of the Missouri Pacific.[17]

Another man who clung to the idea of a ship channel during the eighties was Eber Worthington Cave. After interesting Charles Mor-

---

[16] Houston *Chronicle*, October 14, 1903; Houston *Post*, April 8, 1908; S. O. Young, *True Stories of Old Houston and Houstonians*, pp. 92–93; E. N. Gray, *Memories of Old Houston*, n.p.

[17] S. G. Reed, *A History of Texas Railroads*, p. 324; Walter P. Webb and others, eds., *Handbook of Texas*, I, 204–205.

gan in the channel, Cave began a long association with Morgan's transportation empire, serving for about a quarter of a century as treasurer
of the Houston and Texas Central Railroad. Even after Morgan's abandonment of the channel, Cave continued to be one of its most ardent
and eloquent advocates. Jesse A. Ziegler recalled in his old age how he
had sat at Cave's feet as a boy and listened enraptured to Cave's "fairy
tales" of the bayou. "I thought he was rubbing 'Aladdin's lamp' too
strongly, but I enjoyed them all the more," Ziegler wrote in his memoirs. "He was a man of untiring energy and a most forceful speaker.
He could present a subject as clearly and convincingly as any man I
ever knew."[18]

Helping Cave collect data in support of the channel throughout the
eighties was George W. Kidd, pioneer secretary of the Houston Cotton
Exchange. "They often compiled data and statistics, searching every
nook and corner for information which they sent to Washington," recalled Ziegler. "All information was sent to Charles Stewart, congressman for a decade in Washington, and it was through his influence that
the project was finally recognized." Others whom Ziegler remembered
as supporting the channel during its period of eclipse were William D.
Cleveland and H. W. Garrow, both active in the Cotton Exchange;
Captain R. B. Talfor, resident assistant engineer of the United States
station at Galveston; and Joseph Chappell Hutcheson, who followed
Stewart to the House of Representatives.[19]

The devotion of these and other men to their city and cause became
a matter of jest to some visitors. "After you have listened to the talk of
one of these pioneer veterans for some time," wrote one humorist, "you
begin to feel that the creation of the world, the arrangement of the
solar system, and all subsequent events, including the discovery of
America, were provisions of an all-wise Providence, arranged with a
direct view to the advancement of the commercial interests of Houston."[20]

[18] Jesse A. Ziegler, *Wave of the Gulf*, p. 313.
[19] *Ibid.*, p. 313.
[20] Alexander E. Sweet and J. Armoy Knox, *On a Mexican Mustang Through Texas from the Gulf to the Rio Grande*, p. 49.

That same humorist made a great show of looking for the Port of Houston. "Do you let strangers see it every day, or only on Sundays, or how? Does it keep open all the season?" he asked. "I yearned to see that seaport, even if I had to employ a detective to hunt it up. I knew it was in Houston concealed somewhere, but I was afraid it would be removed to a place of safety before I could see it." When at last he found it, he gave a description well calculated to amuse Galvestonians:

The Houston seaport is of a very inconvenient size;—not quite narrow enough to jump over, and a little too deep to wade through without taking off your shoes. When it rains, the seaport rises up twenty or thirty feet, and the people living on the beach, as it were, swear their immortal souls away on account of their harbor facilities. The Houston seaport was so low when I saw it, that there was some talk of selling the bridges to buy water to put in it.[21]

On one occasion Houstonians joined with Galvestonians in laughter about their city's pretensions as a port. Sampson Heidenheimer, a Galveston merchant, shipped six barge loads of salt to Houston. These were caught in a cloudburst that dissolved the salt into the bayou. "Houston at last has a salt water port," chortled the Galveston *News*. "God Almighty furnished the water; Heidenheimer furnished the salt."[22]

Houstonians too had their fun at Galveston's expense during the 1880's. Although the favorite topic of conversation on the island was the condition of the outer bar and the theme song of islanders was "when we get deep water," the practical results obtained during the decade were disappointing. "When it comes to eating up money without furnishing any practical equivalent, the bar will rival a four-horse daily paper in a one-horse town," commented one journalist. According to a story told him by a Houston man, local journalists were the only persons or agencies that had succeeded in deepening the Galveston bar: "When a reporter goes out with some interested parties to inspect

[21] *Ibid.*, p. 51.
[22] Harris County Houston Ship Channel Navigation District, *The Dramatic History of the Port of Houston*, Episode 6, n.p.

the bar, contractors furnish champagne. If he enjoys himself very much, the depth of water on the bar has been known to increase to sixteen feet; but this is only on extraordinary occasions."[23]

But in the early nineties deep water at Galveston ceased to be a jesting matter in Houston. In response to the persistent agitation on the part of Westerners, Congress authorized the spending of $6,200,000 for the completion of the Galveston jetties in 1890. By 1893 the bar had fourteen feet of water; by 1895, almost eighteen; and by 1896, when the jetties were completed, twenty-five feet, a depth that opened Galveston as a deep-water port. This was of great import to the economy of the Trans-Mississippi West, but it had dire implications for the profitable barging operations on Buffalo Bayou. So long as deep-draft ships had to anchor outside the Galveston bar to load and unload, barges could carry cargo to Houston almost as easily as to Galveston; but if ocean vessels could load and unload directly at the wharves at Galveston, the barges would become obsolete. Moreover, deep water at Galveston threatened Houston's position as a railroad center. As the success of the jetties seemed imminent, various roads at Houston began considering spurs to Galveston, and shortly after the opening of the deep-water port, Southern Pacific acquired two hundred acres on the island waterfront and made plans for operations there.

Deep water at Galveston brought Houston to a major crisis in its economic development. Houstonians could either sit still and watch many of their commercial advantages disappear, or they could build a channel that would again put their town on par with Galveston. The decision was not a hard one. One writer put it simply, "As the city could not be moved to the 25-foot channel recently completed, it was necessary to have that channel extended to the city."[24] With this purpose in mind, Houstonians launched a deep-water movement of their own in the late 1890's.

The movement began quietly. Just before retiring from the House of Representatives in 1896, Joseph C. Hutcheson introduced a bill requesting a survey for a twenty-five-foot channel to Houston. The bill

[23] Sweet and Knox, *On a Mexican Mustang*, p. 34.
[24] Hardy and Roberts, *South-East Texas*, I, p. 269.

passed the House, and Robert Quarles Mills, senator from Texas, took
it through the Senate. Before Congress adjourned Hutcheson arranged
for members of the Rivers and Harbors Committee to visit Houston
and inspect Buffalo Bayou the following winter.

All this was done with so little fanfare that Thomas Henry Ball, a
thirty-seven-year-old attorney from the pine-covered hills of Hunts-
ville, knew nothing about it when he first considered running for the
office Hutcheson was giving up. When Ball drew his tentative platform, it contained no mention of the waterway. R. M. Johnston, man-
aging editor of the Houston *Daily Post,* called attention to this omis-
sion, but, as Ball knew nothing of the project, he was reluctant to mention it, feeling that it compared in importance to a post office in Hunts-
ville or Navasota. At Johnston's insistence, Ball discussed the matter
with a group of Houstonians: Captain Hutcheson, William D. Cleveland, Horace Baldwin Rice, William M. Read, H. W. Garrow, Charles
H. Milby, Thomas W. House, Jr., Ed Sewall, and Eber Worthington
Cave. After talking to these men, Ball changed his mind. "My confer-
ences with them awakened me to the great possibilities of such a waterway," he wrote later. Thus began Tom Ball's association with the Port
of Houston, an association that would endure for almost forty years.[25]

Ball was elected to the House of Representatives in the fall of 1896
and joined with Houstonians in awaiting the visit of the Rivers and
Harbors Committee, a visit regarded as a major event in the campaign
for deep water. "The coming of this committee presents to Houston
the finest opportunity she has ever had to improve her advantages,"
commented the *Daily Post.*[26]

But as the great day approached, those planning the congressmen's
visit grew anxious and then glum. The year 1896 had been one of
unusual drought. Spring rains had been scanty and fall ones had failed
to materialize. By the end of the year Buffalo Bayou had dwindled to
a trickle. When about two weeks before the scheduled visit the rains
still had not come, the local deep-water committee held a gloomy conference and then sent a telegram to Washington asking that the com-

[25] Ball, *Port of Houston,* pp. 5–6.
[26] *Daily Post,* January 26, 1897.

mittee cancel its visit.[27] To the consternation of the Houstonians, word came back that the telegram had arrived too late: The congressmen were already on their way.

But the congressmen proceeded slowly across the country, inspecting other rivers and harbors on the way, and, while they were en route, Houstonians were treated to what they could only regard as a special blessing of Providence on their deep-water dreams. A blue norther swept over Texas, bringing general rains to the state and a Texas gully-washer to the Buffalo Bayou watershed. The bayou rose in its banks and then overflowed. By the time the visitors arrived, the sun had not shone in ten days. "This little bayou of ours that was usually only a few feet deep in the city was, at that time by the grace of God, five feet above every bank from here to Galveston!" Joseph C. Hutcheson recalled on his eightieth birthday.[28]

With profuse—if insincere—apologies for the weather, Houstonians took their guests on a tour of the bayou. But even with the bayou in a state of flood, some knowing Texans observed with amusement how careful the Houstonians were to present the stream in its best light. Tom Ball, for example, noted that the tour did not begin at the foot of Main Street, but that the reception committee "spared the time" for the visitors to go to Charles H. Milby's home at Harrisburg, there to begin their cruise. "I noticed too that our courteous entertainers did not begin to call attention to Buffalo Bayou until we reached the better stretches thereof," commented Ball.[29]

Another local citizen, Jesse A. Ziegler, later recalled the curious behavior of Eber W. Cave when soundings were being made of the bayou. Dissatisfied with the procedure, Cave grasped the lead line and gave it a whirl. Then he exclaimed, "Six fathoms, eight fathoms, ten fathoms, by the Mark Twain." But he took good care when gathering

[27] The local committee was made up of M. W. Garrow, W. M. Read, W. D. Cleveland, R. D. Gribble, W. A. Childress, E. W. Cave, and Charles H. Milby.

[28] I am indebted to Mrs. Lawrence S. Bosworth, daughter of Captain Hutcheson, for some of the details of this story. See also, Palmer Hutcheson, "Earliest Efforts to Secure 25-Foot Channel Described," *Houston* (November, 1937), pp. 3–4; *Daily Post*, February 2, 1897; Ziegler, *Wave of the Gulf*, p. 314.

[29] Ball, *Port of Houston*, p. 7.

up the slack line that the congressmen did not see the markings on the line.[30]

The Houstonians' efforts were not in vain. W. B. Hooker, chairman of the congressional committee, expressed pleased surprise at the size of the stream. "I had thought it was a small insignificant stream that was dry half the time and that it had to be navigated by locks and dams," he said. Other congressmen were similarly impressed. "That bayou, which I thought was more of a good-sized river than anything else, will some day be the making of this place," said Albert S. Berry of Kentucky, while D. S. Alexander of New York commented: "It is a remarkable stream and should be improved. A magnificent stream!"[31]

After stopping at Clinton to sample Captain John J. Atkinson's famous fish chowder and at the San Jacinto Battleground to relive the glories of 1836, the congressional party returned to Houston, where Captain and Mrs. Hutcheson had planned a reception. As the exact date of the congressmen's arrival had been uncertain until they actually arrived, the reception was of necessity an impromptu affair, but it was long remembered as one of the most festive and significant social occasions in the city's history. Neighbors and friends flocked to the Hutchesons' spacious home at 1417 McKinney to help Mrs. Hutcheson with the decorations and refreshments. "The front steps and gallery had been lined with palms and carpeted, and within the decorations were very elaborate," reported the *Daily Post*. "The hall was itself a bower of green, palms, ferns and smilax being used wherever space permitted. All the windows were darkened and soft gas light and hidden music greeted the visitor with a sense of the unusual at the first entrance."[32] From 4:30 in the afternoon until 8:00 throngs of callers filled the house and surrounding walks. Six hundred invitations had been issued, and, commented the *Daily Post*, "most of them were accepted." Without fully understanding all that the Houstonians were celebrating, the visiting congressmen caught the spirit of the occasion. Many afterward recalled the reception as an example of "typical Southern hospitality,"

[30] Ziegler, *Wave of the Gulf*, p. 314.
[31] *Daily Post*, February 2, 1897.
[32] *Ibid*.

and told Tom Ball in Washington that it was the least formal and the most gracious of any gathering they had ever attended. "I will say that this non-political affair did not hurt us when the long struggle for adoption of our deep-water project was begun," said Ball.[33]

After the Rivers and Harbors Committee acted favorably on the channel project, a board of engineers met in Houston in late July, 1897, to consider it. Chairman of the board was Colonel Henry Martyn Robert, who had already won renown in another field by writing *Pocket Manual and Rules of Order,* a work more familiarly known as *Robert's Rules of Order.* Other officers on the board were Major Alexander Macomb Miller and Captain George M. Derby. After inspecting the channel and going over recent surveys, the board divided the channel into three divisions according to the difficulties of dredging. The first division stretched across Galveston Bay from Bolivar Roads to Morgan's Canal; the second, from Morgan's Canal to Harrisburg; and the third, from Harrisburg to the foot of Main Street at White Oak Bayou. The engineers thought that dredging the twenty-five and one-half miles across Galveston Bay would be a relatively simple and inexpensive process because the spoil could be disposed of with little trouble. They estimated that the dredging would cost about five cents a cubic yard and that a channel twenty-five feet deep and one hundred feet wide could be dredged for $1,100,000. For the second division, from Morgan's Canal to Harrisburg, they estimated that the dredging would cost about fifteen cents per cubic yard, a total of $900,000, because of the increased difficulty in disposing of the spoil. For the third division, from Harrisburg to the foot of Main, the cost was even higher per unit because of the extra difficulty in disposing of the spoil and because the narrow, tortuous channel required the removal of at least one bend and the straightening and widening of others. Moreover, in the city limits the stream was constantly shoaling because it received sewage and surface drainage. The engineers estimated the cost of dredging this division at twenty cents per cubic yard for a total cost of $1,700,000. They estimated that the initial overall cost of the channel

[33] Ball, *Port of Houston,* p. 8.

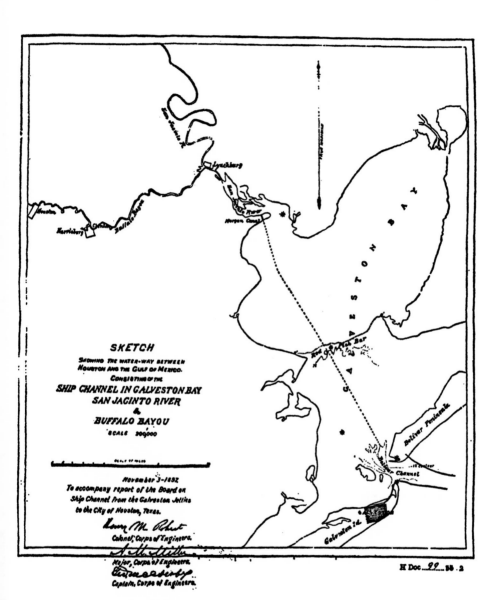

Sketch accompanying U.S. Army Corps of Engineers Report.

would be $4,000,000 and that the annual maintenance would amount to $100,000.

While the engineers were in Houston, Mayor Horace Baldwin Rice, H. W. Garrow, president of the Houston Cotton Exchange, and R. D. Gribble, president of the Houston Business League, presented statistics supporting the economic value of the channel, not only to the city but to the surrounding area and to the Western states. According to figures presented at this time, Buffalo Bayou between January 1, 1869, and July 8, 1897, had carried 5,986,437 bales of cotton, the biggest year being 1894–1895, when 510,878 bales were transported. Figures presented later showed that for the year ending June 30, 1898, Buffalo Bayou had carried 514,024 bales. In the same period there were fourteen steam vessels, thirty-five barges, and sixty-three sailing vessels on the stream. These made a total of 3,525 trips during the year, carrying a total tonnage of 389,574. Other than cotton and cotton products, coal, lumber, building materials, and general merchandise made up the bulk of the cargo transported.[34]

After listening to Houstonians present the advantages of the channel and inspecting it for themselves, the engineers recommended the adoption of the project, providing right of way and land for spoil be furnished the United States free of charge and the city adopt some method of sewage disposal not injurious to the stream. As it later developed, however, the engineers had other reservations about the channel, reservations that delayed congressional appropriations and made Tom Ball's task in Washington more difficult.

---

[34] "Examination and Survey for a Water Route from the Jetties at Galveston, Texas, through and up Buffalo Bayou to Houston," *Annual Report of the War Department, Report of the Chief of Engineers,* 55 Cong., 3 Sess., Vol. II, Part 2, pp. 1515–1526.

VII. DEEP-WATER JUBILEE

~~~~~~

Tom Ball entered the Fifty-fifth Congress with the burden of Houston's deep-water dreams on his shoulders. He was fully aware, on the one hand, of what his constituents expected of him, and, on the other, of his impotence as a freshman Democratic congressman in a period of Republican ascendancy. Houstonians felt that Ball could best serve them on the Rivers and Harbors Committee and frankly informed him of this fact. "Captain Hutcheson stoutly maintained that we could not land the Houston project unless I obtained such a place," Ball recalled in his memoirs.

But such choice assignments were usually reserved for senior congressmen, and Ball took a dim view of his chances. Indeed, he was so pessimistic that when Representative Samuel Bronson Cooper, chairman of the Texas delegation, called a caucus to consider committee assignments, Ball refused to attend. Cooper represented a district that included Sabine Pass and Port Arthur, both places with deep-water aspirations, and, if Texas were given a place on the Rivers and Harbors Committee, he, as Ball's senior, stood to receive it. Knowing this, Ball absented himself from the meeting, feeling that by doing so he could better explain his failure to the home folks. "They would not be satis-

fied to know that I had attended a caucus to compose rival claims, with
the result of having one of my Texas colleagues favored because of
seniority or merit," he wrote.[1] Ball's chances of success were made even
more remote by the fact that the Republicans had increased their majority in Congress in the recent elections and had decided to add one
Republican to each major committee and drop one Democrat.

Fortunately for Ball, the Republicans also decided that the speaker
of the House, Thomas B. Reed, would appoint no committee except
the Ways and Means until after a tariff bill, the famous Dingley Tariff,
had passed. This delay gave Ball and his friends time to maneuver.
Within the Texas delegation his way was cleared by the elevation of
his rival Cooper to the Ways and Means Committee. As Houston's
drive for deep water cut across party lines, influential local Republicans
—among them Charles Dillingham, H. F. MacGregor, R. B. Morris,
and Waller T. Burns—were called to his aid. Ball also took advantage
of a break in Republican ranks caused by Speaker Reed's having been
President William McKinley's opponent for the nomination. Three
Texans who had been ardent Reed supporters were induced to write
letters for Ball. These were George W. Burkett, a Republican candi-
date for governor; Wilbur F. Crawford, Reed's Texas campaign manager; and Robert Bradley Hawley, newly elected representative from
Galveston. Thus reinforced, Ball approached the Speaker about securing the coveted appointment.

"What committeeship have you in mind?" asked Reed.

"The Rivers and Harbors Committee," replied Ball.

"A pretty big committee for a young man in his first term. What
other committees have you in mind?"

"None. If you cannot please me . . . then place me where you can
and you will be pleased."

Reed, a man famous alike for his enormous size and his blunt manner, talked briefly about the friends who had written indorsements of
Ball, and then asked, "Have you any particular steal in view for Texas?"

"No, but I represent a state that has four hundred miles of Gulf

[1] Thomas H. Ball, *The Port of Houston: How It Came to Pass*, p. 8.

coast and only one great harbor," replied Ball. "My district wants a channel that would cost four million dollars." That concluded the interview, and Ball departed feeling no nearer his goal than when he arrived in Washington.

At the night session that closed the first session of the Fifty-fifth Congress, Reed announced his committee assignments. Ball, scarcely daring to hope, listened as the clerk read the list. Upon reaching the Rivers and Harbors Committee, the clerk read first the names of ten Republicans, then the names of six Democrats—and then a seventh. "I caught my breath when he read out Thomas H. Ball of Texas," Ball said. Reed had placed eleven Republicans to six Democrats on every major committee except the Rivers and Harbors, and on that he had omitted a Republican to make a place for Ball. "I did not foresee how important the place was until many unexpected obstacles came as barriers to the success of our deep water-way," Ball wrote.[2]

The prospects of Houston's waterway seemed bright in the period immediately after Ball took his place on the Rivers and Harbors Committee. Chairman of the committee was W. B. Hooker, who in February, 1897, had been favorably impressed by the flooded bayou and well entertained by Houstonians. At the time of that visit he had arranged with Joseph C. Hutcheson for a delegation of Houstonians to come to Washington to present their case before the committee. This delegation, headed by Hutcheson, William D. Cleveland, and H. W. Garrow, arrived in late February, 1898, and included almost every prominent Houstonian of the day.[3] Hutcheson was allotted more than the usual amount of time to speak before the committee and hopes ran high that the engineers' report would be accepted and appropriations made to begin work immediately.[4]

[2] *Ibid.*, pp. 9–10.

[3] Among its members were John Henry Kirby, R. M. Johnston, Charles H. Milby, Charles Dillingham, Jonas S. Rice, H. F. MacGregor, William M. Read, J. M. Dorrance, John F. Dickson, John T. Scott, Frank Reichardt, Justin White, J. W. Jones, G. C. Street, Joseph F. Meyer, Henry Henke, O. T. Holt, W. B. Chew, Waller T. Burns, and Eber W. Cave.

[4] Joseph C. Hutcheson, *Remarks . . . Before the Committee on Rivers and Harbors of the U.S. House of Representatives, March 1, 1898.* A copy of this speech was placed in the files of the Harris County Houston Ship Channel Navigation District

But before the delegation departed from Washington, the adminis-tration decreed that no rivers-and-harbors bill would be passed in that session. This was only the first of many setbacks for the Houstonians. Congress adjourned, and before it convened again, Hooker had re-signed to accept a judgeship, and Theodore Burton of Ohio had taken his place as chairman of the Rivers and Harbors Committee. Burton emerged as the villain of Houston's deep-water story during the next few years. Largely because of his opposition, Ball's first, second, and third terms of office expired without his achieving full congressional recognition of Houston's deep-water channel. "Burton proved himself a relentless and resourceful enemy of the adoption of the engineers' report favoring the construction of the Ship Channel," Ball comment-ed.[5]

Burton's hostility to the project was based on a private conversation with Major Alexander Macomb Miller, who, with Colonel Henry Martyn Robert and Captain George M. Derby, had served on the board of engineers that recommended the construction of the channel in 1897. Miller, who had won widespread respect for his work on the Galveston jetties, confided to Burton and later testified before the Riv-ers and Harbors Committee that he believed deep water possible but not practical for Houston. The engineers could indeed dredge a chan-nel, but he doubted seriously that it would be used to any extent by sea-going vessels. Because these could easily load and unload at Galveston, it seemed unlikely that they would take the time and pay the extra in-surance to traverse a difficult channel some fifty miles inland.

Recognizing Miller's testimony as a threat to Houston's aspirations, Ball demanded that Colonel Robert be called before the committee. Robert, a small, erect man with a stutter, took issue with Miller, ex-pressing the opinion that the project was of great commercial impor-tance not only to Houston, but to Texas and the Trans-Mississippi West as well. But Robert too had reservations about the report he had signed. "The project might well have stopped at Harrisburg or the

by Captain Hutcheson's son, Judge Palmer Hutcheson, on the occasion of the Port of Houston's fiftieth anniversary of deep water, in 1964.

5 Ball, *Port of Houston*, p. 12.

head of Long Reach, instead of at the foot of Main Street, at a saving of around $1,000,000," he told the committee. He explained that the engineers had no option in this matter. Congress had asked them to survey from Bolivar Roads to the foot of Main Street, and they could only report favorably or unfavorably on the subject. "We thought so highly of the proposed channel," said Robert, striking the table with his fist and speaking as rapidly as his stutter would permit, "that we believed the government could well afford to expend the additional million rather than have commerce suffer the loss of the channel, which would provide an inland harbor more secure from storms, and save more than 50 miles in railroad transportation."[6]

Although Robert saved the project from abandonment, he did not convince Chairman Burton. Throughout Ball's first three terms of office, Houston's ship channel received only token appropriations and the work proceeded slowly, the engineers modifying the twenty-five-foot depth to eighteen and one half in 1900. Ball had not intended to serve more than three terms, but with the channel project still pending, he agreed to stand for office once again in 1902. When Congress convened in December of that year, he girded himself for a showdown with Burton. Going to both the Democratic and Republican members of the Rivers and Harbors Committee, he enlisted their support until he was assured that he had the strength to override the Chairman's opposition.

By this time another ally, nature, had also given powerful though tragic assistance to Houston's deep-water project. In early September, 1900, a tropical storm accompanied by a six-foot tidal wave devastated Galveston Island, taking an estimated six thousand lives and laying waste to the city. The founding of the city had been delayed by a storm in 1837, and its subsequent history was marked by many others. Customarily, Galvestonians dated events by storms, and after 1900 the one of that year became the historical dividing line of time on the island. Thereafter, all events were dated as happening either Before or After the Great Storm, much as the Christian era is dated by the birth of Christ.

[6] *Ibid.*, p. 15.

Although knowledge of Galveston's exposed position was nothing new, the disaster enhanced the value of a port protected from the sea and gave strength to Ball's arguments in the House of Representatives. Backed by a majority of the Rivers and Harbors Committee, Ball laid his request before Chairman Burton: first, sufficient funds to restore the port of Galveston to its pre-1900 condition; and, second, unconditional recognition of Houston's proposed channel and an appropriation of one million dollars to begin work from Houston to the Gulf. Although still not convinced of the soundness of the Houston project, Burton conceded defeat.[7]

With the one million dollars made available at this time work on the channel continued throughout 1903 and 1904. When Charles Crotty, a young veteran of the Spanish American War, went to work as a civilian employee of the United States Army Engineers on April 29, 1904, he found them still working on the eighteen-and-one-half-foot modification of the original project. This depth had almost been achieved across Galveston Bay, and three dredges were at work at other points, one at Harrisburg, one at Lynchburg, and one near Morgan's Point. On the bayou the dredging was confined to the straighter reaches, following the deepest water of the natural channel and stopping at the lower end of Harrisburg Bend.

Crotty's introduction to the channel was a rude one. When he applied for employment at the engineers' office at Galveston, he learned that the only job available was a temporary one as surveyman with a field party on Buffalo Bayou at a salary of fifty dollars a month. He accepted this position and was then called into the private office of Commodore E. M. Hartrick. "Young man," said Hartrick, "you are going out to a malarial swamp where men do not last very long, but if you will get a quart bottle of good whiskey, put in it all the quinine it will absorb, and take a tablespoonful before each meal and two before going to bed, you will probably last the two months."

Crotty replied that he was a teetotaler and could not take the whiskey and that he had served with the U.S. Army Engineers in Cuba and in the Philippines without suffering from malaria.

[7] *Ibid.*, p. 22.

"I don't care whether you take the whiskey or not," said Hartrick, "but take the quinine, or I'll not be responsible for your health."

With these words ringing in his ears, Crotty took the night train for Deepwater Station, where a wagon from the field party met him. "Through a drizzling rain and mud of a pasture road the little mule team finally carried me to the tent camp on Buffalo Bayou at Deepwater Landing, at about ten o'clock that night, where Mr. [F. C.] Stanton provided me with a cot in a leaky tent," he recalled years later.[8]

Crotty not only survived his two months on the bayou without whiskey or quinine, but his temporary job became his life's work. With one interruption—when he entered military service during World War I—his connection with the Houston Ship Channel was continuous from the time he began work as a surveyman in 1904 until he retired as assistant director of the Port of Houston on June 1, 1944. Because of his ability, patience, and knowledge of the channel from its inception, Captain Crotty (the title was acquired during World War I) became an institution in the Navigation District during the first half of the twentieth century. "All officials have leaned upon him heavily," Tom Ball wrote in 1936, "and when . . . matters came up with which they were not thoroughly familiar, it became the habit to say, 'See Crotty,' or 'Ask Crotty'."[9]

Charles Crotty's first assignment on the channel ended in the fall of 1904 when the million-dollar appropriation was exhausted. At that time army engineers and Houstonians alike took stock of what had been accomplished and what was yet to be done to bring deep water to the foot of Main. Clear to all was the fact that the four million dollars mentioned in the engineers' report of 1897 would never complete the task. Prices in general were advancing; dredging had proved more expensive than anticipated; and virtually nothing had been done to ease the sharp bends on the upper bayou. This latter was of no small conse-

[8] Charles Crotty, "Houston Ship Channel, Texas, Construction and Development," p. 2, MS, Charles Crotty Collection. I am indebted to Mrs. Crotty, now of Kerrville, and Mrs. C. M. Wildman, Captain Crotty's niece, of Houston, for making this collection available. The above manuscript is part of a history of the Port of Houston that Captain Crotty began writing about 1946 but did not complete.

[9] Ball, *Port of Houston*, p. 55.

quence, for, while the largest ships of the previous century had been less than 300 feet long, the larger new ones were often 350 feet or longer. This meant that unless the sharper bends were eased or cut these vessels could not traverse the channel, and it would be obsolete before it was completed. For these reasons the engineers sent a board to Houston in November, 1904, and revived an old question: Exactly where was the proper head of navigation on Buffalo Bayou?

From the time the Allens had proclaimed it to be White Oak while the Harrises promoted Bray's, the question had been a controversial one, and it was no less so in 1904. One group of citizens, headed by William D. Cleveland, still contended for the traditional head as proclaimed by the Allens, but others were more willing to settle for some location downstream. Tom Ball, by this time in private law practice in Houston, remembered with misgivings that Colonel Robert had testified before the Rivers and Harbors Committee that the engineers would have stopped the project at Harrisburg or the head of Long Reach had the choice been theirs. Going to Washington, Ball conferred with his friends in Congress, and, returning home, he advised the deep-water leaders in private that unless they agreed on some downstream terminus they were likely to lose the project altogether.

Other factors helped reconcile them to this truth. The suburbs of Houston were already spreading toward Harrisburg, and, with improved transportation, the miles between the two points were shorter than when only a horse trail through the wilderness connected them. Moreover, there was the matter of right of way and spoil ground. Local interests had agreed to furnish these to the government free of cost when the project was initiated. As a deep-water channel promised to enhance the value of adjoining lands, most landowners downstream donated the required land or sold it at a nominal cost. But in the vicinity of Houston the price of land was advancing rapidly, and owners were demanding full market value. Thus carrying the project to the foot of Main would lay a burden on local interests aside from the cost to the federal government.

Even after the leaders of the deep-water project reconciled themselves to a terminal below White Oak, the controversy boiled as to

Courtesy Mrs. Rhoda C. Hubbard,
Santa Barbara, California
Nicholas Clopper, from a portrait painted on wood about 1800. Clopper and his sons, pioneers of the Buffalo Bayou trade, were among the first to visualize the potential of the bayou as a route to interior Texas.

Sidney Sherman, a hero of San Jacinto, had the channel surveyed in 1847, hoping that ocean vessels could meet rail transportation at Harrisburg.

Courtesy Victor M. Helm
Photographer, Houston
Captain Thomas Wigg Grayson, master of the Steamboat *Laura*, which made the first voyage up Buffalo Bayou to the newly founded city of Houston.

Courtesy Houston *Chronicle*
One of the distinguished passengers aboard the *Laura* on her first trip to Houston, Francis Richard Lubbock was later governor of Texas during the Confederacy.

Buffalo Bayou in its natural state was bordered by heavy vegetation. Until early in the twentieth century, it looked much as it did in 1827 when Joseph Chambers Clopper wrote that most of its course was "bound in by timber & flowering shrubbery which overhang its grassy banks & dip & reflect their variegated hues in its unruffled waters."

This picture, purportedly of the city of Houston, appeared in a book written by an Englishwoman, Matilda Charlotte Houstoun, in 1844 and gave rise to an erroneous impression. The artist apparently took to heart Mrs. Houstoun's report that the city was "built on high land, and the banks, which are covered with evergreens, rise abruptly from the river."

Courtesy Houston Chamber of Commerce

The San Jacinto Monument, a landmark on the channel, marks the place where Sam Houston's army won Texan independence in 1836. The battle had the side effect of calling attention to Buffalo Bayou as a trade route. The Battleship *Texas,* center, was retired to permanent dock at the battleground after World War II.

The Allen brothers, John Kirby and Augustus Chapman, the founders of Houston, laid out the new city in the summer of 1836 at a point they believed to be the head of navigation on Buffalo Bayou.

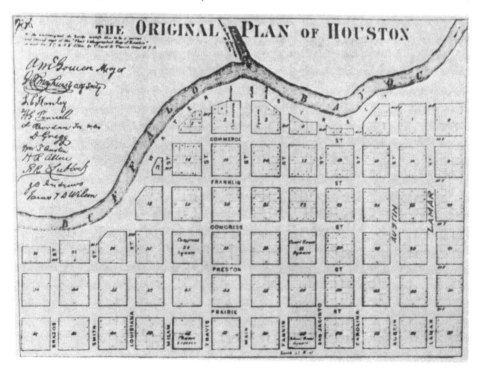

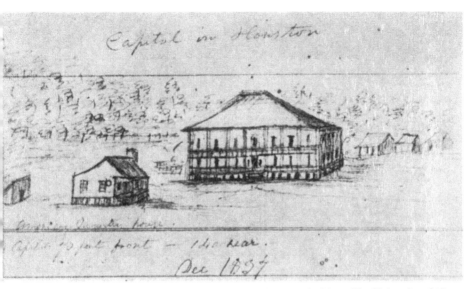

Mary Austin Holley made the first known sketches of Houston when she visited the infant city in December, 1837. "Capital in Houston" was made from the home of her hostess, Mrs. A. C. Allen. The sketch "Houston contains three hundred houses, first house built in Jany 1836" shows one of the tents that prompted one early visitor to call Houston a "city of tents" and another to compare it to a Methodist camp-meeting ground.

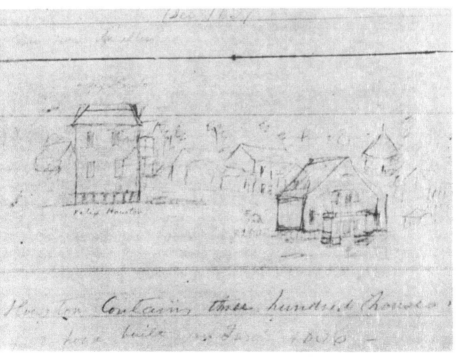

Main Street, Houston, in 1856. "The principal thoroughfare, opening from the steamboat landing, is the busiest we saw in Texas," wrote Frederick Law Olmsted, who visited about this time.

Main Street, probably between Preston and Congress, during the Civil War.

The Port of Houston about 1866, looking north from Allen's Landing, as depicted years later in an advertisement of Ziegler's Warehouse. Trestle bridge over White Oak Bayou is seen with heavily laden cotton barge under tow beneath and another on Buffalo Bayou.

Main Street, looking north from Preston, about 1885, when paving stones had been delivered for surfacing the street.

Courtesy Judge Wilmer J. Hunt

John Thomas Brady, Sidney Sherman's son-in-law, inherited the vision of deep-water vessels meeting rail transportation at Harrisburg, and chartered companies to build belt-line railroads from Harrisburg to Houston.

Courtesy *Southern Pacific Bulletin*

Commodore Charles Morgan, whose steam packets served Texas ports as early as 1837, dredged a canal across Morgan's Point and sent ocean vessels to Clinton, a few miles below Houston, in 1876.

Courtesy *Southern Pacific Bulletin*

The *Morgan*, one of Charles Morgan's "little red sidewheelers," reputedly was the first vessel to pass through the cut he dredged across Morgan's Point.

Passengers on Buffalo Bayou in the early 1880's sometimes amused themselves by shooting at alligators that rolled into the water from cypress stumps or rotten logs upon the approach of the steamboat. From Alexander E. Sweet and J. Armoy Knox, *On a Mexican Mustang* (1883).

The Sternwheel Packet *St. Clair* loading cotton at Houston about 1868. The picture first appeared in Frank Leslie's *Illustrated Newspaper,* on September 27, 1890.

Steamboat *Lizzie* at the foot of Main Street in 1876. Following the Civil War, riverboats like the *Lizzie* not only connected Houston with ocean vessels at Galveston but were popular with excursioners, who found the cruise "a delightful experience."

Leaders in Houston's deep-water project. Top: Horace Baldwin Rice, mayor of Houston; Thomas H. Ball, U.S. congressman and counsel for the Port. Bottom: Henry Martyn Robert, head of the U.S. Engineers' surveying team; Joseph Chappell Hutcheson, U.S. congressman.

The Steamship *Dorothy* of the Bull Line, Captain Walter L. Farnsworth, master, made a trial run up the ship channel a full month before it was officially opened.

A delegation of prominent Houstonians gathered at the Rice Hotel on the occasion of the *Dorothy's* arrival and then visited the vessel. Left to right: Mrs. J. H. Carroll, Mrs. G. W. Hawkes, Mrs. J. Shelton, J. R. Clark, Captain Walter L. Farnsworth, Mrs. Farnsworth, J. H. Carroll, who was the ship's agent, Captain Charles Crotty, and Captain S. Talliferro.

The Steamer *Satilla* of the Southern Steamship Company was the first deep-water vessel to dock at the Port after its official opening.

The Turning Basin in 1913. At that time many Houstonians believed that eventually deep water would be brought to the city's historic head of navigation, the foot of Main Street.

De Marter Photo
J. Russell Wait, Port director from 1931 to 1947, guided the Port through the difficult years of the depression and World War II.

Benjamin Casey Allin, engineer, world traveler, and former army officer, served as Houston's first Port director, from 1919 to 1930.

The *Merry Mount*, loaded with 23,719 bales of cotton, sailed from Houston directly to Europe in November, 1919, thus ushering in a new era for the Port.

Cotton created jobs and accounted for much of the prosperity of the Port during the 1920's.

Loading a cargo of cotton for Europe at Port of Houston. By 1930 the Port led all others in cotton exports. Note "gangways" up which bales were hauled by dragline from ship's booms.

Jesse H. Jones, banker, businessman, and civic leader, helped raise the private financing for dredging the original ship channel and throughout his life was an ardent supporter of the Port of Houston.

Ross S. Sterling, a founder of Humble Oil and Refining Company, served as navigation and canal commissioner from 1911 until 1930, when he was elected governor of Texas. From 1924 he served as chairman of the commission.

Robert J. Cummins, a consulting engineer, served longer on the Port Commission than any other member.

William Lockhart Clayton, a founder of Anderson, Clayton and Company, the world's largest cotton marketing firm. Clayton's firm built Long Reach terminal, near the Turning Basin, in 1923.

Liners are shown in the late thirties at the Clinton Street Wharf, which served the Morgan Line-Southern Pacific Railroad combination whereby passengers and freight could move from the West Coast by rail to Houston and then by coastal steamer to New York.

Cecil Thomson Studios, Houston

An earlier view of the Clinton Wharf, probably in the early or middle twenties, showing also the Carnegie Steel Company's warehouse and dock. Both coastal steamers and barges could bring steel from the East and interior points for Southwestern distribution.

Pipelines between oil fields and channelside industries have contributed to the growing tonnage of the Port of Houston. The above picture shows the construction of the original Houston Pipe Line Company line from the South Texas fields to Houston in 1925.

The fleet of Central Freight Lines in 1932, when trucking was a new and revolutionary factor in the transportation picture of the Port of Houston as well as of the nation.

Courtesy Humble Oil and Refining Company

Humble Oil and Refining Company's Baytown docks in 1920 shortly after the refinery began operations, with *S.S. Baytown*, first tanker owned by Humble, in foreground. The channel became an oil-refining center during the 1920's.

Courtesy Humble Oil and Refining Company

Aerial view showing portion of Humble's Baytown refinery and Enjay Chemical Company's plant in 1967, with supertankers on channel at left.

Allen's Landing, looking south down Main Street, as it appeared about 1910 from the mouth of White Oak Bayou. Both steam and sail vessels still used the wharf, and the viaduct over Buffalo Bayou had not been built.

Allen's Landing as it appeared in the early twenties, also looking south on Main Street from across Buffalo Bayou. By then the viaduct over the bayou and the Southern Pacific Building, right background, had been built.

Allen's Landing in mid-1967, at dedication ceremonies following its restoration into a park area as an historic site.

The men responsible for the role of the Navigation District in the restoration of Allen's Landing are shown before the granite marker of the Main Street Wharf set in 1917. Center foreground are W. N. Blanton, Port commissioner for thirteen years, and Howard Tellepsen, commission chairman. Others, from left, are Executive Director J. P. Turner; Commissioners W. D. Haden II, E. H. Henderson, R. H. Pruett, W. C. Wells; and Travis Smith III, director of Planning and Development of the Navigation District.

Courtesy Travis L. Smith III, Houston

The Master's ticket of Travis L. Smith, who was later to own and operate seven steamers on the Brazos as the Columbia Transportation Company, licensing him for Galveston Bay and tributaries, West Galveston Bay, and the Brazos River.

Courtesy Travis L. Smith III, Houston

Called "the fastest and most beautiful sternwheeler ever brought to Texas," the *Hiawatha* of the Columbia Transportation Company ran on the Brazos River between Columbia and Valasco from 1892 to 1895, a sometimes competitive shipping route for cotton with the riverboat service from Houston and Harrisburg to Galveston on Buffalo Bayou to the north.

The Cruiser *Houston* came up the channel in November, 1930, to mark a decade of phenomenal growth for the Port.

The cotton float in the downtown parade celebrating the visit of the Cruiser *Houston*, depicting Houston's dramatic growth as a cotton port.

The U.S. Frigate *Constitution*, better known as *Old Ironsides*, passing the San Jacinto Battleground in 1932. More than 100,000 visitors went aboard the old vessel while she was in port.

Manchester Terminal at the junction point of Sims Bayou at top center and the tanker berths of the Sinclair Refinery at bottom. Buffalo Bayou originally went to the left of the wooded point in the center. The new channel on the right was cut during the first channel dredging in 1912–1914 to remove the sharp bend in the bayou. In 1965–1966 the whole point was dredged out to make a second turning basin.

The channel became an arsenal of democracy during World War II when Brown Shipbuilding Company built the above yard at Greens Bayou. Built from scratch, the yard constructed more than five hundred vessels for the U.S. Navy.

Photo by Aerial Photo Service, Dallas

Liberty ships under construction in 1941 at the Houston Shipbuilding Corporation subsidiary of the Todd Shipbuilding Corporation. After World War II the site was purchased by the Phillips Petroleum Company and renamed Adams Terminal.

Fireboat *Port Houston,* that served the Houston Fire Department on the Houston Ship Channel for many years.

Captain and Mrs. Charles Crotty in the wheel house of the Navigation District's fireboat *Captain Crotty,* named after the former Corps of Engineers officer and assistant Port director in recognition of his service to the Port of Houston from 1904 to 1944.

Pervin and Associates Photography, Houston

The Navigation District's dry bulk materials handling plant on Greens Bayou and the Houston Ship Channel. The plant has an average cargo handling rate of 1,000 tons per hour, and in 1966 moved more than 1,177,000 tons of material.

Pervin and Associates Photography, Houston

The Navigation District's 6,000,000-bushel grain elevator at the Turning Basin is one of five elevators now lining the ship channel to give Houston the greatest shipside grain storage capacity of any port in the nation, with a total of 27,500,000 bushels.

The Port of Houston about 1930, looking upstream toward the Turning Basin, which is lined by the public docks. The Long Reach Docks, now owned by the Navigation District, are upper center, and in lower left center are the two wharves of the Sprunt Terminal, now the Petty Terminal. In lower left foreground are warehouses of the Gulf Atlantic Warehouse Company, former owners of Long Reach.

The Manned Spacecraft Center of the National Aeronautics and Space Administration located near the Bayport Terminal on Galveston Bay. The Center houses research facilities and offices for the United States man-in-space program and is the control center for all United States manned spacecraft flights.

Courtesy Houston Chamber of Commerce

This aerial photograph of downtown Houston graphically portrays the growth of the central business district in recent years and also demonstrates the accessibility provided by the downtown freeway loop. Houston's 244-mile, $500 million master freeway plan features inner and outer loops connected by radial freeways.

Pervin and Associates Photography, Houston

The $3.5 million World Trade Building was completed by the Navigation District in 1962 to fill the need for a center of international commerce for Houston. Here are located foreign consulates, steamship offices, freight forwarders, importers-exporters, and others involved in world trade. Its entire fourth floor houses the famed World Trade Club, where business-men meet from all over the globe.

Howard T. Tellepsen, chairman of the Navigation and Canal Commissioners since 1956, has guided the Port of Houston during the era of its greatest progress.

J. P. Turner, executive director of the Navigation District since 1957. Under his supervision the Port's greatest building and expansion program was executed.

The Inspection Vessel *Sam Houston,* show-window of the Port of Houston, has carried more than 350,000 visitors down the ship channel to show them the wonders of the modern Port and the sprawling, multi-billion-dollar industrial complex which lines its banks and has made Houston great.

exactly where the terminal should be. Some contended for Bray's Bayou; others for Sims; and still others for the head of Long Reach, a strip of the bayou that obtained its name because it was the longest and straightest stretch above Lynchburg. After examining the bayou and holding public hearings in Houston, the engineers recommended the head of Long Reach as the most feasible location. It was below any bridge over the waterway; the existing railroads and highways seemed to favor it; and it offered ample room for wharves, warehouses, and trackage. The board also recommended that the Turning Basin be six hundred feet in diameter on the bottom rather than five hundred as previously provided.[10]

When funds became available in March, 1905, Charles Crotty assisted in laying out the Turning Basin at the designated spot. At that time the area still retained its primitive appearance. "On the south side the sloping banks were sheltered with large magnolia, pine and oak trees," he recalled, "while the north bank was steep and set with pine and heavy underbrush which required extensive clearing even to survey."[11] A contract was let the following year to the Atlantic, Gulf and Pacific Company of New York for dredging the basin and the channel above Harrisburg Bend. As Crotty recalled, the company's dredge *Washington* started work on September 3, 1906, and completed the contract on August 4, 1908.[12]

The decision of the engineers in late 1904 by no means laid to rest the matter of the location of the Turning Basin. In the following decades the issue cropped up time and again to influence bond issues, inspire speculation, and figure in local and national politics. Property owners upstream persisted in their efforts to extend deep water, while old residents continued to argue that the proper head of the Houston Ship Channel was in Houston. To newer residents this argument lost meaning, for Houston extended its limits to include Harrisburg in 1926. When in the early 1930's the old question again became an

[10] "Galveston Ship Channel and Buffalo Bayou, Tex.," *Rivers and Harbors Com. Doc.*, 61 Cong., 2 Sess., No. 35; Ball, *Port of Houston*, p. 35.
[11] Crotty, "Houston Ship Channel," p. 5.
[12] Charles Crotty to J. Russell Wait, August 26, 1943, HCHSCND files, C-13-C.

issue, J. Russell Wait, newly arrived in the city as Port director, gave a classic answer when asked by army engineers, "Do you think the terminal should be moved to Houston?" "What do you mean 'moved to Houston'?" he responded. "Gentlemen, the turning basin is now four miles within the Houston city limits."[13]

The city dredged a barge canal between the Turning Basin and the foot of Main Street in 1913–1914, and in 1921 the United States Engineers adopted a project for deepening this channel to ten feet and widening it to sixty feet. As late as the 1940's there was still talk of deepening a portion of this barge channel for ocean vessels. Property values continued to rise, however, and local interests became more and more reconciled to the head of Long Reach as the permanent head of the deep-water project.

In addition to locating the Turning Basin, the engineers' report of 1904 provided for cuts at Clinton, Irish, and Harrisburg bends. Contracts were awarded to Bowers Southern Dredging Company for cutting across Irish and Clinton bends. Work started on Irish Bend in the spring of 1905, and the cut, eighteen and one-half feet deep and one hundred feet wide, was completed late that year. Work was completed on the Clinton cut early in 1906. Two government-owned dredges, the *General H. M. Robert,* a small pipe-line dredge, and the *Colonel A. M. Miller,* a new twenty-inch dredge, made the Harrisburg cut, the work beginning early in 1906 and being completed the following year.[14]

As earlier, property owners along the channel were generous in providing right of way and spoil ground. When the cuts were made, this sometimes involved sacrifice and inconvenience on the part of the owner. For example, the Direct Navigation Company, then a subsidiary of Southern Pacific, had built a marine ways for the building and repair of tugs and barges at Clinton. When it developed that the proposed easement of the bend would completely destroy this facility, the railroad agreed to move it to a point downstream if local interests would

13 As related by J. Russell Wait to the writer, December 29, 1965.

14 Crotty to Wait, August 26, 1943, HCHSCND files, C-13-C; "Galveston Ship Channel and Buffalo Bayou, Tex.," *Rivers and Harbors Com. Doc.,* 61 Cong., 2 Sess., No. 35.

pay the cost of removal. "However, so far as I can recall," said Charles Crotty, "the bill was never presented, and the railroad donated some 15 or 20 acres for the cut."[15]

A similar spirit was displayed by a group of citizens in regard to the Irish Bend cut. As this cut would form an island and isolate about fifty or sixty acres of land, the owner felt he could not afford to donate it. To facilitate matters, Charles H. Milby, Andrew Dow, William D. Cleveland, Charles Dillingham, Charles Clarke, Thomas W. House, and Eber W. Cave joined together, purchased the land and donated the right of way to the government. They held the remainder until 1920 when they sold it to the Navigation District at cost plus taxes and interest. During this period Sinclair Taliaferro did most of the legal work in connection with acquiring right of way and spoil ground. Others instrumental in accomplishing this task were John G. Tod, Jr., Charles H. Milby, Sam Allen, Justin C. White, B. A. Riesner, and Horace Booth.[16]

The eighteen-and-one-half-foot project was almost completed by 1908 when prevailing hard times caused a sharp reduction in all river and harbor appropriations. From that year until 1912 little was done on the channel aside from maintenance and the dredging of the Upper Clinton, or Fidelity, cut in 1910–1911.[17]

Nor, in spite of the efforts and dollars expended, had the general nature of the channel trade changed by this time. Tugs and barges still carried all but a small percentage of the traffic, and cargoes, as in 1890's, still consisted chiefly of bulky, low-grade freight. For the year 1910 the city wharfmaster, Maurice Murphy, reported that the bayou carried a total of 2,030,646 tons with a value of $45,210,430, of which 1,295,690 tons valued at $37,439,120, passed over the city wharves. Most of the remainder was handled by the Direct Navigation Company over its wharves at Clinton. As in the past, cotton was the most valuable product and there was a considerable amount of lumber.

[15] Crotty, "Houston Ship Channel," p. 11.

[16] Ibid.; Ball, Port of Houston, pp. 13–14, 29.

[17] Crotty, "Houston Ship Channel," p. 7; Crotty to Wait, August 26, 1943, HCHSCND files, C-13-C.

But two products that had not figured in nineteenth-century statistics appeared on the 1910 report. The first was rice, which became an important product of the Texas coastal plains about the turn of the century; and the second, petroleum, which would figure prominently in the channel's future. The famous Spindletop oil field had blown in near Beaumont in 1901, bringing with it a new era for Texas and especially for the Houston area and its waterway. Although petroleum accounted for only a fraction of the channel's commerce in 1910, it would replace cotton as the number-one product within a few years. Murphy listed the following as the chief products carried on the channel in 1910:[18]

Product	Tons
Cotton	92,151
Rice	30,000
Lumber and shingles	420,400
Hardware and machinery	26,000
Groceries	32,000
Shell	420,000
Petroleum	11,000
Sand	760,000
Grain	36,000
Furniture	1,200
Beer and ice	4,640
Fruits and vegetables	5,000

That the channel trade remained much as it had been at the end of the nineteenth century was not due to lack of effort on the part of local citizens. After the completion of the Turning Basin, the city built two slips on the basin's northwest end. These were completed in late 1909 at a cost of more than $125,000. To make use of the depth available at this time, Houstonians, attempted to develop a trade with Mexican ports. They brought up the channel as a part of the No-Tsu-Oh Carnival of 1909 a small Swedish steamer, the *Disa*, that customarily called at Mexican and Central American ports. The *Disa* thus became the first sea-going vessel to make use of the new Turning Basin. In addi-

18 *Texas Almanac*, 1911, pp. 123–124; Houston *Daily Post*, January 17, 1909; January 1, 1911.

tion to a small cargo of bananas, the *Disa* brought King Nottoc XI, ruler of the carnival, to the Turning Basin, where he changed to a smaller vessel to accompany a flotilla up the bayou to the foot of Main Street, there to begin the street parade. A large crowd went to the Turning Basin on November 8 to greet the ruler, in private life Captain James A. Baker, Jr., and hail the arrival of the *Disa.* Some hopeful citizens suggested that the *Disa's* voyage signaled the opening of the channel to ocean vessels, but their predictions were premature. Houston had an outlet to the sea, but that outlet was still far from deep enough to carry the type of vessels then in coastal and foreign service at other Gulf ports, vessels that usually drew from twenty to twenty-five feet of water.[19]

At this point Horace Baldwin Rice emerged as the new leader of the Houston deep-water movement. A nephew of William Marsh Rice, who had figured prominently in the city's commercial life in the previous century and whose fortune founded Rice University, Horace Baldwin Rice served as mayor of Houston from 1896 to 1898 and again for four terms from 1905 to 1913. Rice purchased a large yacht, the *Zeeland,* that was used principally to show the channel to prominent visitors. "It is a well known fact that he used the larger part of his private fortune in promoting the interests of the city and the Ship Channel," commented Tom Ball.[20]

Impatient at the slow progress on the channel after 1908, Rice first consulted with a number of channel enthusiasts and then called a public meeting at the office of the Houston Business League. At this meeting Rice proposed that the city take over and complete the channel project, a suggestion that brought enthusiastic indorsement from several other speakers. Tom Ball, going against the tide of popular opinion, stood to call attention to some special difficulties. "I saw that objections to his plan would not appeal to those present . . .," he wrote. "However, I felt it my duty to tell the assembly of some of the difficulties which would confront Houston.[21] One of these was that the

[19] Crotty to Wait, June 16, 1939, HCHSCND files, Q-8; Crotty, "Houston Ship Channel," p. 7; *Daily Post,* November 7, 8, 1909.
[20] Ball, *Port of Houston,* p. 43.
[21] *Ibid.,* p. 30.

city lacked corporate power outside its limits; another, that the cost of maintenance would be burdensome aside from the cost of construction. Ball concluded his speech by agreeing to abide by the decision of those present. When Rice called for a vote, the assembly gave almost unanimous approval to the plan to construct the channel. John T. Scott then moved and the group so voted that Ball be appointed counsel without pay to work out the plan. "You can, if you will, find a way to show how the objects . . . can be accomplished," Scott told Ball with a laugh.[22]

Ball did indeed suggest a plan. Houston was not the only Texas coastal city that wanted access to the sea. Beaumont also wanted a deepwater channel, and leaders there had already decided that the most feasible way to get it was to form a navigation district. Under the state constitution the legislature was authorized to create drainage, conservation, and other special districts, each district to have the power to initiate improvements and pay for them by issuing bonds upon the approval of its voters. Although no navigation district had yet been formed, Beaumont leaders had formulated plans for one and had presented a bill permitting its creation to the legislature. At a meeting held in the mayor's office on January 18, 1909, Ball called attention to what Beaumont leaders had done and suggested that Houston join them in shaping the bill and securing its passage. Acting on this suggestion, Mayor Rice appointed Ball, W. H. Wilson, and T. H. Stone to work with Beaumont leaders.[23]

The bill met with little opposition. As passed by the thirty-first legislature in 1909, it provided for the creation of navigation districts upon the approval of the voters, the districts to have the power to "make improvement of rivers, bays, creeks, streams and canals running or flowing through such districts or any part thereof." When so authorized by a vote of the electorate, such navigation districts could issue bonds to pay for the improvements. The law provided that the districts be governed by a board of three navigation and canal commissioners, these to be appointed by the county commissioners' court and to have the power to adopt any approved survey made by the United States

22 *Ibid.*
23 *Ibid.*, p. 32; *Daily Post*, January 2, 11, 19, 1909.

government engineers.[24] Under the bill and its subsequent amendments, not only Houston and Beaumont, but Orange, Corpus Christi, and other Texas cities obtained ports.

At the same meeting that Ball recommended the creation of a navigation district, he made another suggestion. Why not send a delegation to Washington when Congress convened and offer to share with the government the cost of a deep-water channel? "I felt sure that should we propose to create a navigation district . . . with power to issue bonds for one-half the amount necessary to complete the 25-foot project, Congress would jump at the offer," he wrote. This suggestion too was accepted, and in December, 1909, another large delegation from Houston again went to Washington to appear before the Rivers and Harbors Committee. Mayor Rice headed the delegation, and it included many veterans of the cause who had made a similar journey in 1898.[25]

The committee gave the Houstonians a sympathetic hearing. The hostile Burton had been succeeded as chairman by D. S. Alexander, who had visited Houston and been impressed by the bayou at the time of the providential rain of 1897. Alexander and other committee members expressed amazement upon hearing of the proposal of the citizens to match dollars with the federal government. The Houstonians explained that work need not begin until they had created the navigation district, voted for and sold bonds, and placed one-half the amount for the twenty-five-foot channel with the Secretary of War. They assured the committee further that no railroad or private company would be permitted to monopolize the waterfront. After plying the Houstonians with questions, the congressmen voted unanimously to accept their proposal—taking into consideration, no doubt, that many hurdles were yet

[24] W. W. Herron, *Supplement to Sayles' Annotated Civil Statutes of the State of Texas 1908–1910*, pp. 308–324.

[25] The National Rivers and Harbors Congress was also meeting in Washington at this time, so Houston delegates accomplished a double purpose. Houston delegates to the congress were J. S. Cullinan, Sam T. Swinford, Ike M. Standifer, C. C. Oden, D. E. Garrett, J. N. Murphy, F. A. Heitmann, Adolph Boldt, J. Z. Gaston and R. M. Johnston (*Daily Post*, December 7, 1909). Ball recalled that in addition to himself the delegation also included John T. Scott, S. F. Carter, William D. Cleveland, Jonas S. Rice, H. W. Garrow, B. F. Bonner, Sinclair Taliaferro, H. F. MacGregor, Justin White, John H. Kirby, T. H. Stone, Tom Lucas, and Horace Booth (Ball, *Port of Houston*, p. 31).

to be passed before the government would be called upon for its half of the cost.[26] This so-called Houston Plan of sharing the cost of projects with the government set a precedent. "Prior to Houston's offer, no substantial contribution had ever been made by local interests to secure the adoption of their projects," wrote Ball, "and no project has since been adopted by the national government without promise of local contributions and assurances that the waterfront would not be privately controlled."[27]

Elated at the backing of the Rivers and Harbors Committee, the delegation returned home to persuade the citizens of Harris County to create the Harris County Houston Ship Channel Navigation District and vote bonds in the amount of $1,250,000 to pay for the District's share of the waterway. This promised to be no simple task, for the parts of the county that were far removed from the channel often felt little interest in it and traditionally opposed bond issues. Indeed, leaders for a time considered not including all of the county in the District. After deciding to include all of it, they launched a campaign such as the county had seldom, if ever, seen before. Alexander Sessums Cleveland, president of the Chamber of Commerce, appointed a committee to oversee the campaign and promised to carry it to every precinct in the county. Jake F. Wolters, chairman of the speakers' committee, enlisted representative businessmen and sent them to speak at various meetings. At one large rally in the city auditorium, the press reported, no less than three dozen prominent citizens had been invited to speak. Although women could not vote at this time, they too were urged to come to the meetings to learn what the channel could mean to the county. This was the "most momentous epoch in the history of Texas since the Battle of San Jacinto," said the Houston *Daily Post*, while Mayor Rice declared a half holiday on election day, Tuesday, January 10, 1911, and asked that all business in the city be suspended "while the voters in solid array march to the polls."[28]

The voters were not uniformly enthusiastic about the Navigation District. Tom Ball recalled one amusing incident when F. A. Heitmann

---

26 *Daily Post*, December 7, 11, 12, 14, 16, 19, 1909.
27 Ball, *Port of Houston*, p. 32.
28 *Daily Post*, January 1, 8, 10, 1911.

spoke to an unreceptive audience in the northeast section of the county. "What are you men folks going to do about it?" Heitmann asked, striking the table. "Are you not willing to help Houston, which pays 85 per cent of our county taxes to build your roads and improvements, become a great city and market for your products?" Seeing that he was getting little response, he changed tactics. "I am going to appeal to the women here, and say to them that the average increased taxes paid by property owners in this precinct will not be more than the cost of a 'pair of pullets'. If you men are unwilling to pay that price, I am going to ask all the ladies to stand up and agree, if necessary, to bring the pullets to market." The women stood, and this precinct joined the rest of the county to pass the bond issue. Countywide the issue carried by a majority of sixteen to one.[29] Three years later the voters approved bonds in the amount of $250,000 to match an equal federal appropriation to buy two dredges for maintaining the channel and basin.

But still all the problems of financing the waterway were not resolved. After the navigation bonds were prepared, burdened with the name Harris County Houston Ship Channel Navigation District Bonds, they were indifferently received by the buying public. Most buyers had never heard of navigation bonds, and bankers and brokers hesitated to handle them because of the small commissions received and because the law provided they could not be sold for less than par and accrued interest. At this point, Jesse Holman Jones, a man who had already made his mark on Houston, took a hand. After discussing the problem in conference with Mayor Rice, Ball, William T. Carter, Sr., T. C. Dunn, and Camille G. Pillot, Jones offered to ask the Houston banks to take the bonds in proportion to their capital and surplus. His task was made easy by the fact that the presidents of most of Houston's banks had been active in the deep-water movement. For example, Jonas S. Rice was president of the Union National Bank; John T. Scott, of the First National; Charles Dillingham, of the South Texas; W. B. Chew, of the Commerce National; and Samuel Fain Carter, of the Lumberman's National. In less than twenty-four hours Jones obtained the promise of Houston bankers to accept the bonds. "The next morning, Mr. Jones

[29] Ball, *Port of Houston*, p. 34.

reported that every bank in the city would buy its share," wrote Ball, and this 'trouble knot' was cut."[30]

After the creation of the Harris County Houston Ship Channel Navigation District, the county commissioners, in accordance with the provisions of the law, appointed the governing body. The first three canal commissioners were Charles Dillingham, Camille G. Pillot, and Ross S. Sterling. Tom Ball agreed to serve as counsel and Stuart A. Giraud as Secretary. All served without pay although, as Ball observed, "the duties of the board were onerous and required frequent meetings." Colonel Dillingham was elected chairman of the first board, but he resigned in 1916 because of ill health. Sterling then became chairman, and Ball was appointed to the board.[31]

Before deep water became a reality, another governing body was created to manage municipal facilities on the channel. The original navigation act gave the District the right to improve the waterway but no authority over the waterfront. As work proceeded on the channel, the need of docks, wharves and other public facilities became obvious, and the city undertook to supply the need. Ben Campbell, who succeeded H. Balwin Rice as mayor in 1913, called a city election that authorized a bond issue for three million dollars to provide for the facilities. The city council then passed an ordinance creating a city harbor board of five members to be appointed by the mayor and to have jurisdiction over city property on the waterfront. Jesse H. Jones became the chairman of the first city harbor board, and the other original members were Roy Montgomery Farrar, John T. Scott, Camille G. Pillot, and Tom Ball. Ball resigned in May, 1914, and was replaced by Daniel Ripley. This board worked with city engineer E. E. Sands to plan the city's harbor facilities.[32]

A traditional jealousy between city and county authorities carried over into relations between the city and District boards. Their jurisdic-

[30] *Ibid.*, p. 34.

[31] *Ibid.*, pp. 34–35; Minutes of the County Commissioners' Court, Vol. P., pp. 455, 520–521, 548–551; Navigation and Canal Commissioners, "Notes on Minutes," March 23, 1916, July 26, 1916, March 12, 1919, HCHSCND files.

[32] E. E. Sands, "A Report on the Proposed Development of Houston Harbor," June 10, 1915, MS, Jesse Holman Jones Papers; Minutes of the City Council, City of Houston, Vol. Q, p. 353; Ball, *Port of Houston*, pp. 44–45.

tion sometimes overlapped, and, in order for one body to know what the other was doing, it became customary for one of the canal commissioners to serve also on the harbor board. The two boards eventually began meeting together and were finally consolidated into a single and more satisfactory governing body. Although the division of authority proved impractical, these early boards began the development of the channel. They also set the precedent that capable citizens give their services without pay to the governing of the waterway. All of the original members of the two early boards were outstanding, but two men, Ross S. Sterling and Jesse H. Jones, best exemplify the caliber of men whom the citizenry expected to serve on the channel's governing body. Sterling, one of the founders of Humble Oil Company, later became governor of Texas, while Jones, after acquiring a legendary fortune based on Houston real estate, became a political figure of national importance during Franklin Delano Roosevelt's administration.

While local citizens were creating the Navigation District and working out the details of its administration, army engineers were considering another problem. In Galveston Bay the channel shoaled rapidly due to cross currents. Thus, the engineers suggested a new route, one that used part of the existing Texas City Channel and then followed the shoreline to Morgan's Point. By placing all the excavated material on the bay side in a continuous ridge, they proposed to protect the channel from the action of waves and the dangers of shoaling. This route to Bolivar Roads was about two miles longer, but the engineers felt that the reduction in maintenance costs would justify the increased distance. When bids were taken, the new route proved more costly by about $100,000 than the old. The engineers were inclined to favor the new one in spite of the additional cost, but local interests vigorously protested any change in the route. The original route was retained, but army engineers had lingering regrets that the channel did not hug the coastline.[33]

When all details of financing and the matter of the route had been settled, work began on the twenty-five-foot project. In early 1912 District engineer Major Earl I. Brown called Charles Crotty into his office

[33] Crotty, "Houston Ship Channel," pp. 12–13; "Galveston Harbor and Adjacent Waterways, Tex.," *House Doc.*, 62 Cong., 3 Sess., No. 1390.

and asked how long it would take to make an estimate and prepare the specifications for dredging the Houston Ship Channel to the specified depth. "About thirty days to make a survey to determine present condition and another ten to fifteen days to write specifications," replied Crotty. "Use available data and have specifications on my desk in one week," said Brown. This was done, and, strangely enough, the final total of cubic yards dredged, nearly 23,000,000, differed only 1,341 from the estimates made in that week.

A contract was awarded in June, 1912, to the Atlantic, Gulf and Pacific Company for a turnkey job, the channel to be finished full depth and width for the entire length from Bolivar Roads to the Turning Basin before acceptance. "Our survey party took to the field about the last of April 1912 to lay out the line of channel to be dredged," recalled Crotty, "placing range beacons, cross sectioning the stream each 100 feet at 10 ft intervals, platting the lines and cross sections, making up estimates of quantities to be excavated, and marking out the locations of suitable dumping grounds." Commodore E. M. Hartrick, then semi-retired because of age and failing eyesight, spent most of his time with the party as consultant, while Crotty was in active charge. This party remained in the field until the contract was completed.[34]

The contractor placed the large dredge *Texas* on the job on June 15, 1912, even before the final contract was signed. He later added five more dredges, the *George W. Catt, Pensacola, Houston, Galveston,* and *Washington.* "These huge suction plants with pipe lines 22 to 30 inches in diameter were scattered along the stream, their cutters like great egg-beaters cutting into the silt and clay at the bottom of the channel and into the banks where straightening and widening was needed," wrote Crotty.[35]

Throughout 1912, 1913, and 1914 as the men worked on the channel they kept up on the news from two other projects, both akin to the

---

[34] Crotty, "Houston Ship Channel," p. 10. As Crotty recalled, other members of this party were C. M. Wood, Henry E. Shudde, Eric T. Davis, J. G. McKenzie, and A. A. Riley.

[35] *Ibid.,* p. 10.

channel project in nature and related to its future. The first was the Gulf Intracoastal Waterway, a canal older in the dreams of Texans than the Houston Ship Channel. First approved as a project in 1873, the waterway was revived in the early twentieth century largely through the efforts of C. S. E. Holland. Under the supervision of the United States Army Engineers, a two-hundred-mile segment below Galveston was completed in 1913. This waterway connected with the Houston Ship Channel and developed simultaneously with it.

The second project, the Panama Canal, was farther removed but no less related to the development of the channel. Another old dream come true, the Panama Canal linked the Atlantic and Pacific oceans and gave the Gulf of Mexico ready access not only to the Pacific Coast States, but also to the Far East. The men working on the channel read monthly reports from the Canal Zone with interest and were sometimes pleased to learn that they had excavated more dirt during a certain length of time than workers on the Isthmus.[36]

The contractor had agreed to complete the channel in three and one-half years from starting, but the work went faster than expected. By September, 1914, only two years and three months from starting, it was completed. Before it was accepted, Charles Crotty's party made a rapid survey of the entire channel to see that it was indeed the required depth and width for the entire length from the Turning Basin to Bolivar Roads. As the channel filled in some places while being dredged in others, one of the contractor's dredges followed the surveyors to take care of shoals. "For about two weeks about sixty men were employed from daylight to dark cross-sectioning the stream and platting the results," wrote Crotty. "The last shallow spot was found just above Harrisburg, and as the dredge *Texas* swept up this shallow section for a few hundred feet the engineers followed with the sounding, and when all was clear the whistle blew a long, long blast of victory." The time was 11:15 on the morning of September 7, 1914.[37]

This first long blast of victory was followed by a formal celebration incorporated with the No-Tsu-Oh Carnival of that year. Patterned after

36 *Ibid.*
37 *Ibid.*, p. 13.

New Orleans' Mardi Gras and filling a week in November, No-Tsu-Oh had first been celebrated in 1899. Traditionally, an outstanding civic or business leader ruled as king, while the season's most beautiful and blue-blooded debutante reigned as queen. The carnival was characterized by much backward spelling. No-Tsu-Oh, for example, was Houston backward, while its monarch was King Nottoc, cotton backward. During carnival week Harrisburg became Grub-Sir-Rah; all Saxet was invited; and the Negro citizens held their own celebration called De-Ro-Loc Carnival and ruled by King La-Yol-E-Civ-Res. Houstonians did not altogether abandon No-Tsu-Oh nor backward spelling in 1914, but they named the celebration the No-Tsu-Oh Deep-Water Jubilee, with emphasis on the last three words, and replaced King Nottoc with King Retaw I. Previously the carnival had been stereotyped, copied from others, and lacking in meaning, observed the Houston *Daily Post*, but for 1914 it would be a distinctively Houston celebration.[38]

Houston's leaders planned a celebration such as the city had never seen. The Turning Basin was decked in holiday attire, being surrounded by streamers, banners, and flags. Forty blocks of the downtown streets were strung with incandescent lights, still a novelty, while the wires supporting the trolley wires were strung with red, white, and blue streamers. The press watched the preparations with anticipation. "Inasmuch as there are four of these wires to the block, the streets will be a maze of brilliant color," wrote a reporter for the *Post*.[39]

Figuring prominently in the preparations for the Jubilee were the Red Roosters, a group of high-spirited young men from prominent families. Organized in August, 1913, to add merriment to the No-Tsu-Oh of that year, the Roosters had delighted the crowds by their burlesque of events of the carnival. For example, they were ruled by a High Cockalorum and Little Brown Hen. The Roosters themselves enjoyed their pranks so much that they decided to make their organization permanent. Departing from the characteristic backward spelling, they

38 *Daily Post*, November 3, 1914; B. H. Carroll, Jr., *Standard History of Houston*, pp. 282–283.
39 *Daily Post*, November 1, 1914.

derived their name by changing the first letter of the word boosters to an *r*. The two words were synonymous, they explained. The purpose of the Red Roosters, according to their bylaws, was to "promote and encourage social intercourse between the members, advertise Houston and her deep-water port." They took as their motto "First for Houston; one for all, all for one." This group became official boosters of Houston and Southeast Texas during this period. "Since the Roosters were hatched they have taken part in the entertaining of every convention of consequence that has been held in Houston and also have visited several cities advertising the Deep Water Jubilee," said the *Post*. Membership was limited to two hundred, and there was a long waiting list before the organization was a year old. Appropriately enough, Clarence Kendall, a descendant of General Sidney Sherman, was president of the Red Roosters in 1914.[40]

As their major stunt of the Deep-Water Jubilee, the Roosters planned a Zulu float in which "200 howling savages elaborately dressed with a ring of grass around their bodies" were scheduled to participate. The *Post* hailed this float in advance as the most original ever seen in Houston:

On the float will be a Zulu grass hut in which will be seen a number of captive missionaries. At regular intervals, a missionary will be plucked from his prison and plunged into a huge black pot under which a fire will be burning. The cooks will stir the pot with their spears and will occasionally reach down and pick out nice juicy ribs which they will hand to the prancing savages that will howl around the float.[41]

In addition to the Red Roosters, others added individual touches to the Deep-Water Jubilee. The Traveling Men, another club, promised to present as their queen "the most physically perfect and beautiful woman in Tekram"; that daredevil of the air, DeLloyd Thompson, arrived to thrill the crowds with his airplane stunts; and Judd Mortimer Lewis, later named the first poet laureate of Texas, wrote a poem in honor of the occasion.

[40] *Ibid.*, November 8, 1914.
[41] *Ibid.*, November 1, 1914.

As the great week approached, the Deep-Water Jubilee vied with
the war in Europe for newspaper headlines in Houston papers. The
festivities began with the arrival on Monday morning of King Retaw I,
in real life Eugene Arthur Hudson, founder of the Hudson Furniture
Company. Half a dozen bands heralded his arrival and a group of
Agricultural and Mechanical College cadets escorted him through the
streets. That afternoon the Agricultural and Mechanical College met
Rice Institute in a football game (final score: A. and M., 32; Rice, 7),
and the remainder of the week was marked by other festivities, among
them an elaborate Ships of All Nations Pageant, a floral parade, and
various stunts by such organizations as the Traveling Men and Red
Roosters. The week ended with a ball and the presentation of the
queen, Miss Frankie Carter,[42] daughter of Mr. and Mrs. William T.
Carter.

The formal opening of the channel came on Tuesday morning, November 10, when the celebrants gathered at the Turning Basin. Head-
ing a group of dignitaries present for the occasion were Governor
Oscar B. Colquitt, Governor-elect James E. Ferguson, and Lieutenant
Governor-elect William P. Hobby. As a special feature, the planners
had arranged that President Woodrow Wilson push a pearl-topped
button in Washington, to set off a cannon on the banks of the Turning
Basin and thus signal the opening of the channel. The local manager
of Mackay Telegraph-Cable Company, F. C. Lacy, had arranged for
this device, and the Southern Pacific Railroad Company had cooperated
by lending one of its wires. Technicians gave assurances that the device
would work, but still those responsible for the celebration awaited the
moment with some anxiety. This was laid to rest when at twelve o'clock
Washington time, eleven o'clock in Houston, the President interrupted
a Cabinet meeting to press the button. At Houston the cannon boomed.
Miss Sue Campbell, daughter of Mayor Ben Campbell, stepped to the
platform of a ship in the Turning Basin, took several white roses from
a basket on her arm, and dropped them into the water. "I christen thee
Port of Houston and hither the boats of all nations may come and re-

[42] Later Mrs. R. D. Randolph, liberal Democratic leader in Texas.

ceive hearty welcome," she said. The band struck up the "Star-Spangled Banner," a twenty-one-gun salute sounded over the Turning Basin, and the crowds cheered. Some two thousand miles away in the White House President Wilson wondered if he had indeed set off the cannon. "Did she fire?" he asked an aide as he resumed his seat at the Cabinet meeting. The aide sent the question by wire to Houston, and the answer came back, "The ship channel is open."[43]

[43] *Ibid.*, November 11, 1914; Houston *Chronicle*, November 10, 1914.

VIII. REACHING FOR THE SEA

~~~~~~

DURING THE DEEP-WATER JUBILEE HOUSton's newspapers sometimes carried double headlines of equal size, one
telling of events in the local celebration and the other of the war in
Europe. For example, on November 9, 1914, the *Daily Post* carried
the headlines:

KING RETAW WILL OPEN JUBILEE TODAY
ALLIES' POSITION IS SAID TO BE HOPELESS

Although the headlines seemed so unrelated as to be ludicrous in juxtaposition, the war in fact had profound implications for the new-born
port. For those who had waited long for deep water it was bitter irony
that only weeks before the twenty-five-foot depth became a fact a war
should break out that would paralyze world commerce for the next
four years. The same newspaper that hailed the arrival of the first
deep-draft vessel on the channel also reported a $58,320,619 decrease
in United States export trade due to the war;[1] and the same papers that

[1] Houston *Daily Post*, September 26, 1914.

hailed the inauguration of regular coastwise service to Houston reported that Great Britain had placed cotton on the contraband list and gave the grim statistics for Houston's first year as a deep-water port. Whereas citizens had confidently expected a sharp increase, channel trade in fact dropped almost one half, the figures being 1,860,452 short tons for 1913 to 1,070,700 for 1914. Cotton, still the channel's most valuable cargo, dropped one third, thus accounting for most of the decrease, but, because of generally adverse conditions, lumber also showed a decrease.[2]

The development of the Port was hindered not only by the war but also by the natural reluctance of ocean vessels to venture into new and untested waterways. Even before the final depth was achieved, Joseph H. Carroll, a local wholesale coal and coke dealer who customarily received cargoes at Texas City, began efforts to bring large vessels up the channel. When steamship owners protested that they had no information about the waterway, he made a trip to New York, taking blueprints of it to them. As a result of his efforts and under the agency of Blakely Smith & Company, the first two ocean vessels made use of the new channel. On September 26, 1914, the schooner *William C. May*, 184 feet long, 37 feet of beam, and drawing 16.5 feet of water, docked at the Southern Pacific wharves at Clinton with a cargo of pipe from Philadelphia. This vessel received no official welcome, but on October 12 a party of dignitaries went to the San Jacinto Battleground to meet the second deep-water vessel, the Bull Line steamer *Dorothy*, and congratulate Carroll for his efforts on behalf of the Port. The *Dorothy*, 290 feet long, 40 feet of beam, and drawing 19 feet of water, was commanded by Captain W. L. Farnsworth and brought 3,000 tons of coal from Philadelphia to Clinton. The captains of both these vessels confessed that they came up the channel with misgivings, fearing that they would not find the promised depth. But neither ran into difficulty and both professed to be pleased with the waterway.[3]

[2] *Ibid.*, August 15, 1915; "Houston Ship Channel, Tex.," *House Doc.*, 65 Cong., 3 Sess., No. 1632.

[3] Charles Crotty to J. Russell Wait, June 16, 1939, HCHSCND files, Q-8; Houston *Chronicle*, October 12, 13, 1914; *Daily Post*, September 26, October 13, 1914.

Nevertheless, other vessels were slow to follow them. The United States revenue cutter *Windom* made several trips up the channel in the fall of 1914; on December 10 the schooner *Francis Hyde* brought in a cargo of 1,400 tons of phosphate rock to the recently completed Armour Fertilizer Works just below the Turning Basin; and on December 18 the schooner *Pleroma* brought a cargo of 150,000 coconuts from Central America.[4] But this was the extent of ocean-going traffic during the year of the Deep-Water Jubilee. Movements were just as sporadic during the early part of the following year. On June 15, 1915, the Gulf tanker *Winifred* arrived with the first cargo of foreign oil from Mexico; the *New Orleans* made several trips bringing general merchandise; and possibly a few other sea-going vessels ventured up the channel. But on the whole the traffic was discouraging. Faced with the European war, the timidity of large vessels, and the lack of public shipping facilities, Houston's leaders realized that the development of a port required more than a specified depth of water. Thus, the energies that had previously been directed toward putting dredges to work on Buffalo Bayou were turned to the attracting of vessels to the channel.

As a first step the Houstonians attempted to secure a regular coastwise service for the port. Largely through the good offices of Colonel R. H. Baker and his son Burke Baker, the Southern Steamship Company, a subsidiary of the Atlantic, Gulf, and West Indies Lines, became interested in the potential of Houston. On May 13, 1915, a representative of the company arrived in Galveston, where Burke Baker and a small committee met him and brought him to Houston on Horace Baldwin Rice's yacht, the *Zeeland*. H. C. Schumacher, president of the Chamber of Commerce, presented Houston's claims for service and appointed a committee consisting of Burke Baker, Alexander Sessums Cleveland, R. H. Spencer, D. D. Peden, and C. L. Desel to negotiate in the matter. When the company did not immediately schedule the service, Cleveland and Spencer went to New York. With them they carried a bond signed by a hundred citizens, promising to pay a thousand dollars each to the line if any losses were incurred in giving

4 Crotty to Wait, June 16, 1939, HCHSCND files, Q-8.

Houston the desired service. The company refused the bond, and inaugurated service without it.[5] The company's first vessel to Houston, the *Satilla*, 312 feet long and drawing 22 feet of water, left New York early in August, loaded with seventy-five carloads of general merchandise.

As the first public wharves were scheduled for completion in time for the *Satilla*'s use, Mayor Ben Campbell arranged for what the newspapers called a "monster celebration" of the occasion. He declared August 19, the date set for the *Satilla*'s arrival, a holiday, and the city planned the biggest barbecue ever attempted in the county. Barbecue pits two blocks long were dug near the Turning Basin and arrangements made to feed ten thousand people. In addition, plans called for a parade, a speaking, a watermelon feast, and a free dance sponsored by the Red Roosters, "Houston's famous funmakers." The speaking was scheduled for the new warehouse at the Turning Basin with Tom Ball serving as master of ceremonies, and Lieutenant Governor William P. Hobby, Colonel C. S. Riche, and others addressing the assembly. A separate celebration, to be attended by Governor James E. Ferguson, was planned for the San Jacinto Battleground.

But before the great day arrived, a Gulf storm slammed into the Texas coast, bringing death and destruction in its wake and refreshing memories of the Great Strom of 1900. Thanks to the seawall and to the raising of the city of Galveston by filling, the island escaped another major disaster, but the causeway to the mainland was washed away and the island isolated for several days. At Morgan's Point water covered the flats to a depth of four or five feet and wrecked the quarterboat that had served as headquarters for Charles Crotty's survey party during the dredging of the channel. Commodore E. M. Hartrick, who refused to leave the boat, was drowned, while other members of the party narrowly escaped. Crotty and his wife lived about two blocks from the bay. When water began rising dangerously about midnight on August 15, they and a group of neighbors grasped a long rope and, guided by a single flashlight, made their way to higher ground. "The

---

[5] Thomas H. Ball, *The Port of Houston: How It Came to Pass*, pp. 45–47.

water was about ankle deep when we started, with a terrific wind and rain beating in our faces," Crotty wrote. "By use of the flashlight we were able to see the telephone poles and keep on the shell road, but the water rose so rapidly that it was waist deep before we reached the rising ground, with drift, logs, dead animals, etc., swirling around us."[6]

As soon as the immediate danger passed, Captain Sinclair Taliaferro took a tug down the channel from Houston to check on the losses and re-establish communications. Crotty joined him at Morgan's Point and they decided to try to get through to Galveston. All along the channel buoys and beacons had been swept away, and the two dredges, *Sam Houston* and *San Jacinto*, that had been working at Red Fish reef, were badly damaged. But the first concern of Taliaferro and Crotty was for the depth of the channel. Through the years the channel had gained a reputation for silting, and many pessimists had predicted that the first bad storm would mean the end of the twenty-five-foot depth. As they made their way to Galveston, the men took soundings with a lead line to see if the channel had shoaled. To their surprise they found that it seemed deeper than before the storm. A few days later when the water was normal, a survey showed that the channel had indeed retained its full depth. "This hurricane dispelled the fears of many Houstonians that the channel would be filled up by such a storm," commented Crotty, "and, perhaps, disappointed some of the Port's competitors who hoped and expected it would be filled."[7]

The storm postponed indefinitely the "monster" celebration planned for the *Satilla*. The ship rode out the storm in the Gulf, arriving at Bolivar Roads on August 20. Upon assurances that the channel had not been damaged, the ship came to the Turning Basin, where a crowd of about two thousand citizens welcomed it quietly on August 22.[8] Thereafter, Southern Steamship Company vessels became increasingly a common sight on the ship channel. Although the war created adverse conditions and the Houston run lost money at first, the company continued the service, thus winning for itself a special and enduring place in the

[6] Charles Crotty, "Houston Ship Channel, Texas," p. 16, MS, Charles Crotty Collection.

[7] *Ibid.*, p. 17.

[8] *Daily Post*, August 23, 1914.

affections of ship-channel enthusiasts. By 1918 most of the tonnage in and out of the ship channel other than crude oil was carried on Southern Steamship vessels, among them the *Algiers, Altemaha, Ockmulgee,* and *Ossabaw.* These vessels were from 281 to 300 feet in length and drew from 18 to 22 feet of water.[9]

The Southern Steamship service was one of the few bright spots in channel traffic during the war years. Tonnage figures told a gloomy story, and even by 1920 the total tonnage amounted to only 1,210,204 as compared to 2,030,646 for a decade earlier. These figures brought many I-told-you-so's from those who had little faith in the channel. One Houston professional man remarked while watching the loading of an early vessel that one could "make a better living in Houston for the next twenty years selling snow shoes" than by handling all the ships that came into port. Roy Montgomery Farrar heard a prominent railroad man refer to the channel as "a huge economic mistake," and Galvestonians, who for two generations had derided the idea of deep water at Houston, were in their heyday. One islander told Farrar that the Houston waterway was "the damndest fake out of doors," while Benjamin Casey Allin, the first Port director, and Blakely Smith, a Houston shipping agent, attended a banquet at Galveston where the speakers tried to outdo each other in making fun of Houston's channel. One speaker suggested that hinges be put on large vessels so they could turn the bends on the bayou, and T. R. Hancock, manager of the Texas City Terminal, proposed that Houston fill in the bayou, pave it as a highway, and thus profit from the ocean traffic at Galveston. Yet another speaker summed up the island's general attitude toward Houston's pretensions as a port. "If you people at Houston could turn the channel into a pipeline and suck as hard as you can blow, you'd have deep water at Houston," he said.[10]

But in spite of tonnage figures and derision, the future of the channel was already becoming apparent by the end of World War I. The war had proved the usefulness of the internal-combustion engine, thus

9 "Houston Ship Channel, Tex.," *House Doc.,* 65 Cong., 3 Sess., No. 1632.

10 *Daily Post,* June 4, 1922; Benjamin Casey Allin, *Reaching for the Sea,* pp. 96–97; R. M. Farrar, *The Story of Buffalo Bayou and the Houston Ship Channel,* n.p.; and as related by Blakely Smith to the writer, February 12, 1966.

creating a demand for petroleum, and by 1918 the farsighted had recognized the peculiar advantages of the channel as a location for oil refineries. By that time the Petroleum Refining Company had a refinery
in operation on the north side of the channel near Galena; Sinclair Oil
Company had a refinery under construction on the south side; Humble
Oil and Refining Company had bought 1,500 acres near Goose Creek;
and the Empire Oil and Gas Company had bought a thousand acres
near the San Jacinto Battleground. In addition, rumors were rife that
other oil companies had purchased or were negotiating for sites. As
early as 1905 Joseph Stephen Cullinan had marked Houston as the
executive center of the petroleum industry for the Southwest, and by
1918 he had marked the channel as an oil-refining center. In a letter to
Colonel J. C. Sanford dated August 9, 1918, Cullinan listed the re-
quirements of oil refineries: deep water, abundant fresh water, large
acreage, and protection from floods and tropical storms. He pointed
out that only two areas on the Texas Gulf Coast offered all these. One
was the Houston Ship Channel, and the other the Neches and Sabine
channels south of Beaumont and Orange respectively. Moreover, refineries in these areas were assured of a long working life because of
the abundant crude-oil supplies nearby and because additional supplies
could easily be obtained from Mexico and Central and South
America.[11]

By 1918 most of the petroleum on the channel was transported by
oil barges measuring from 125 to 200 feet in length, from 30 to 38
feet in width, and drawing from 6 to 14.5 feet loaded. In areas affording deeper water, however, large tankers, drawing as much as 30 feet,
had come into use and had proved the most economical means of transporting oil. Thus, oil interests on the channel felt themselves at a disadvantage. The Petroleum Refining Company, for example, reported
the loss of a $1,312,000 order because the customer's vessels drawing
27 feet could not negotiate the channel. While the war was still in
progress and at a time when even the twenty-five-foot depth was
poorly utilized, oilmen, headed by Cullinan and Ross S. Sterling, led a
movement for deeper water. In response to their request, army engi-

---

[11] "Houston Ship Channel, Tex.," *House Doc.*, 65 Cong., 3 Sess., No. 1632.

neers approved a depth of 30 feet in 1919. Congress made appropriations for the project in 1921, and the new depth was achieved in
1925.[12]

Oil refineries and other industries on the ship channel foretold a
basic and significant change in Houston's commerce. From its founding, the city had been a distribution center, its prosperity largely dependent on the handling of cargoes destined for other places. In a historical analysis of the city's commerce in 1910 Dermot H. Hardy and
Ingham S. Roberts wrote, "Houston became not an ultimate market,
where commodities were brought to be converted by manufacture or to
be consumed; but rather the convenient point where commerce is collected for wider transmission and where imports are distributed to
smaller communities." At the time they wrote, Hardy and Roberts
found the intermediate relationship to trade still the basic characteristic
of Houston's commerce.[13] But eight years later twenty-two industries
were located on the channel below the Turning Basin and sixteen
above, and perceptive observers saw that Houston was destined to be
an industrial as well as a distribution center. "The future of the Houston Ship Channel appears to lie in the direction of industrial development as its banks furnish very favorable locations for industries which
would thus be given the advantage of water transportation," wrote
Major R. C. Smead in a report to the Secretary of War made in 1918.[14]

The future of the Port was not readily apparent to Benjamin Casey
Allin when he reported to work for Ross S. Sterling on March 16,
1919. A native Chicagoan and world traveler who had come to Camp
Logan, Texas, as a United States Army officer, Allin had decided that
the oil industry offered the greatest opportunity to a young man with
his way to make. Thus at war's end he sought an introduction to Sterling and was promised employment by him. But when Allin reported
for work, Sterling had a surprise in store. On March 2 Congress had
approved thirty feet of water for the Houston Ship Channel, and on
the same day it had adopted a policy with profound implications for

---

[12] *Ibid.; Chronicle*, July 1, 1925.
[13] Dermot H. Hardy and Ingham S. Roberts, *Historical Review of South-East Texas*, I, p. 242.
[14] "Houston Ship Channel, Tex.," *House Doc.*, 65 Cong., 3 Sess., No. 1632.

American shipping. The war had left the government with a large surplus of ships and Congress proposed to put these to work in the United States merchant marine and encourage the development of American ports. "Plans have been changed," Sterling told Allin, referring to events in Washington. "What we want you to undertake is development, construction, and operation of the Port of Houston."[15] Allin, an engineer with railroad experience, protested that he knew nothing whatever about port operations, that he had never held public office and never wanted to. Sterling quieted these protests and sent him to inspect the ship channel and talk to the navigation and canal commissioners and members of the harbor board.

The physical aspects of the Port did not impress Allin favorably. City terminal facilities at that time consisted of a creosoted-timber dock, 650 feet long, with a single-story, reinforced-concrete warehouse; a concrete dock, 777 feet long, with a similar warehouse; a creosoted-timber cotton dock, 800 feet long, with three cotton storage sheds covering 5.75 acres; an open concrete dock, 1,303 feet long; a concrete warehouse covering 5 acres; and 7.7 miles of terminal railway that connected with main lines of the railroads entering Houston. Allin was critical of the fact that all these facilities were concentrated in one area near the Turning Basin, thus creating a "masterpiece of congestion where cargoes could pile up one atop the other." Moreover, the warehouses built for channel cargoes were filled to the rafters with condemned World War I airplanes, and the two dredges for which Houston had paid one-half the cost had been dispatched to parts unknown while the channel shoaled.[16]

Unimpressive as were the Port facilities, Allin glimpsed the future as he talked to local leaders. When he wrote his memoirs some thirty-five years later, he paid special tribute to the foresight of Roy Montgomery Farrar, John T. Scott, and Jonas Shearn Rice, but he reserved his highest praise for Sterling. "He needed no stimulant to bring out the hardy qualities of his personality . . .," Allin wrote, "and he compelled the respect of men for the high personal principles by which he

---

15 Allin, *Reaching for the Sea*, p. 84.
16 *Ibid.*, p. 86; "Houston Ship Channel, Tex.," *House Doc.*, 65 Cong., 3 Sess., No. 1632.

lived." Sterling was further distinguished in Allin's memory for the grand scale of his thought in all matters pertaining to the growth of Houston and especially in the development of the city as a port. "If Houston today is the biggest city of our biggest state, it certainly owes much of the swift and solid character of its growth to Ross Sterling," he wrote in 1956.[17]

Sterling and other Houstonians called Allin's attention to the budding petroleum industry on the channel and also the city's potential as a cotton port. Houston was already the largest spot cotton market in the world and second only to New Orleans in the volume of cotton orders handled. But cotton ordered from Houston was not shipped from there. With the deepening of the channel and the increase in the merchant marine, Houston could look forward to a large cotton-export business. The city could build its port on oil and cotton, and, looking at a map, Allin saw that its location would bring other cargoes. "The city lies at the seaward, western side of the broad Mississippi Valley stretching from the Great Lakes to the Gulf, bounded by the Rockies on the west and the Appalachian chain on the east," he wrote. "Within this area 1,500 miles wide lies most of the agricultural wealth of the country; the cities cradled within it produce a high percentage of the nation's manufactures."[18] Inspired by the vision of the Port's future, Allin cast his lot with the Port of Houston. As Port director for the next twelve years, he helped translate the vision into reality and saw the Port come from a standing start to rank among the top in the nation. His responsibilities increased so rapidly that he induced Charles Crotty to resign his position with the United States Engineers to become assistant Port director on April 19, 1920.

Originally, Allin and Crotty were employed jointly by the navigation and canal commission and the city harbor board, but the two bodies were consolidated in 1922. From the first the divided authority had proved impractical. In some instances the jurisdiction of the two boards overlapped, thus arousing jealousy between county and city; and in other instances neither body had the power necessary for the proper development of the channel. For example, the Navigation District had

---

[17] Allin, *Reaching for the Sea*, p. 83.
[18] *Ibid.*, p. 85.

no authority whatever to build waterfront facilities, and, as traffic began increasing at the end of the war, it became obvious that the city could not adequately finance the facilities needed for the Port's growth.

Moreover, there was the touchy question of the development of the waterfront outside the city limits, a question closely related to the old matter of the location of the Turning Basin. This question came to the forefront when the state legislature passed a law in 1913 permitting the city to extend its limits for police but not taxation purposes for 2,500 feet on either side of the stream for twenty miles downstream. The matter became a burning issue in the spring of 1917 because of a gift to the city of land at Manchester. In the fall of 1914 Joseph R. Cheek and associates offered to give the city twenty acres of land with 1,500 feet of channel frontage on the condition that the city build a wharf on part of the frontage. Mayor Ben Campbell, believing he had the approval of other city officials, accepted the offer, but later when he moved to build the wharf the city harbor board protested vigorously that Manchester was outside the tax boundaries of the city and therefore the city should not build there. Houstonians divided sharply on the issue. Jesse H. Jones, chairman of the harbor board, led the opposition and suggested that instead of downstream expansion deep water be extended toward Main Street. Oilmen as a group supported Mayor Campbell. Hugh Roy Cullen, for example, wrote a letter to the *Post* in favor of building the wharf, while Joseph S. Cullinan urged not only that the city build at Manchester but that it develop all the channel "from Houston to Morgan's Point." In the heat of the controversy Jones and three other members of the harbor board—Camille G. Pillot, Roy M. Farrar, and Daniel Ripley—resigned, leaving John T. Scott as the lone board member.[19]

The city accepted the gift and along with it the obligation to build a wharf at Manchester, but three years later the issue was reopened with renewed bitterness. The harbor board proposed to buy additional property for development at Manchester and asked for a bond issue to pay

[19] *Daily Post,* April 3, 6, 7, 8, 16, 22, 25, 1917; *Chronicle,* April 16, 1917; Ball, *Port of Houston,* p. 45; Minutes of the City Council, City of Houston, Vol. 5, p. 360.

for the purchase. This request led to one of the bitterest elections in the Port's history. Jones gave vigorous opposition to the bond issue in the pages of his Houston *Chronicle,* while the *Daily Post,* Roy G. Watson, publisher and president, supported the issue. The voters agreed with Jones and defeated the bonds by a margin of three to one.[20]

The bitterness engendered by this election caused some citizens to fear that the United States government would refuse further assistance to the Port. As the administration and financing had also proved unsatisfactory, leaders suggested basic changes in the structure of the Navigation District. "A way must be found to create a port and industrial district that will be self-supporting, self-extending, capable of floating securities upon its own values, instead of upon the public credit, and paying its expenses and debts out of its own revenues," said a *Post* editorial. "This plan will relieve the municipality and its current revenues of all port burdens, and it will relieve the port of the burden and embarrassment of ward rivalries, speculative rapacity, personal grudges, popular prejudice, mossbackism, and political demagogy."[21]

In order to accomplish these purposes, leaders proposed in early 1921 that the powers of the Navigation District be enlarged and that the District and city boards be combined. Soon after taking office Mayor Oscar Holcombe brought city and county officials together, and in a meeting that lasted through the night and into the morning hours they agreed on a reorganization of the Navigation District. At their request the state legislature passed a bill on August 21, 1921, that gave the District wide power to acquire wharves, warehouses, and any other facilities or aids to commerce incident to the development of the Port or the channel. The bill also provided for the consolidation of the two authorities into a single board of five members called the Board of Navigation and Canal Commissioners. Two members would be appointed by the county commissioners' court; two by the city council; and the county commissioners and city councilmen would jointly ap-

[20] *Daily Post,* November 2, 3, 4, 5, 6, 10, 1920; *Chronicle,* November 2, 4, 6, 7, 9, 1920.
[21] *Daily Post,* November 11, 1920.

point the chairman. The term of office would be for two years, with the terms expiring in alternate years.[22]

Voters approved these changes early in 1922, and in May the two original boards were combined. E. A. Peden was appointed first chairman of the new commission. Other members were Ross S. Sterling, Roy M. Farrar, Robert J. Cummins, and D. S. Cage. Tom Ball was appointed counsel for the District. Peden resigned on October 13, 1924, at which time former mayor Ben Campbell became a member and Sterling became chairman. The only other change on the Port Commission, as the new board was popularly called, during the twenties occurred when Farrar resigned on June 1, 1925, and was replaced by William T. Carter, Jr. The new commissioners continued the tradition of serving without remuneration.

In accordance with the powers granted by the new act, the Navigation District leased all city waterfront facilities and late in 1922 won the voters' approval of a four-million-dollar bond issue for the building of new wharves, a grain elevator, additional channel railway, and other channel improvements. Throughout the twenties the District expanded services and engaged in a continual building program without ever quite catching up with the demand. From 1922 to 1924 four new concrete wharves with a total length of 2,140 feet were built on the north side of the Turning Basin; in 1926 a public grain elevator with a capacity of a million bushels was completed; during 1928 two other wharves, totaling 940 feet in length, were constructed. In addition to this new construction, the older facilities were enlarged and improved. By 1930 the District could boast that it had 7,401 feet of public wharves with berths for seventeen vessels.[23]

During this same period the District made significant strides in providing public belt railway service on equal terms to all industries located on the channel. By an agreement with the railroads entering Houston, the District contracted to construct railroad trackage to serve the channel but to place control of this trackage under a neutral organi-

[22] D. A. Simmons, "Organization of Navigation Districts in Texas," *Houston Port Book* (November, 1941), pp. 17–18.
[23] "Description of the Port," *Houston Port and City* (May, 1930), pp. 13–19.

zation, the Port Terminal Railroad Association. By the terms of the agreement the association was placed under a board of control consisting of representatives from each of the trunk lines or member lines serving the city, while the chairman of the Port Commission was also to serve as chairman of the board of control. The Port Terminal Railroad Association took over the operation of the public belt railway on July 1, 1924. As industries multiplied and new wharves were built, the publicly owned railroad was extended on both sides of the channel. By 1930 it stretched for 42.01 miles on the north side and 30.36 on the south for a total of 72.37 miles.[24]

Officials considered port promotion one of their important activities during the twenties. When Allin accepted the position of director, he visited several other ports to inspect their operations. His findings convinced him that port promotion was a neglected activity and that most authorities proceeded on the false assumption that once built, a port would inevitably be used. Because of Houston's inland location both he and the Port Commissioners felt that promotion would have to be a continuous activity there. This belief led to the creation of the Houston Port Bureau under the sponsorship of agencies interested in the Port's development, among them the City of Houston, the Port Commission, Houston Merchants' Exchange, Houston Chamber of Commerce, Houston Cotton Exchange, and the Maritime Committee of the Houston Cotton Exchange. The Houston Port Bureau began operations on June 1, 1929, by establishing offices at New York, Kansas City, Dallas, and Houston. Originally designed as a solicitation agency, the bureau proved a flexible agency that was reorganized from time to time during the following decades to meet the special needs of the times.[25]

The policy of construction and promotion paid off handsomely during the twenties. Cotton, the historic cargo of the bayou, accounted for much of the Port's growth. Through the influence of Daniel Ripley, a

[24] "Description of the Port," *ibid.* (May, 1931), p. 16; "Annual Railroad Inspection, Port Terminal Railroad Association," *ibid.,* p. 21; Ball, *Port of Houston,* pp. 69–73.

[25] *Daily Post,* May 15, 1929; "The Houston Port Bureau, Its Purpose and Accomplishments," *Houston Port and City* (May, 1930), p. 25.

veteran steamship operator, the United States Shipping Board vessel *Merry Mount* arrived in Houston in November, 1919, to take the first cotton directly to Europe. The *Merry Mount*, loaded with 23,719 bales, left Houston on November 15, while jubilant cotton men watched from the shore and looked forward to a bright new day.

But even after the *Merry Mount*'s successful voyage, regular export service was delayed because of rumors that the vessel had encountered difficulties in navigating the channel. According to A. Munkewitz, master of the *Merry Mount*, "The ship came down the ship canal in fine shape. Above Morgan's Point she took the bank a couple of times, but really never stuck." Word went to the shipping board, however, that "the ship went aground seven times and had it not been for the assistance of the tugs there is no doubt but that the ship would have had a serious time of it." Irate Houstonians charged that this report was maliciously manufactured in Galveston, but nevertheless it caused the shipping board to hesitate before sending other vessels to Houston. Only after local interests had protested vigorously and insured the steamship *Montgomery* at their own expense did American and foreign vessels begin regular export service to Houston.[26]

After the safety of the channel had been proved, the facilities for handling both cotton and cotton exports increased rapidly. In 1922 Alexander Sprunt & Son, a cotton firm that had operated barges on the channel since 1866, built the Ship Channel Compress Company. The following year the Houston Compress Company, owned by Anderson, Clayton and Company, acquired southside frontage about half a mile below the Turning Basin and built the facility known familiarly as Long Reach, a facility that remained for decades the largest private terminal on the channel. A few years later Manchester Terminal Corporation built another private terminal designed primarily to handle cotton. By 1930 the Houston Compress Company had berths for six vessels; the Manchester Terminal Corporation, for four; and the Ship Channel Compress Company, for two. Cotton exports increased from

---

[26] A. Munkewitz to Messrs. Daniel Ripley & Co., November 15, 1919 (copy furnished by R. Starley Tevis); unsigned memorandum dated April 29, 1924, also furnished by R. Starley Tevis; Houston *Post*, November 3, 16, 1919.

275,879 bales in 1920 to 2,069,792 a decade later,[27] at which time Houstonians could say with pride that their port led all other United States ports in cotton exports. For the season ending July 31, 1930, Houston led its nearest competitor by 276,000 bales.[28]

During the decade 1920–1930 petroleum also fulfilled all the hopes held for it as a cargo on the channel. By 1927 eight refineries with a capacity of about 125,000 barrels of crude oil daily were in operation along the waterway. About half the crude oil reached Houston by pipeline, and the remainder came by tank cars, tankers, and barges. An average of three tankers, each carrying from 25,000 to 115,000 barrels, passed through the channel daily to handle petroleum products. By 1930 Humble Oil and Refining Company had private berths for four vessels; Texas Company, for four; Shell Petroleum Corporation, for three; Sinclair Refining Company, for three; and Clarion Oil Company, Gulf Refining Company, Crown Central Petroleum Corporation, American Petroleum Corporation, and Gulf Pipe Line Company had berths for one vessel each. By that year twenty-seven tanker lines were in operation at the Port and more than 3,920,100 tons of petroleum products were exported.[29] As oil boosted the total tonnage carried on the channel, rival ports noted with condescension that this was *liquid cargo*. "And even today, when Houston is second only to New York in total tonnage handled," Allin wrote in 1956, "New Orleans taunts the Texas metropolis with the fact that three out of four tons

[27] Cotton exports for the intervening years were as follows:

1921	455,015 bales
1922	771,894
1923	1,004,680
1924	1,288,280
1925	1,918,314
1926	2,071,005
1927	2,158,475
1928	2,326,372
1929	1,998,739

(HCHSCND, Annual Report, 1930, p. 33-A).

[28] *Ibid.*, p. 33-A; J. V. Scott, "Cotton and the Port of Houston," *Houston Port and City* (November, 1930), pp. 32–33.

[29] *Ibid.*, p. 23-A; "Oil Transportation Through the Ship Channel," *Houston Port and City* (November, 1927), p. 31.

handled on the Houston docks are liquid cargo—oil. This is a hollow taunt. We like it that way."[30]

No grain was shipped out of Houston in 1919, but from the opening of the new grain elevator on July 1, 1926, grain became increasingly an important cargo on the channel. Originally constructed with a storage capacity of a million bushels, the elevator was designed so it could easily be enlarged as the volume demanded it. Grain poured into Houston from the vast grainlands stretching north from Texas to Canada, and within only a few years the elevator became inadequate. In the first year of its operation it handled 3,045,482 bushels, and in the nine months from July, 1929, to March, 1930, it handled 4,947,515 bushels. Citizens voted a bond issue on March 22, 1930, to increase the elevator's capacity to 3,500,000 bushels.[31] The American Maid Flour Company, which built a plant on the channel in 1922, had additional storage for a million bushels of grain.

In addition to the cargoes that acounted for the spectacular growth of the Port, Houston received some unusual cargoes during this period. One of the most unusual was that carried between Houston and New Orleans by ships of the Bowie Line. Longshoremen customarily greeted these ships with derisive crowing, as live chickens were the exclusive cargo of the line. "It was one of those waterfront legends to which sea people are more commonly addicted than most, that Bowie Line crews were fed only eggs laid enroute, and chickens killed enroute," recalled Allin. "Thus, the longshoremen claimed, the Bowie Line operated without crew maintenance costs, and rolled up fabulous profits. But this Bowie Line diet, and the cargoes carried by its ships, it was further said, made it necessary to give all orders by crowing or cackling."[32]

Another unusual cargo Allin recalled was a shipment of hundreds of bales of human hair from China, this to be used in that pre-nylon day to make filter cloths for the production of peanut butter. Still another cargo Allin remembered belonged peculiarly to the prohibition era. Allin went aboard a Luckenbach ship to welcome it to port only to be

[30] Allin, *Reaching for the Sea*, p. 85.
[31] George S. Colby, "Tripling Houston's Grain Facilities," *Houston Port and City* (May, 1930), pp. 22–23.
[32] Allin, *Reaching for the Sea*, pp. 108–109.

greeted like a long-lost brother by the son of the line's owner. The skipper, engine-room gang, and galley crew met him with equal warmth. Never, he told himself in amazement, had he seen so happy a ship. The happiness was explained when he inspected the hold and found row after row of gleaming champagne bottles. The vessel and its cargo had been acquired from Germany in connection with the peace settlement, but because of prohibition none of the cargo could be legally cleared at any port in the United States. Thus, wrote Allin, "all the cargo had to be consumed on board, making the Paul Luckenbach a kind of champagne version of the Flying Dutchman."[33]

The prosperity of the Port brought corresponding prosperity to the men who worked there. In the year of the Deep-Water Jubilee, longshoremen received thirty cents an hour for day labor, forty cents for night, and a work shift consisted of ten hours. Even these jobs were scarce, and, when the *Satilla* arrived, two union groups battled each other for the privilege of unloading it. At that time the Turning Basin was out in the country, so laborers customarily walked from the end of the street-car line at Harrisburg at 75th Street. Work on the docks was done manually with the assistance of little equipment, the most common piece of equipment being a four-wheel truck called a "backbuster." This truck was usually loaded with about 1,600 pounds of cargo and pulled by two men. Lunch Women, so-called, brought baskets of food on horseback to the docks and sold lunches for twenty cents each. As there were no sewers or running water, there was, of course, no modern sanitation. "In fact there wasn't even old time sanitation," says the writer of a brief but lively history of I.L.A. Local 872. "No one had time to think about constructing privys—not while he could be earning 30¢ an hour for loading fertilizer."[34]

As ships became more numerous, jobs became more plentiful and wages and working conditions improved. By the end of the twenties longshoremen were drawing eighty cents an hour and skilled workers such as cotton screwmen were making more. Galveston longshoremen taught those at Houston the process of "screwing cotton," that is, fit-

[33] *Ibid.,* pp. 110–111.
[34] Charles J. Hill, "A Brief History of I.L.A. Local 872," *Personal Telephone Directory and Local History of I.L.A. 872,* p. 5.

ting more cotton bales into a ship's hold. Customarily thirty cotton bales were stacked across a ship but by "screwing" thirty-five could be pushed into the same space. This practice was followed throughout the twenties, when the demand for cotton in foreign countries put a premium on shipping space. The job of "screwing cotton" was a hot, difficult one, but it paid time and a half.[35]

The elite among those who earned a livelihood from Port operations were the pilots who guided ships in and out of the Port. In the first years after the achievement of deep water, pilots were employed by the Houston Chamber of Commerce and steamships were not charged for the service. This situation was changed in 1919 by the organization of the Houston Pilots with a complement of three men. Each pilot was commissioned by the governor of Texas, and after 1923 the pilots on the channel were appointed by and came under the jurisdiction of the Port Commission. Because piloting requires the greatest experience and wisest judgment of any form of navigation, the pilots were carefully chosen, usually from among tug-boat captains or others thoroughly familiar with the channel. Only after an exacting apprenticeship under an experienced pilot were new pilots appointed.[36] As the Port grew busier, the number of pilots increased until by 1965 there were thirty-nine.

By the end of World War I Galveston had a harbor thirty feet deep and still ranked first on Houston's list of commercial competitors. But during the 1920's the booming Port of Houston passed Galveston first in tonnage carried and then in total value of cargo, and, as 1930 approached, Houstonians began to look farther afield and more and more to think of New Orleans as their greatest competitor.

This did not mean that the old rivalry between the two Texas cities died easily or quickly. Indeed, after Houston acquired deep water, the rivalry blazed brighter than ever over the perennial matter of freight rates. From the time Texas acquired its first railroads centered at Houston, the matter of rates between Houston and Galveston, the so-called

35 *Ibid.*, p. 9.
36 "Houston Pilots Assure Safe Channel Passage," *Houston Port Book* (Spring, 1953), p. 49.

Houston-Galveston differential, had been a sensitive subject. Because the first railroads all led to Houston, the practice evolved of basing rates on the distance to or from that place. But the water route between Houston and Galveston offered competition not encountered elsewhere. Thus, rates between those two places tended to be lower than for similar distances where there was no rail-water competition. For example, in 1872 the rate for carrying a bale of cotton from Hempstead to Houston, a distance of about fifty miles, was $1.25, while the rate for carrying the same bale from Houston to Galveston, also about fifty miles, was $1.00. Although Galveston was fifty miles farther from almost all inland points than Houston, the cross-fire of competition between rail and water transportation resulted in the practice of figuring rates from the interior to Galveston by taking the Houston rate and adding a fixed amount, or differential, that was considerably less than the distance between the two cities justified. By 1888 the differential on first-class freight was ten cents. Thus, a hundred pounds shipped from Palestine to Houston, a distance of about 150 miles, cost sixty-four cents, while a hundred pounds shipped from Palestine to Galveston, a distance of about 200 miles, cost seventy-four cents. The differential served to equalize the cities as shipping points, so that whether the inland producer shipped from Galveston or Houston the ultimate cost of transportation was practically the same, and businessmen in the two port cities competed on an equal basis for trade with the interior.[37]

After the creation of the Railroad Commission of Texas in 1891, Galveston launched efforts to have the differential removed, and from then until the 1930's the matter was constantly before the Railroad Commission, the Interstate Commerce Commission, and in and out of the courts as the two port cities jousted for advantage. The bitterness engendered sometimes found expression in petty ways. For instance, during one No-Tsu-Oh week Galveston papers refused to carry any news whatever about the carnival, and on another occasion delegates from the two cities came to blows in a hotel lobby at Washington during a National Rivers and Harbors Congress. Harvey H. Haines, traffic

[37] Hardy and Roberts, *South-East Texas*, I, pp. 258–262.

manager of the Galveston Chamber of Commerce, bloodied the nose of Houston's Colonel Ike M. Standifer, and Standifer in turn shattered his cane over Haines' head.[38]

The opening of Houston as a deep-water port intensified the controversy over rates. During the early years of the twentieth century Galveston enjoyed rates on coastwise traffic that placed her on parity with Houston and obtained equalization on many import and export commodities. But when the Southern Steamship Company began its Houston service, it made the same rates to Houston as to Galveston, and other shipping lines followed this precedent. Thus Galveston merchants found themselves at a disadvantage in trading with the interior, and they redoubled their efforts to secure equal rail rates between Galveston and Houston and all inland points in Texas. During the 1920's the two port cities spent thousands of dollars in airing their differences before various commissions and courts, and the issue eventually became a political one involving shippers, consumers, producers, the state and federal governments, and other communities.[39]

But even as the battle raged, two new factors, automotive and air transportation, began to figure in the old controversy and to shorten the miles between Houston and Galveston as earlier improvements in transportation had shortened those between Houston and its ancient rival Harrisburg. Moreover, as the city of Houston extended its limits and industries built along the Houston Ship Channel, the number of miles between the two ports actually became less. A younger generation began thinking of the *Greater Houston-Galveston Bay Area* and considering New Orleans as that area's competitor. The Interstate Commerce Commission took note of this new concept in 1930 by expressing the opinion that "Houston, Galveston and Texas City should be considered as one terminal district or port." The disastrous depression of the early thirties further emphasized the common interests of the area and pointed up the folly of the ruinous economic battle between the two ports. In early 1931 private cotton interests of Houston, Galveston, and Texas City grew weary of the fight and quietly met in conference to settle their differences. "The Houston-Galveston cotton in-

[38] *Daily Post*, November 10, December 10, 1909.
[39] S. G. Reed, *A History of Texas Railroads*, pp. 644–651.

terests felt it would be to the best interests of all to combine after the long and futile rate warfare of the past years," commented Kenneth E. Womack, spokesman for the Houston Cotton Exchange, in announcing the terms of the settlement.[40]

This action by cotton men opened the way for further negotiations and for the signing of the Houston-Galveston Equalization Agreement on March 16, 1933. The agreement was based on recognition of the common interests of the area. "It is recognized and accepted as inevitable that in the course of time the cities of Houston, Galveston and Texas City will be physically merged, and that these three ports are already merely one shipping district serving the same territory," the agreement read in part.[41]

The agreement gave Galveston interests almost all they wanted by providing for equalization on import, export, and coastwise shipments. Only interstate domestic shipments and intrastate shipments were left to be equalized.[42] But while Galveston seemingly won the battle, Houston could afford to be generous by the 1930's. In reality, the commercial supremacy enjoyed by the island during the nineteenth century had passed to the inland city at the beginning of the twentieth. In large measure, simple geography accounts for the shift in supremacy. The island was confined by its seawall, while Houston could spread over miles of prairie in every direction. Moreover, Houston had its long, protected channel frontage to attract oil refineries and other industries. But historians have sought other reasons to explain Galveston's comparative decline. Some have blamed the Great Storm and fears of other disasters from the sea for creating a conservative turn of mind among islanders. Others have pointed to the shortsighted policies of the Galveston Wharf Company and its continuing control of the island's waterfront. Still others have suggested that Galveston's leaders deliberately turned their backs on the twentieth-century variety of progress, and,

[40] Houston *Press*, February 10, 1931; Lloyd C. Philips, "The Houston-Galveston Equalization Agreement: A Basis for the Merging of Houston-Galveston into One Port District for Unified Reporting" (unpublished paper).

[41] Philips, "Houston-Galveston Equalization Agreement," p. 11.

[42] In 1952 the Interstate Commerce Commission equalized domestic rates by regrouping the Southwest and placing Galveston in the Houston group.

in this connection, have made much of the comment of a prominent islander to his son as they talked of the general exodus from the island after the Great Storm. "Remember," he said, "the fewer the people, the better the fishing."[43]

Galvestonians are inclined to attribute the island's loss of commercial supremacy to the aggressiveness of Houston's "political port," and in fact the loss occurred almost simultaneously with the Great Storm and Congress' acceptance of Houston's deep-water aspirations. Throughout the nineteenth century Galveston led Houston in population, but in 1900 Houston for the first time surpassed the island, the statistics being 37,789 for Galveston and 44,633 for Houston. During the next decade Galveston's population dropped more than 800 to 36,981, while Houston's almost doubled to 78,800. Thereafter, Galveston grew slowly into a self-contained island metropolis where the nineteenth century lingered long, while Houston spread out over its surrounding prairies to become the perennial boom town of twentieth-century Texas. Before Houston began operations as a deep-water port, Galveston's leaders had adopted a conservative, nonaggressive policy. "Then, as now," Allin wrote in recalling 1919, "Galveston was a solidly established, conservatively and semi-privately operated port whose directors did not seek a mounting volume of traffic, but only the maintenance of its steady level of operations."[44]

By 1930 Houstonians could look back on a decade of fantastic port development. Not only had the Port of Houston surpassed all its Texas rivals, but it ranked third in foreign exports in the United States, being surpassed only by New York and Los Angeles.[45] Almost eighty shipping lines called regularly at the Port, carrying in that year 15,057,360 tons of cargo valued at $500 million.[46] Moreover, the industrial com-

---

[43] Quoted in Howard Barnstone, *The Galveston That Was*, p. 192. Also see *ibid.*, pp. 13–15; Earl W. Fornell, *The Galveston Era*, p. 4.

[44] Allin, *Reaching for the Sea*, p. 88.

[45] The statistics for 1930 were as follows:

	Tonnage of Foreign Exports
New York	7,862,282
Los Angeles	5,854,936
Houston	4,165,243

[46] See Appendix C.

plex that lined the channel had grown each year until more than forty industries lay below the Turning Basin, and more than twenty-five above. In the same period, the city of Houston had grown from third to first in size in the state and to second in size in the South.[47]

To dramatize the decade's eventfulness, Port officials invited the cruiser *Houston* to visit the city for Navy Day, October 27, 1930. The visit held special meaning to many citizens, for they had been instrumental in the naming of the vessel. When Congress authorized the construction of eight large cruisers to be named for various United States cities, William A. Bernrieder, secretary to Mayor Holcombe, City Councilman H. A. Halverton, and Colonel Ike S. Ashburn, of the Chamber of Commerce, launched a drive to have one named for Houston. Through Dr. E. E. Oberholtzer, superintendent of schools, they enlisted the aid of the city's schoolteachers, who had their students write the Secretary of Navy urging that he name one of the ships the *Houston*. Other organizations—civic, social, political, veteran, business, commercial, and juvenile—joined in the drive and flooded the Secretary with letters and telegrams. The communications overwhelmed his office staff until, at last, before making the public announcement, he informed Mayor Holcombe that the Houstonians had won their campaign and asked the Mayor to stop the letters.[48]

After the cruiser's completion and the public announcement of its name, a large delegation of Houstonians traveled to Newport News, Virginia, where on September 7, 1929, they watched Miss Elizabeth Holcombe christen the vessel with a bottle of Buffalo Bayou water. Miss Mary Ellen Bute served as Miss Holcombe's maid of honor, and Miss Charlotte Williams, a granddaughter of Sam Houston, attended as a special guest of the city of Houston.

The announcement that the cruiser would visit the city created widespread interest, for, aside from the citizens' special interest in the vessel, it would be the largest ever to navigate the ship channel, being six hundred feet long and sixty-four in the beam. Port officials planned a

---

[47] "Description of the Port," *Houston Port and City* (May, 1931), p. 14; November, 1931, pp. 39, 22–26.

[48] Ball, *Port of Houston*, pp. 107–108; Scrap Book of the *U.S.S. Houston* (made available by William A. Bernrieder, Houston, Texas).

full week of celebration, complete with a parade, a banquet at the Rice Hotel, and a series of private festivities. Houstonians collected fifteen thousand dollars to buy a silver service to present to the cruiser. As the ship nosed its way up to the Turning Basin, crowds lined the banks of the channel to welcome it, and approximately a quarter of a million persons visited it during its week in port. A high moment of the celebration came when Senator Tom Connally addressed the banquet at the Rice Hotel and predicted that within another decade the Port would rank second in the nation.

The celebration caused those who could remember the beginnings of the Port to look both backward and forward. Ex-Mayor Ben Campbell and Joseph S. Cullinan reminisced about the difficulties that had been overcome in obtaining deep water and exchanged letters agreeing that a history of the Port should be written. "Those of us living now know when the foundation of the ship channel was laid, of the effort it has required to nurse the project and put it on a sound and dependable basis," wrote Cullinan.[49] But John Henry Kirby, who had been instrumental in removing Morgan's infamous chain in 1892, still looked to the future. "Why, my friends," he told those gathered at the Rice Hotel banquet, "we are only getting started!"[50]

[49] Cullinan to Campbell, December 27, 1930, Joseph Stephen Cullinan Papers.
[50] Peter Molyneaux, "Houston: An Example of Progress," *Houston Port and City* (November, 1930), p. 24.

IX. "A CHANNEL PARVENU"

$\sim\sim\sim\sim\sim\sim\sim\sim\sim\sim\sim\sim\sim\sim\sim\sim\sim\sim\sim\sim\sim\sim$

T$_{HE}$ VISIT OF THE CRUISER *Houston* IN THE fall of 1930 marked the end of one era and the beginning of another for the Port of Houston. The preceding year the stock market had crashed, thus bringing to a dramatic end the fat decade of the twenties and thrusting the American people into the lean years of the thirties. At the time of the cruiser's visit, business at the Port still reflected the prosperity of the previous decade, and leading citizens were still considering investments to increase tonnage, but already the paralyzing effects of the Great Depression were spreading through the sinews of the nation's economy and foretelling the dreary years ahead.

Along with this new economic background, the year 1930 brought new leadership to the forefront at the Port of Houston. Early in the year Ben Campbell and D. S. Cage retired from the Port Commission, and later in the year Ross S. Sterling, after being elected governor of Texas, offered his resignation as chairman of the board. Together these three veterans represented almost forty years of experience on the various governing bodies of the Port. All had served on the old harbor board prior to 1922. In addition, Campbell had served as mayor during some crucial years of Port development, and Sterling had been an original member of the old navigation and canal commission when the District was first created in 1911. In 1930 the Port lost not only these experienced leaders but also its first director. A delegation from Stockton, California, inspected the Port during the visit of the cruiser *Houston* and persuaded Benjamin Casey Allin to accept the task of building a port at the West Coast city. The next few years saw still further changes in leadership. Tom Ball, who had grown old while the Port grew large, retired as counsel in July, 1931, after handling an unfortunate land deal for the Port. He was replaced by his partner, David A. Simmons. Two years later William T. Carter, Jr., another name long associated with Port development, retired from the Port Commission. Thus, by 1933 only Robert J. Cummins remained of the men who had been most closely associated with the Port's direction during the twenties. For years Cummins represented a link between the old and new. Beginning his service as a member of the harbor board on May 5, 1921, he had become a member of the consolidated commission in 1922. When he retired, in 1946, he had given a quarter century of service and had set a record for tenure on the Port Commission.

As in the past, new men stepped forward to fill the void in leadership at the Port of Houston. In accordance with the provisions of the law, the city council and the county commissioners' court jointly elected Joseph W. Evans, a man prominent in cotton circles, to the chairmanship. Customarily addressed as Colonel because he was a native of Kentucky, Evans had come to Houston at the turn of the century. In addition to making a name for himself in the cotton business, he had won a reputation for civic leadership in the city. His long tenure as chairman of the Port Commission enhanced that reputation. For fifteen years he left his personal business largely in the hands of his staff while he devoted himself to shaping Port policy to meet the emergencies created by depression and war. Kenneth E. Womack, another influential member of the Cotton Exchange, and Stephen P. Farish filled the other vacancies on the Commission in 1930. Farish retired in 1932, at which time W. A. Sherman began a decade of service. Other new faces on the board during the 1930's were H. C. Cockburn, who served from 1933 to 1937, and his successor, William Walcott Strong, a representative of organized labor whose appointment spoke significantly of changing times.

The most urgent task facing the new chairman and commissioners in 1930 was the selection of a Port director to replace Allin. This was no simple matter for there was no agency that trained men for such a position. Allin had felt himself completely unprepared for it and had searched in vain for a body of Port doctrine to guide him. In his own words, he had "played by ear" in developing the Port, learning by experience as he worked.[1] But Allin had started with the Port from a standing start and grown with it. By 1930 the Port had become a complex business operation, involving not only the diverse activities connected with the shipping but also relations with industry, railroads, labor organizations, the federal, state, and local governments, and the public.

Recognizing the demanding nature of the position, the commissioners felt fortunate in securing the services of J. Russell Wait, a man with an engineering degree from Lehigh University and practical experience as director of the ports of Charleston and Beaumont. Wait came to the job with unusual recommendations. "Not even his enemies will say anything detrimental to him," Colonel Evans said to R. Starley Tevis, a newspaperman covering Port activities, in announcing Wait's appointment. One frank acquaintance, upon being asked his opinion, informed the commissioners that Wait feared no interest, served none, and finished the job for the public "even when wrong."[2]

Along with unusual recommendations, Wait brought to the job a high ideal of public service. He conceived of the Port as a business in which the taxpayers were the stockholders, the commissioners the directors, and himself the manager. "I am engaged in an enterprise by law administered in behalf of the public by a Port Commission of five outstanding citizens, non-political and serving without pay," he once wrote:

It is my conception that these men are the trustees or board of directors representing all the stockholders, and that they employ me to administer the of-

---

[1] Benjamin Casey Allin, *Reaching for the Sea*, pp. 98–99, 87.

[2] R. Starley Tevis, "This Man Wait," *Houston Port Book*, XXV (November, 1947), 26.

fice of General Manager and Director in a manner which is proper and in accord with the law and as the stockholders—the entire citizenship as owners—would have it administered, if it were a privately owned business.[3]

In accordance with this philosophy, Wait had a portrait of Sam Houston painted (paid for by personal funds, he always emphasized) that represented the composite taxpayer of Harris County. This picture hung behind his desk as a constant reminder of those for whom he worked. During his seventeen years, lacking one month, as Port director he defended Sam Houston against all who seemed to infringe on the old hero's rights. This meant that on occasion Wait did battle with capital, labor, industry, shippers, railroads, rival ports, the Houston Taxpayers' Association, city fathers, the Houston Pilots' Association, Governor Miriam A. Ferguson's husband, the United States Engineers, the United States Navy, and the United States Army. Although he sometimes fought singlehanded, no one ever suggested that any of his battles were unevenly matched. Wait was called by various names—a tsar, a communist, a militant idealist, a belligerent democrat, an iron man, a fly in the ointment, and assorted colorful names belonging peculiarly to the waterfront. But all considered him a worthy opponent, and he won nationwide respect for his port management. Both his ability and the growing prestige of the Port were recognized by his election to the presidency of the American Association of Port Authorities in 1934. At a dinner given for him on that occasion by civic leaders, S. G. Reed, a railroad man who had fought a running battle with Wait, paid him tribute. "I have fought some mighty good fights with Mr. Wait," said Reed, "but he is a clean fighter."[4]

The Port had need of a good, clean fighter in the early thirties. The stock market crash had seemed far removed from Houston at first, and during the first half of 1930 statistics showed that 30 per cent more tonnage passed through the Port than in the same period for the previous year. But during the last half of the year tonnage dropped, so that the year as a whole showed slightly less than a 10 per cent increase over the previous one. The next year for the first time since real Port devel-

[3] J. Russell Wait, "Who Is the Boss?" *Lehigh University Bulletin* (Spring, 1938), p. 4.
[4] Houston *Chronicle*, November 16, 1934.

opment began at the end of World War I tonnage figures showed a decrease. For 1931 tonnage dropped more than 3 per cent below 1930, and for 1932 it dropped almost 12 per cent below the same year. But the year 1932 marked the depth of the depression insofar as tonnage was concerned. In 1933 the figures spurted upward to a new high and the following years saw further increases. Not until 1939, however, did the value of the cargo surpass the high set in 1930.[5]

That the depression came late and left early at the Port of Houston speaks of the basic soundness of the Port's economy and its good management. But the Great Depression did not leave the Port unscathed. For a generation of officials the symbol of the early thirties became a big, new grain elevator standing empty on the channel. During the late twenties the elevator had done a capacity business and early in 1930 when the depression still seemed remote the electorate had voted bonds to triple its size. But the enlargement was no more than completed before conditions had reversed. The depression spread over the entire world; so countries that had been buying grain no longer had money. Moreover, almost simultaneously with the advent of hard times, Congress had enacted the Hawley-Smoot tariff, raising import duties to a new high. In protest against these duties nations that did have money refused to purchase United States products. Thus an elevator that had handled 2,967,981 bushels of grain in 1932 stood silent and with only a maintenance crew the following year. "The grain elevator has been inactive because of unforeseen world grain conditions and grain production conditions beyond the control of this management," said the Annual Report of that year. "The same conditions face all Gulf Coast elevators. All such properties are inactive as a result."[6]

Not until 1938 was grain again exported from the Port of Houston.[7] The empty elevator was long remembered along the channel. As white elephants went, one official reflected years later, none was whiter or larger than an empty grain elevator.

Nor was the empty elevator the only evidence of the depression on

[5] HCHSCND, Annual Reports 1931, 34A; 1937, 53; 1939, 39a.

[6] *Ibid.*, 1932, p. 19; 1933, p. 18.

[7] *Ibid.*, 1938, pp. 8–9. In 1935 and 1937, however, there was an unusual import movement of grain from Argentina (*ibid.*, 1935, p. 22; 1937, pp. 37–38).

the waterfront. As tonnage dropped and ships became scarcer, there were fewer jobs and more men to fill them. Suddenly the depression that had once seemed remote became an intensely personal thing to men on the waterfront as well as to many other Houstonians. The local newspapers told of the upside-down times in stories of babies starving to death in East Texas and of milk being poured out in the streets of Houston because producers refused to sell for less than four cents a quart.[8] At first the men who earned a livelihood on the channel gathered at union halls where they played dominoes, pitched horseshoes, and played softball while they waited for ships to arrive. But as time wore on the intervals between ships became longer; the pay scale dropped; and families grew hungry. Then a series of labor disputes exploded along the waterfront. "It becomes almost an annual duty to record some destructive strike on the Houston waterfront," Director Wait wrote wearily in his Annual Report of 1936.[9]

Wait attributed the strikes to New York thugs intent on extorting money from the steamship lines. Others saw the hand of communists who hoped to undermine the capitalist system, while still others, among them the respected churchman William States Jacobs, saw the strikers as symbolic of workingmen everywhere. In a measure, all these voices were right. What happened on the channel was indeed symptomatic of what was happening with variations throughout the country; and, as in other places, idle men with hungry families made a ready audience for troublemakers.

The longest and ugliest strike, one called by longshoremen against the steamship lines, threatened throughout 1935 and finally developed in the fall. Beginning at New Orleans, it spread to other Gulf ports, causing Houston longshoremen to walk off their jobs on October 11. In this as in the other strikes of this period, the operators of Port facilities, both public and private, were not principals in the dispute, but their businesses were directly affected and they were caught in a difficult position between disputants. At the same time that the longshoremen announced their intention of striking, the steamship lines, backed by all local interests concerned with keeping the Port open, announced

---

[8] For example, see Houston *Post*, January 4, February 15, 1932.
[9] HCHSCND, Annual Report, 1936, p. 5.

their intention to break the strike. Busloads of strikebreakers were brought in from East Texas and quartered on public wharves. With violence clearly in the offing, Port officials threw up a fence to protect public property from destruction and the city deputized a special force to police the waterfront. Frank Hamer, a former Texas Ranger captain who had won renown the previous year for tracking down desperadoes Bonnie Parker and Clyde Barrow, was hired to head the special force. Hamer's arrival aroused bitterness on the part of union leaders, who charged that a "hired killer" had been brought in to quell them. The following weeks were uneasy ones, marked by outbreaks of violence and rumors of even greater violence. Director Wait heard once that a truck loaded with dynamite was en route from San Antonio to blow up the entire waterfront. On another occasion, word came that someone had been hired to kill William L. Clayton, whose company owned Long Reach Docks, and Wait and Colonel Evans rushed to Clayton's home to warn him. Nor were all the rumors unfounded. In all, some fourteen men died in Texas and Louisiana as a result of the strike, and there were many other instances of men being beaten and property destroyed.[10]

The longshoremen's strike lasted ten weeks and was followed the next year by a nine-week seamen's strike. At the end of both strikes, no one was sure who had won. Certainly, the Port of Houston had gained nothing. "The cost to the Port of Houston of this strike cannot be estimated in money," Wait wrote at the end of the seamen's strike, "but it was very large in the aggregate and consisted of loss of payrolls, the diversion of much tonnage to other transportation agencies, and the tying up of shipping over a long period of time. Several steamship lines, offering a regular weekly coastwise service, abandoned all sailings for four months."[11]

The labor troubles of the thirties brought demands that a representative of labor be placed on the Port Commission. As the commissioners served without pay and the position was a demanding one, it had become traditional that only men of independent means and a civic

[10] *Ibid.*, p. 5; *Post*, October 1, 5, 7, 9, 11, 12, 14, 18, 19; November 3, 4, 9, 10, 11, 12; December 2, 10, 13, 20, 1935.
[11] HCHSCND, Annual Report, 1936, p. 5.

turn of mind be appointed. But the upheavals of the decade brought charges that the commissioners were antilabor. Some years later a resolution adopted by the board set forth its policy: "The Board is not procapital. It is not pro-labor. It is not pro-steamship. It is not pro-railroad. In fact, it must not at any time take positions that favor one group against another."[12] This was substantially the policy laid down by the commissioners during the thirties and a policy to which Wait was dedicated. But Wait considered strikes against the interest of his stockholders, the taxpayers, and he was determined to protect the Port against all losses—either a loss of business or a loss of property through violence. To him, organized labor represented one more special interest trying to infringe on Sam Houston's rights. Thus, although Wait on occasion fought capital, industry, and railroads as vigorously as he did labor, he emerged from the labor troubles with a reputation for being antilabor.

Labor leaders began a campaign to "tame Wait," and in response to their agitation, the city appointed William Walcott Strong, president of the Texas Allied Printing Trades Council and a man active in the labor movement for thirty years, to the Port Commission on June 1, 1937. Wait regarded the appointment as a personal affront and was prepared to be hostile. But to his surprise he was completely disarmed when he met the unassuming man who became organized labor's first representative on the Port Commission. The two men immediately respected each other, and in the years that followed a rare friendship grew between them. "W. W. Strong was one of the big men in my life," Wait recalled years later. "He was a man of character, integrity, sincerity, principle." When after ten years Strong retired from the board because of ill health, there was widespread agreement that he had represented organized labor at its best, served his cause with dignity, and done a good job for the Port. On that occasion Wait wrote a letter of commendation that became the basis of an editorial in a local paper. And two years later, after Wait too had severed his connection with the Port, he drove from Freeport to act as pallbearer at Strong's funeral and write finis to the unlikely friendship between organized labor's

---

[12] Resolution adopted at board meeting, October 31, 1945, and widely printed. See *ibid.*, 1945, p. 6.

Port commissioner and the manager who never lived down his reputation for being antilabor.[13]

In addition to a new era in labor relations, the depression brought to the Port of Houston an era of sharp competition with other Gulf ports, more especially that old aristocrat of the Gulf, New Orleans. As cargoes grew scarce and prices dropped, the slightest advantage in rates became enough to divert traffic from one port to another. This meant that land as well as water forces affected the ports' business. "Today the port has become a land phenomenon . . .," one analyst of the shipping industry commented in 1937, "and the main factors that control its destiny are railroad transportation rates, terminal charges, local industries, flexibility of operation, and availability of shipping service."[14] Recognizing this, Wait joined with the managers of the three private terminals-for-hire on the channel to set uniform tariffs and thus avoid a cannibalistic competition within the Port. The four men—Wait for the public terminal, Henry Ahlers for Sprunts, Harrison J. Luhn for Long Reach, and R. M. (Daddy) Bain for Manchester—became known along the channel as the Four Horsemen during the early thirties. Although they kept a weather eye on each other to be sure that all adhered strictly to the published tariffs, they presented a united front as they sought to attract business to the Port of Houston.

A new factor, trucking, figured prominently in the transportation picture of Houston as well as throughout the nation in the early thirties. Earlier, automotive transportation had supplemented the railroads, making short hauls where there were no rails or delivering goods between rail terminals and customers. But with better roads and technical improvements such as the balloon tire, trucks suddenly emerged as formidable competitors to the railroads about the time the depression began. Trucks offered flexible, pick-up-and-delivery service that the railroads could never match. Moreover, the trucking industry, unlike

---

[13] As related by J. Russell Wait to the writer, July 27, 1965; and by Mrs. Strong to the writer, March 9, 1966. See also, Houston *Post*, February 24, 1949; June 1, 1937.

[14] "Eight U.S. Ports," *Fortune Magazine*, XVI (September, 1937), 92. Also see Earl Charles Thibodeaux, "The New Orleans-Houston Port Rivalry" (Ph.D. Dissertation, Columbia University, 1952).

the railroad, was virtually unregulated in 1929. The economic conditions of the time gave further impetus to the new industry. With smaller inventories and orders, there was a demand for less-than-carload cargoes which trucks could handle more economically than railroads. Because used trucks were plentiful, and because a man with little training and a minimum of capital could easily go into the trucking business for himself, the industry became a haven for men displaced by the depression. These men, known as wildcat truckers, were often interested only in paying immediate operating expenses and earning a bare subsistence, and they cut prices to a point that railroads—and even established trucking lines—could not meet. The railroads, joined by a few trucking lines, protested against the unregulated competition, with the result that the State of Texas enacted legislation to regulate trucking in 1932. As a signal that the new industry had taken its place in the national economy, the federal government enacted regulations in 1935. By then trucking coupled with the depression had dealt a severe blow to railroading. Nationwide, the ton miles carried by rail dropped from 450 billion in 1929 to 235 billion in 1932.[15]

Trucking played an especially important role at the Port of Houston. During the early years of the depression trucks heavily loaded with cotton began rolling in from North Texas, Oklahoma, and Arkansas. The truckers, operating on a slender margin of profit, subscribed to no nonsense about the miles between Galveston and Houston being nonexistent. Ignoring the traditional Galveston-Houston differential, they treated the fifty miles between the two ports the same as fifty miles anywhere else. Thus, Houston obtained the advantage of its interior position, and, as more and more trucks rolled in from the north, Houstonians became less interested in the old equalization battle with Galveston and more willing to let the island have its way about rail rates.

The same trucks that neutralized the old rivalry with Galveston intensified that with New Orleans. The trucks bringing cotton from Oklahoma and Arkansas diverted traffic from New Orleans, something that port did not accept meekly. In retaliation two railroads serving New Orleans, the Texas and Pacific and the Louisiana and Arkansas,

[15] Merrill J. Roberts, "The Motor Transportation Revolution," *Business History Review*, XXX (March, 1965), 54–95.

cut rates so that by the mid-thirties the Louisiana port had been equalized with Houston and other Texas ports on practically all export, import, and coastwise tonnage. This same period saw a revival of barge traffic on the Mississippi River and its tributaries, a circumstance that gave New Orleans a tremendous advantage over its competitors. Barges carried enormous cargoes of bulky freight at rates no other transportation agency could meet. Moreover, the barge-rail rate structure gave New Orleans a rate advantage that extended into New Mexico. For example, the all-rail rate from Tucumcari, New Mexico, to Houston was $2.42; to New Orleans, $2.76; and to Memphis, $2.62. But the rail-barge rate from Tucumcari through Memphis to New Orleans was $2.41.[16]

Inequities such as this and the vicious competition of the period caused a reorganization of the Port Bureau. Originally set up as a solicitation agency, the old bureau was absorbed in the Houston Port and Traffic Bureau on June 1, 1936, with Harold B. Cummins as general manager. "Its prime function is to keep informed on rate adjustments initiated by hostile transportation agencies," explained Wait in his report of 1936. "These make continual efforts to divert tonnage to and from the interior and heretofore there has been no single agency responsible for combatting such activities."[17]

Wait, Cummins, and C. E. Holloman, manager of the traffic department of the Houston Chamber of Commerce, bombarded the Interstate Commerce Commission and other regulatory bodies with complaints about inequities in the rate structure. Yet until the approach of World War II began to burden all transportation agencies and relax the competition between Gulf ports, Houston did not receive the advantage of her location insofar as rail rates to the North and West were concerned. The Port of Houston showed increased tonnage each year after 1932 and maintained its relative standing among the nation's ports, but Wait fretted continually over the source of that tonnage. "Houston is geographically situated as the center of a very vigorous industrial and petroleum development," he wrote in explaining the increased tonnage of 1936. "Both are responsible for a large water-

16 HCHSCND, Annual Report, 1937, pp. 5, 16–17.
17 Ibid., 1936, p. 2.

borne commerce, and it is this commerce which the statistics reveal as increasing, but there was no increase in the tonnages to and from the interior of the vast Southwest."[18]

Despite the conditions created by the depression, improvement of the ship channel continued throughout the thirties. At the beginning of the decade Houston had already taken its place among the nation's ports, but still seamen were inclined to look askance at the channel. They had to "climb a tree" for cargo, some captains complained, as they made their way to Houston for cotton. These complaints were reflected in the regulations of the Board of Cotton Underwriters in New York, which limited the amount of cotton that could be loaded on ships at Houston and forbade night navigation on the channel.

Serious as were these restrictions, it was not a cargo vessel but the historic old United States Frigate *Constitution,* better known as *Old Ironsides,* that dealt the single most humiliating insult to the channel in the early thirties. The vessel, a veteran of the War of 1812, had been reconditioned by the contributions of school children throughout the United States. Before sending it to a permanent berth, the Navy sent it on a cruise to selected ports so that as many of the children as possible could see it. Houston officials, always on the lookout for good publicity, arranged for their city to be one of *Old Ironsides'* ports-of-call and made elaborate plans to welcome it. School children from surrounding towns planned excursions to Houston while the vessel was in port, and on the day set for its arrival, February 24, 1932, an estimated 150,000 lined the channel, while a party of dignitaries boarded a small ship to greet it.

But when Captain L. J. Gulliver, commander of *Old Ironsides,* reached Galveston Bay, he suddenly had misgivings about risking his priceless antique on the Houston Ship Channel. Unlike countless other sea captains who had navigated the route in the preceding hundred years, Captain Gulliver was concerned not with *depth* but with *height.* The three masts of his old ship soared some 188 feet into the air, and his pilot informed him that power lines near Baytown crossed the chan-

[18] *Ibid.,* p. 1.

nel at about that height. Unwilling to risk an encounter with the lines, he turned the vessel toward Galveston.

Director Wait had gone to considerable trouble to ascertain that the lines would accommodate the frigate and had sent this information along with diagrams and charts for the Captain's information. But this information had not reached Captain Gulliver. Wait, aboard a small ship with a party of newsmen, spotted the masts on the horizon and then realized to his dismay that they were going in the wrong direction. He ordered his ship to follow the frigate into Galveston harbor, and, upon overtaking it, clambered aboard like one of the Barbary pirates of the vessel's earlier history. "I've heard of the wooden navy, but I didn't know it was run by blockheads," he began as he reached the deck. He continued in language enriched by his years on the waterfront, to remind those present of the charts he had sent, the crowds waiting along the channel, the dignitaries gathered in welcome, and the Captain's orders directing him to go to Houston *not* Galveston.[19]

All this was to no avail. The *Constitution* would not budge, Captain Gulliver informed Wait politely, until the United States Engineers' office at Galveston gave assurances that the power lines would clear the masts. Wait called in the Engineers, but by the time they had spoken affirmatively, it was too late an hour for the frigate to continue its voyage and the disappointed crowds had melted away. But the following day *Old Ironsides,* aided by several tugs, went under the power lines— with at least three feet to spare—and began a festive four-and-a-half day visit at the Turning Basin. The number of visitors broke previous records while the old ship was in port. A total of 110,406 people went aboard, 28,247 of them in a single day.[20]

Old Ironsides was probably the only vessel during the thirties that hesitated to visit Houston because of the height of the channel. Other

[19] This occurred the year before the two ports signed their peace pact. "It was a damn filthy Galveston pilot that caused it," said Wait when he recalled the incident thirty-three years later. Then after some reflection he added, "I'd have done the same thing if I'd been in his shoes."

[20] *Post,* February 21, 25, 26, 1932.

vessels were more concerned about depth and width, and, as ships—
especially petroleum tankers—became larger and more numerous, the
channel again became inadequate. In 1932 the United States Engineers
approved a project for deepening the channel to thirty-two feet and
widening it to four hundred feet through Galveston Bay and three hundred feet in the cut through Morgan's Point. Three years later, they
increased the project depth to thirty-four feet and provided for further
widening with suitable easing of bends above Morgan's Point.[21]

Another significant improvement of the 1930's was the installation
of lights to provide for night navigation. The United States Lighthouse
Department, under the direction of E. S. Lanphier, superintendent of
8th District, put a series of thirty-two channel lights into operation on
October 26, 1933, between Lynchburg and the Sinclair refinery. These
lights were about twenty-five feet above water and used acetylene gas.
About the same time, additional improvements were made on the range
beacons between Morgan's Point and Lynchburg. With the improved
lighting, the New York underwriters removed their restrictions on cotton ships, and the channel was used on a twenty-four-hour basis. In
1930 a total of 110 vessels navigated the channel at night. By 1936 the
number had increased to 943. In the same period the total number using the channel increased from 4,223 to 5,460.[22]

Flood water posed a serious threat to the Port's progress in the mid-
thirties. In the past occasional floods had hampered navigation on the
channel, but as the city grew and more drainage water was turned into
Buffalo Bayou, the problem became progressively more acute. In 1929
a flood had damaged the Turning Basin, and in December, 1935, the
worst flood on record made the entire city a disaster area. Twenty-five
blocks of the downtown district and a hundred blocks of the residential
were flooded to depths ranging from four to twelve feet; eight people
lost their lives; and property damage ran into the millions.[23]

The Turning Basin and channel shoaled badly during the flood and

[21] "Houston Ship Channel, Tex.," *Rivers and Harbors Committee Doc.*, 72 Cong.,
1 Sess., No. 28; 74 Cong., 1 Sess., 58.

[22] HCHSCND, Annual Report, 1933, pp. 5–6; 1936, p. 10; 1935, p. 2.

[23] "Houston Ship Channel and Buffalo Bayou, Tex.," *House Doc.*, 75 Cong., 2
Sess., No. 456; *Post*, December 8, 9, 10, 11, 1935.

did not quickly return to normal. Many people had dumped old automobiles and other junk on the banks of streams emptying into the channel, and the flood washed these into the mainstream. This material impeded dredging operations and damaged dredging equipment. For eight months after the flood the Turning Basin was not its full depth, and for several months it was only twenty-one feet deep. "During this time was witnessed the spectacle of boats being handled stern first downstream," wrote Wait. "Vessels were grounded in the Turning Basin, a new and not profitable experience."[24]

The flood of 1935 convinced Houstonians that the ship channel could no longer serve as a drainage ditch for the city. Shortly after this flood Albert Thomas was elected to the United States House of Representatives and began a thirty-year tenure during which flood control was a matter of continuing concern. Port authorities joined with him, a committee of influential citizens, and the United States Engineers to formulate a plan to protect both the city and the channel from further disasters. The plan eventually adopted called for the retention of water by two upstream dams and the diversion of excess water to Galveston Bay by streams other than the ship channel.[25]

The year 1936 held special significance for the channel. A hundred years earlier Sam Houston's army had won Texas independence at San Jacinto and called attention to Buffalo Bayou as a route to the interior. In commemoration of the events of 1836, the entire state entered into a centennial year of celebration with special attention being given to the San Jacinto Battleground. Through the years the state had acquired the battleground as a state park, and in 1936 this park was landscaped with

---

[24] HCHSCND, Annual Report, 1936, p. 3. See also, *ibid.*, 1935, pp. 5, 8–9.

[25] "Houston Ship Channel and Buffalo Bayou, Tex.," *House Doc.*, 75 Cong., 2 Sess., No. 456; HCHSCND, Annual Report, 1936, p. 3; 1940, pp. 6, 14.

See also "Notes on Flood Problems in Vicinity of Houston"; W. N. Blanton to Albert Thomas, February 22, 1937; Thomas to Charles Crotty, May 27, 1939; Thomas to J. L. Schley, June 5, 1941; Thomas to Robert R. Casey, August 8, 1951; Thomas to Rowland R. Hughes, September 20, 1954, Albert Thomas Papers. Mr. Thomas' long tenure in office was ended by death while this book was in progress, and it was announced that his papers would be deposited at Rice University. I am indebted to Mrs. Thomas, who succeeded her husband in office, for permitting me to use those papers bearing on the Port of Houston before they were made generally available for research.

new drives, esplanades, reflection pools, terraces, and markers. Toward the end of the year the foundation was laid for an imposing monument. When completed three years later, the monument, a shaft topped by a Texas star, reached 570 feet into the air, and the base housed a museum for Texas relics. Not only was the monument a fitting memorial to the battle, but it also became a landmark to navigators of both sea and air in the area. As further recognition of the Texas centennial, President Franklin Delano Roosevelt visited Houston in June and took a cruise from the Turning Basin to the battleground, where he made a speech.[26]

The year 1936 was also a significant one for the channel in more practical ways. The reciprocal trade agreements negotiated by Cordell Hull had given new life to foreign trade, and in 1936 Congress passed an act assuring the future of the United States merchant marine. Of more specific interest to Houston, Champion Paper and Fibre Company bought a 160-acre site on the channel at Pasadena and began construction on a paper pulp mill designed to cost $3,500,000 and employ from three to five hundred men. The mill was not only a new type of industry for the channel, but it was the first major plant to be constructed there since Shell Petroleum Company had begun its large refinery in 1929. Thus, the coming of Champion marked an official end of the depression on the channel.[27]

By the following year the channel had recovered much of the buoyancy that characterized it in the twenties, and a writer from *Fortune Magazine* ranked the Port second only to New York in tonnage and importance. Expressing amazement that the waterway was manmade, the writer called the Port a "channel parvenu" that was challenging the "river aristocrat," New Orleans, for Gulf trade. "If you want proof of the fact that natural advantages no longer make a port, try piloting a freighter from Galveston to Houston," he wrote:

For twenty-five miles you will negotiate a man-deepened channel through Galveston Bay. And then for another twenty-five you will poke your way through a meandering, landlocked, man-dredged bayou in which you can't turn around until you reach the Turning Basin, heart of Houston's water-

---

[26] HCHSCND, Annual Report, 1936, p. 13; 1939, p. 14; *Post,* June 11, 12, 1936; "San Jacinto Memorial," Jesse Holman Jones Papers.
[27] HCHSCND, Annual Report, 1936, p. 1.

front. . . . By this time you will have passed mountains of old railroad ties, bedsprings, alarm clocks, auto fenders, and I beams, representing some 200,000 tons of stored scrap iron. And you will have realized how all the dredging, the thirty-odd wharves, the nineteen newfangled locomotive cranes, the $4,000,000 grain elevator, and other developments can represent an investment of federal, county, and private funds amounting to $250,-000,000. And you will have been told that Houston—although naturally an oil center and an anomaly as a seaport—has, until this year, been leader for twelve years in cotton shipping; its 1936 cotton exports being valued at $84,000,000.[28]

The scrap iron stacked at the waterfront represented a significant export cargo for the Port during the mid-thirties. In 1937 alone seventy-six vessels took some 289,024 tons of scrap from the Port of Houston, most of it destined for Japan. Similar cargoes went from other American ports as the world rearmed and nations without iron-ore reserves sought to make up for the lack. The depression-ridden American people suddenly found their cast-off automobiles, old bedsprings, and other junk metal looking like gold, and, without asking questions, they gathered up their scrap and cashed in on the windfall. "No one . . . seemed to know what the Japs were planning on doing with the 'junk' scrap iron," comments the historian of I.L.A. Local 872, "and as long as the work load was increasing, no one in the entire nation seemed to care."[29]

But the American people could not long ignore the ominous meaning of the ships loaded with scrap iron. Adolph Hitler's troops marched into Poland in September, 1939, thus setting off World War II. By the next summer all Europe was involved, and Denmark, Norway, Holland, Belgium, and France had fallen to the Axis powers. On December 7, 1941, Japan attacked Pearl Harbor, and the United States and the Far East became involved in the conflict.

The hostilities had immediate effect on operations at the Port of Houston. "When Germany declared war on Poland, many strange ef-

---

[28] "Eight U.S. Ports," September, 1937. Courtesy of *Fortune* Magazine.

[29] Charles J. Hill, "A Brief History of I.L.A. Local 872," *Personal Telephone Directory and Local History of I.L.A. 872*, p. 14; HCHSCND, Annual Report, 1937, pp. 33–34; J. Russell Wait, "Scrap Iron and Steel," *Houston Port Book* (May, 1937), p. 17.

fects were noted in shipping," said Wait. "Insurance soared. Cargo rates soared. Ship strikes for wage increase and bonus because of war risk were numerous. Then followed the Government decree against American vessels entering the war zones."[30] The major portion of the United States merchant marine was government-subsidized and government-owned, and, as the threat to the United States became more apparent, these vessels were taken from coastwise service and assigned tasks more directly connected with defense. Five steamship lines discontinued service to Houston in 1940, and, after the United States entered the war, all regular sailings were suspended. For the first time since the historic visit of the *Satilla* in 1915, the Southern Steamship Company did not offer regular service to Houston. "Commercial operations have been practically abandoned as we have known them in the Port of Houston for 20 years . . .," commented Wait. "Old methods of operation will never return. . . . We must revamp to face new conditions."[31]

War conditions immediately relieved the competition among Gulf ports and caused them to draw together in recognition of their common problems. Because of the vast amount of raw products in the coastal area and the relative lack of industrialization, Gulf ports had traditionally exported far more than they imported, a matter of long-standing concern to all of them. Moreover, Gulf ports had always felt themselves at a disadvantage in competing for world trade with Atlantic and Pacific ports. The war increased this disadvantage, for it became the practice to collect war goods at Atlantic or Pacific ports to be convoyed across the oceans. "At the beginning of this war our ports almost dried up," complained E. O. Jewell, port manager of New Orleans in 1945. "When shippers go south of Norfolk, they feel that they are going into foreign waters. And as far as Washington is concerned, we don't exist."[32] Wartime conditions made it imperative to concentrate shipments on the Eastern and Western coasts, but Gulf ports still felt apprehensive that the diversion of shipping would do them permanent harm. In order to prevent this and promote common

[30] HCHSCND, Annual Report, 1939, p. 7.
[31] *Ibid.*, 1941, p. 45.
[32] *Post*, September 29, 1945.

interests, the Gulf Ports Association was chartered by the State of Louisiana on March 19, 1945. At the second annual meeting of the Gulf Ports Association, held at Houston in September, 1945, the group asked for more influence in national shipping, pointing out that the South and Southwest had never been represented on the Maritime Commission and only poorly represented on the Interstate Commerce Commission.[33] Other aims of the association were to promote world trade, develop foreign and domestic commerce, exchange ideas, and encourage the development of Gulf ports along sound economic lines.

Although the war suspended normal shipping operations, it gave a tremendous boost to industrial development along the Houston Ship Channel. The oil refineries expanded to meet the demands not only for their customary products but for special wartime products. Some facilities were turned to the production of high-grade aviation gasoline, while others produced toluene, a basic ingredient to trinitrotoluene (TNT). The most revolutionary development in the petroleum field, and one that held great significance for the Houston area, was the development of a synthetic rubber. Early in the war, the Japanese took the Malay Peninsula, the United States' primary source of natural rubber, thus making the development of a substitute of first importance. The responsibility for developing the substitute rested largely on Jesse H. Jones, who served simultaneously as chairman of the Reconstruction Finance Corporation and Secretary of Commerce during the war years. By 1943, a satisfactory synthetic rubber had been developed with butadiene, a petroleum by-product, as one of the basic ingredients. Because of the local supply of petroleum and other necessary ingredients, the synthetic-rubber industry concentrated along the Texas Gulf Coast, with two plants located near Houston.[34]

Deep water and the protected position of the channel made Houston an ideal location for other defense industries, especially shipyards.

[33] *Ibid.*

[34] "Statement of Jesse Jones, Secretary of Commerce before the Senate Agriculture Sub-Committee, May 21, 1942," Jesse H. Jones to the President, September 13, 1942, and "History of the United States Government's Natural and Synthetic Rubber Programs," Jesse Holman Jones Papers. See also, *Houston Port Book* (November, 1943), p. 31; H. Stuart Hotchkiss, "Synthetic Product Seen as Stabilizing Factor in Natural Rubber Prices," *ibid.*, May, 1944, pp. 19–20.

Early in 1941 the Houston Shipbuilding Corporation, a subsidiary of the Todd Shipbuilding Corporation of New York, chose Irish Bend Island as the site for a shipyard. The island, created by the straightening of Buffalo Bayou, contained about fifty-five acres, most of them marshy, and all of them undeveloped. Within a matter of a few months, the island had been linked to the mainland by the filling of the old channel and converted into a shipyard with nine marine ways for the building of Liberty ships. The first keels were laid on July 18, 1941, and by October of the following year, twenty-three ships had been launched. Brown Shipbuilding Company built a shipyard on the north side of the channel at Greens Bayou and began building subchasers under contract to the Navy. Although only a few of the workers at the two yards had experience in the field, the two plants made significant contributions to the war effort and won official commendations for efficiency.[35]

About the same time that Irish Bend Island became a shipyard, United States Army Ordnance officials selected a site and purchased nearly five thousand acres with five miles of channel frontage for the San Jacinto Ordnance Depot. This depot bordered the Old River and San Jacinto River areas on the channel and included the site of Lorenzo de Zavala's home. Closely related to this installation was Dickson Gun Plant, a wartime plant that was operated by Hughes Tool Company.[36]

Another contributor to the war effort was Sheffield Steel Corporation, which bought a six-hundred-acre tract on the channel in 1941 and began construction on a $17,000,000 plant. Designed to make use of scrap iron and steel, this plant also used iron ore from East Texas.

These and other defense installations made the channel truly an arsenal of democracy during the war. The number of defense industries and the fact that so many handled explosive materials placed a heavy responsibility on those charged with safety. To prevent sabotage officials carefully screened those who entered the channel area.

The war years brought several changes on the Port Commission. Kenneth E. Womack resigned on May 9, 1941, and was replaced by Thomas H. Elliott. Elliott resigned the following year to enter active

35 HCHSCND, Annual Report, 1941, p. 18.
36 Ibid., p. 19.

service with the Navy, and E. C. Barkley was appointed to the board. Another vacancy was created in June, 1942, when W. A. Sherman retired after ten years of service. Eugene L. Harris, chairman of the Houston Rationing Board during the war, filled this vacancy. Shortly before the war's end Joseph W. Evans resigned as chairman because of poor health.

Although officials gave their first attention to the needs of defense, they also laid plans for the future during these years. From the time Albert Thomas entered the United States House of Representatives in 1937, he had been active in sponsoring resolutions which authorized further development of the channel and in supporting appropriations for the project. During the late 1930's and early 1940's his efforts were abetted by those of Joseph J. Mansfield, representative of the Ninth Texas Congressional District from 1916 and long the chairman of the House Rivers and Harbors Committee. At the request of these two men Congress approved a resurvey of the channel in 1941 with the view of widening and straightening it and easing the bends. Army engineers recommended that the channel be widened to three hundred feet from Fidelity Island to the Turning Basin in 1944, and the following year Congress approved this project.[37]

Navigation District officials made other plans for the future while the war was in progress. In cooperation with local officials they planned the construction of two tunnels under the channel, one at Pasadena and one between La Porte and Baytown. The completion of these tunnels would remove some ferry boats from the channel and thus speed up navigation for ocean vessels.

Other negotiations were carried on for the purchase by the District of city-owned facilities on the channel. These facilities, built by the city between 1909 and 1922, had been leased to the District upon its reorganization in 1922. The arrangement had not been entirely satisfactory, for the city was reluctant to spend money for reconditioning

---

37 J. Russell Wait to Albert Thomas, May 10, 1941; Thomas to Wait, September 22, 23, 1941; Thomas to J. J. Mansfield, August 14, 1939; and "Hearing before the Committee on Rivers and Harbors, January 11, 1938," Thomas Papers. See also, *Houston Port Book* (May, 1941), p. 33; "Houston Ship Channel, Tex.," *House Doc.*, 79 Cong., 2 Sess., No. 737.

the docks, and the District was restricted by law in spending county money on city-owned facilities. As a result the facilities had become obsolete and in sad need of repair. "It was this dual ownership that acted like a brake on the Port of Houston for many years . . .," J. Russell Wait wrote years later. "The real impetus to the development of the Port of Houston did not begin until we had purchased all City-owned port facilities."[38] After much negotiation, the city and District agreed on a price of $1,500,000. Voters approved bonds for the purchase on December 19, 1944, and the facilities were transferred to the District on July 1, 1945.[39] Wait later pointed to this purchase as the most significant event in the Port's history during his tenure as director.

In the same election that they approved the purchase of the city property, the voters approved a contribution of $1,250,000 toward the construction of the tunnels and an additional $2,250,000 for other Port improvements. Thus, at war's end authorities looked forward to a resumption of the Port's shipping activities and made plans for Houston to again take its place as one of the nation's leading ports.

[38] J. Russell Wait to the writer, June 6, 1966.
[39] HCHSCND, Annual Report, 1945, p. 5.

THE DECADE FOLLOWING WORLD WAR II SAW many changes in the leadership of the Port. Upon Colonel Evans' resignation J. Virgil Scott, an experienced terminal operator and banker, was appointed to complete his term of office. Scott held the position until July 6, 1946, when he was succeeded by Wilson G. Saville, the head of a consulting geophysical firm and a man who had served the Army as district engineer at Galveston during the war. Other new commissioners appointed in the immediate postwar period were R. Dowman Ernst, president of Manchester Terminal Corporation, who began two years of service on May 30, 1945; L. G. Sanders, a Goose Creek businessman, who served from July 6, 1946, to October 30, 1950; W. L. Walker, a nationally known cotton broker, who began eight years of service on July 6, 1946; Sewall Myer, an attorney long associated with Port development, whose tenure of six years began May 14, 1947; and Lawton E. Deats, an oilman, whose service dated from September 18, 1947, to January 28, 1953.

Chairman Saville retired in 1950 and was succeeded by Warren S. Bellows, a distinguished civic leader and the president of a construction firm. Bellows resigned after serving four years, and Judge J. S. Bracewell, a prominent attorney, accepted the chairmanship for a year. The early fifties brought other changes in the membership of the Port Commission. Robert Hemphill, a Baytown automobile dealer, began three years of service on October 30, 1950; William N. Blanton, Sr., longtime executive director of the Houston Chamber of Commerce and a man long associated with Port promotion, began a tenure of thirteen years on January 28, 1953; John G. Turney, a well-known engineer, began a decade of service in the same year; and the following year R. Vernon Whiteside, former mayor of Pasadena, and M. A. Rowe, a realtor and former ship captain, were appointed to the board.

The decade following World War II also saw unprecedented changes in the executive management of the Port. In November, 1947, J. Russell Wait resigned as director and manager after holding the position for almost seventeen years. W. F. Heavey, a retired army officer with distinguished service in both world wars, accepted the position on July 16, 1948, and held it until December 16, 1952. He was succeeded by Warren D. Lamport, a man with West Coast shipping experience, who served from December 1, 1953, until August 10, 1956. In the intervals between the service of these men, Vernon Bailey, a veteran of Port service, held the position of acting manager in addition to his regular duties as director of Port operations.

The immediate postwar years brought heavy responsibilities and many frustrations to those in command at the Port. During the war officials had watched glumly as tonnage figures slumped from a record of 28,174,710 tons in 1939 to 25,623,078 tons in 1941 and to 15,047,871 in 1943. Tonnage began rising during the last years of the war, but still officials harbored misgivings about the long-range effect of the war on the Port's shipping operations. The expediencies of war had caused goods to be routed to the Atlantic and Pacific coasts for shipment overseas. Would shippers continue this routing after the war, officials asked, or could they be lured back to Houston? And what would happen to the numerous war-related channel industries at war's end? Would they disappear, or could they be converted to meet peacetime needs?

All misgivings about the shipping and industrial future of the Port were laid to rest during the first three years after the war. As the United

States government acted to rebuild the war-shattered economy of the world, cotton, grain, petroleum products, and other goods flowed through the Port of Houston in large quantities, and tonnage figures broke record after record. In 1946, the first full year of peace, the figure reached the high of 31,837,453 tons. This record was broken in 1947 by 34,323,833 tons, and again in 1948 by 38,904,464. In 1948 for the first time valuation of tonnage went over a billion dollars, and four years later it surpassed two billion. These gains were accompanied by a corresponding jump in the Port's relative position in the nation. In 1948 the Port of Houston became the second port in the United States in tonnage, a position it held through 1954.[1]

But the sudden resumption of shipping and the increases in tonnage brought special problems. First depression and then war had postponed new construction at the Port. Moreover, the emergencies of war had delayed needed repairs and the maintenance of existent facilities and had caused the channel to be neglected so that it had shoaled in places. Thus, the record tonnage taxed the facilities of the Port, and authorities worked under extreme pressure to meet immediate as well as long-term needs.

In 1946 Chairman Saville outlined a program calling for the expenditure of about $37,000,000 for Port improvements. This program included the widening and deepening of the channel by the federal government; the construction of two tunnels under the channel in cooperation with local and state governments; the construction of wharves and other facilities in the amount of $2,337,000; and the improvement of the publicly owned railway system.[2]

Despite the best efforts of those in authority, this program was impeded by postwar conditions. The same factors—depression and war—that had postponed construction at the Port had also postponed it throughout the nation. Thus at war's end there was a pent-up demand for new schools, churches, residences, commercial and industrial buildings. The American people launched a nationwide construction program, and the Port faced a new type of competition. Where in the past

[1] HCHSCND, Annual Report, 1956, p. 6.
[2] "Col. Saville Outlines Port's New Program," *Houston Port Book* (November, 1946), p. 25.

it had competed with other ports for business, it now competed with the entire nation for building material and labor to build facilities to take care of the record business coming its way. This competition caused construction prices to rise sharply, and Port authorities watched in dismay as the $5,000,000 bond issue that had seemed adequate in 1945 shrank in value before the proposed improvements could be made. Prices rose so sharply that contractors refused to make definite bids but instead placed so-called escalator clauses in contracts pegging the final cost to the price of material at the time of delivery.[3]

Although the high price of supplies and a rash of labor strikes delayed construction and tried the patience of Port authorities, the immediate postwar years saw progress at the Port. On March 2, 1945, just before the end of the war, Congress, at the behest of Representative Albert Thomas, approved a project for widening the channel, and on July 31, 1947, the army engineers recommended that the channel be deepened to thirty-six feet for its entire length.[4] While these projects were under way, the Navigation District joined with the local and state governments to build the tunnels provided for in the bond election of 1944. The Pasadena tunnel, named for long-time auditor Harry L. Washburn, was opened to traffic on May 27, 1950, and the Baytown-La Porte tunnel was completed three years later. Of a total cost of about $12,900,000, the Navigation District contributed $1,250,000 to the construction of these tunnels. Port officials considered this an excellent investment, for the tunnels removed ferry boats from the channel at two points, thus expediting navigation and making the north side of the channel more accessible for industrial development. In addition, the tunnels were less vulnerable to attack than bridges in the event of another war.

Another project of this period was the building of a suitable executive office for the Navigation District. When the District was formed, it had been assigned offices in the county courthouse, but as the county

3 J. Russell Wait, "Address to Kiwanis Club of Houston, September 11, 1946." Copy supplied by Lloyd Gregory, Houston.

4 "Houston Ship Channel, Tex.," *House Doc.*, 79 Cong., 2 Sess., No. 737; "Galveston Harbor, Houston Ship Channel, Texas City Channel, and Galveston Channel, Tex.," *House Doc.*, 80 Cong., 2 Sess., No. 561.

and city as well as the Port grew larger, these offices became crowded. The District moved its executive offices from the civil courts building to Wharf No. 13 on the channel in August, 1947. In late 1951 the Port Commission purchased a downtown site at the corner of Crawford and Capitol and authorized the construction of a two-story office building. The executive offices of the District were moved to this new building in 1953.

Another acquisition of these years was a new fireboat. The first fireboat, the *Port Houston,* had been purchased in 1926 and had served well. Indeed, through the years the Port had gained a reputation for safety, this in spite of the fact that much of the material shipped and handled by the industrial complex was inflammable. Always safety conscious, Port officials were further impressed by the necessity of precautions when a waterfront explosion devastated neighboring Texas City on April 16, 1947, killing hundreds of people. Shortly after this tragedy, the commissioners ordered a new fireboat that was smaller, faster, and equipped with more modern means of firefighting than the *Port Houston.* Appropriately, this new boat was named the *Captain Crotty* after Charles Crotty, for many years the assistant director of the Port. Miss Susan Anderson, daughter of Mr. and Mrs. Dillon Anderson, christened the boat at Camden, New Jersey, on March 20, 1950, and after its arrival at Houston, Captain and Mrs. Crotty came from their retirement home at Kerrville for special commissioning ceremonies.

Questions about the Port's industrial future were answered as favorably as those about its shipping future in the immediate postwar years. In the first few months of peace some seventeen government defense installations in the Houston area were declared excess, but the switch from war to peacetime production was accomplished with a minimum of dislocation. The wartime production of synthetic rubber was in fact the forerunner of a significant new industry, the petrochemical, for the channel. Petroleum companies purchased the installations they had been operating for the government and turned to the private production of synthetic rubber and other petrochemicals. In 1947 Phillips Petroleum Company purchased the wartime facilities of Todd-Houston Shipbuilding corporation at Irish Bend and began construction on a giant chemical installation. Other companies built or enlarged facilities so that within five years after the end of the war the chemical industry had accounted for more than a quarter of a billion dollars in new construction in the Houston area. In a book written about this time George Fuermann, a Houston *Post* columnist, called the Port the "First of the Seven Wonders of Houston," and observed that the channel was the "fertilizer, water, and sun" for a new crop, industry, that had joined the older crops, cotton and oil, as a source of Houston's wealth. "To anyone who ever thought about it, the importance to Houston of the Houston Ship Channel is as obvious as the sun on a clear June day," he wrote:

Houston's superlatives have always been given in terms of oil and oilmen, but since 1941 these superlatives have belonged to oil and oilmen least of all. Hand-in-glove with the yeasty processes of World War II and handy natural gas, the Houston Ship Channel has been a spellbinding magnet in fetching new industry, new citizens and new dollars to the Houston area.[5]

But the very success of industry along the channel intensified an old problem, that of pollution. From the time the first sawmills had dumped sawdust on the banks of Buffalo Bayou, the disposal of industrial wastes had posed a problem. With the increase in both population and industrialization, the problem had become more acute until it was the most pressing one that faced local and state authorities in the latter half of the twentieth century. Indeed, the problem did not belong peculiarly to the Houston Ship Channel but was one of nationwide concern as the American people developed a highly industrialized society.

More local in nature was the problem of the ultimate fate of the San Jacinto Ordnance Depot. When the Army acquired this five-thousand-acre tract in 1941, the area had been thinly populated, but by the early 1950's population had increased sharply and there was a heavy demand for industrial tracts along the channel. Although the depot had been established as a wartime installation, the Army showed signs not only of making it a permanent one but of increasing its size. Representative Albert Thomas felt that the depot, because of its nature, should be located in a more thinly populated area, and, moreover, that

---

[5] George Fuermann, *Houston: Land of the Big Rich*, p. 142.

it would hinder the development of the channel by monopolizing a large tract more suitable to industry. Thus, shortly after the war he began persistent and eventually successful efforts to persuade the Army to release the site.[6]

Prosperous though the Port was, it came to another crisis in its development as the shortages of the postwar years disappeared and the world recovered from the ravages of war. In the early fifties tonnage figures leveled off, and in 1953 and again in 1954 tonnage dropped slightly. From 1948 through 1954 the Port had ranked second only to New York in tonnage, but in 1955 Philadelphia and New Orleans crowded Houston down to fourth place.[7] Houstonians had come to take their Port and its phenomenal growth for granted, and these statistics brought home the fact that the Port was facing a new competitive situation. New Orleans, long Houston's foremost competitor on the Gulf, had embarked on a multimillion-dollar expansion program in the early fifties and had sought business with a new aggressiveness. At the same time Corpus Christi and other young but dynamic Gulf ports had also entered vigorously into the contest for business. Moreover, all ports serving the Midwest faced new and formidable competition as the St. Lawrence Seaway, a project begun in 1954, opened the Great Lakes area to ocean-going vessels from the Atlantic Ocean. As work began on this project, Chicago made plans to become the ocean port for the vast heartland of the United States.

The new competition caused Houstonians to give thoughtful consideration to the future of their Port. The industrial complex along the channel and the trade of the immediate hinterland assured the Port of a substantial and steady business, but all Port facilities were already being used at full capacity and the Port was actually turning away business for lack of facilities. If the Port met the new competition, a dramatic expansion program was in order and that quickly. Thus, Houstonians faced a major decision: Should the Port rest on its laurels

---

[6] Albert Thomas to Major General E. L. Cummings, January 18, February 11, 1955; Thomas to W. N. Blanton, February 1, 1955; Thomas to Lloyd Gregory, February 13, 1958; Thomas to Vernon Bailey, January 24, 1957, Albert Thomas Papers.

[7] HCHSCND, Annual Report, 1955, p. 6.

and remain content with the comfortable position it had already obtained, or should it expand its operations to meet the challenge for world trade?

Throughout 1956 civic-minded Houstonians considered this question. At a meeting of the Houston Downtown Rotary Club on June 14, 1956, F. M. Law, a distinguished banker and one of the city's elder statesmen, set forth the problem: "With growing world trade and competition among ports getting tougher and tougher, there will be a necessity for aggressive and well-planned effort to keep the Port of Houston abreast and ahead . . .," he said. "Our Port is losing business every day because its facilities are not adequate to meet the increasing demand. Much business which would like to come here goes elsewhere because they know that facilities are lacking in Houston."[8]

The problem also received attention in academic circles. Dr. Earl W. Fornell, then of Rice University, reviewed the economic decline of Galveston and found a lesson for Houston. The island had lost its position as the greatest seaport of Texas, he observed, because shortsighted leaders had followed a policy of profit-taking and conservative expansion in the face of a growing trade. "The Port of Houston can ill afford to take its present position of leadership for granted," he warned. "What happened to Galveston could well be repeated in regard to Houston if this seaport also, in its turn, fails to expand to meet the needs of the fast-growing Gulf Coast region."[9]

As in other crises in its development, the Port of Houston was fortunate in its leadership. Howard Tellepsen, the young president of Tellepsen Construction Company and a man already noted for his civic leadership and ability to get things done, took the helm as chairman of the Port Commission on May 7, 1956. He joined with the other commissioners—Vice-Chairman William N. Blanton, Sr., John G. Turney, R. Vernon Whiteside, and H. M. Crosswell, Jr., who was appointed to the board on August 29, 1956—in considering the future of the Port. In the previous decade more than nine million dollars of earnings had

---

8 F. M. Law, "Challenge for Houston," *Houston Port Book* (Fall, 1956), pp. 31, 51.

9 Earl W. Fornell, "Geopolitics and the Gulf Coast . . .," Houston *Post*, September 30, 1956.

been reinvested in Port facilities, while something more than six million dollars of bond funds had financed further improvements. The Port was in excellent financial condition and its own earnings would finance a slow growth, but not the immediate expansion that the competition required. The commissioners thus decided to ask the taxpayers to vote a bond issue.

In 1956 the Navigation District tax rate was the lowest on record— 4.4 cents per hundred dollars valuation as compared to 30 cents per hundred in 1923—and the indebtedness of the District was a little more than four million dollars as compared to nearly ten million dollars in 1930. In spite of these figures, the decision to ask for a bond issue was not easily reached. Bonds required the approval of two-thirds of the electorate, and it was never easy to persuade voters to tax themselves. Moreover, two and a half years earlier another request for bonds had led to the bitterest election campaign the Port had seen since 1920. In 1920 the issue had been whether to purchase property at Manchester; in 1953 it was whether to purchase Long Reach Docks.

Long Reach, the largest private terminal-for-hire on the channel, had handled a substantial amount of the dry cargo that passed through the Port since the early 1920's. The owner, Anderson, Clayton and Company, decided in 1952, however, that the countrywide spread of public wharves was making it increasingly difficult for private wharfingers to operate. Consequently, the company began negotiations to lease the docks to the United States Air Force for storage purposes, a move that would take the docks from normal shipping activity and reduce the already inadequate facilities of the Port. The board had just purchased from Houston Endowment, Inc., a Jesse H. Jones interest, a tract of 226 acres directly across the channel from Long Reach and made plans for building docks there. But it was the opinion of many leaders, among them Port Commission Chairman Warren S. Bellows, that these docks could not be built quickly enough to make up for the loss of Long Reach to the Port. Thus, it was proposed that the development of the Houston Endowment property be postponed and that the District purchase Long Reach. The board began negotiations with Anderson, Clayton and Company, and reached a tentative agreement to pay nine million dollars for the facility. Then a bond election was called, asking for eighteen million dollars to purchase the docks and construct other facilities.[10]

The proposal to buy Long Reach stirred up a hornet's nest of powerful opposition. As in the Manchester fight thirty-three years earlier, Jesse H. Jones led the opposition, charging in the pages of his Houston *Chronicle* that the proposed price was too high. The other local papers followed the *Chronicle*'s line, and the issue divided the Port commissioners and others long influential in Port affairs into two hostile camps. After a bitter campaign the voters not only turned down the proposal to buy Long Reach but also refused bonds for the other construction.[11] The memories of this campaign were still fresh in 1956, so it was with some reluctance and only because they felt that the very future of the Port depended on it that the commissioners again asked the voters for bonds.

The campaign of 1956 was characterized by a united leadership and much serious discussion of the Port's future. Ben Belt, president of the Chamber of Commerce, appointed F. M. Law to conduct the campaign, and other leaders joined in to present the case of the Port to the voters. Thoughtful news articles reviewed the history of the Port, pointing out how the destinies of Port and city had been interwoven. The site of the city had been chosen because of its position in relation to navigation, and through the years Port and city had developed together. As the Port grew, so grew the city; as the Port prospered, so prospered the city. Dr. F. A. Buechel, statistician of the Houston Chamber of Commerce, pointed out that the Port by the very fact of its existence attracted industry. "Basic industries determine the growth of any city," he wrote. "Following this is the growth of secondary industries that find a market due to the basic industries. This brings on a growth of retail stores, professional services, and other factors that make a city grow. We have the basic industries here because we have the port."[12]

[10] HCHSCND, Annual Report, 1952, p. 12; "Commissioners Move to Guard Port's Future," *Houston Port Book* (October, 1952), p. 29. See also, E. V. Huggins to Albert Thomas, November 26, 1952, and W. J. Nelson to Thomas, August 20, 1952, Thomas Papers.

[11] Houston *Chronicle,* September 8, 9, 10, 1953; *Post,* September 9, 1953; Houston *Press,* September 10, 1953.

[12] *Post,* January 22, 1957.

Other writers hammered home the fact that the future of the Port was at stake, that the real question to be decided was whether the Port of Houston—and by implication, the city—was to continue to grow as it should. "This is no ordinary election," said a writer for the *Post*. "It is a bread-and-butter matter affecting the future of the community."[13]

With the responsibility for the Port's future resting on their shoulders, the voters went to the polls and gave a resounding mandate for expansion. The returns showed that something more than the necessary two-thirds of the electorate approved the bond issue, and the commissioners were jubilant. "Today marks the start of a great new era for the Port of Houston," said Chairman Tellepsen, when he heard the results.[14]

At the same time that the commissioners were considering a bond issue, they were again facing the problem of finding an executive director and manager for the Port. As the Port grew larger and its operations more complicated, the position became increasingly more demanding. Thus, the commissioners were elated when almost simultaneously with the passage of the bond issue Jerry P. Turner, then director of the Alabama State Docks at Mobile, accepted their unanimous offer to become executive head of the Port of Houston. A native of Chicago, Turner was a man thoroughly experienced in the handling of Gulf shipping. He had learned every phase of the business in twenty-seven years at Mobile and from 1951 had been general manager of that port. He had also won national recognition in his field, having served as president of both the American Association of Port Authorities and Gulf Ports Association. On February 4, 1957, Turner began his service as director of the Port of Houston, a service that would be marked by spectacular growth and progress. "It was a lucky day for the Port of Houston when we employed Jerry Turner," said Chairman Tellepsen when Turner had been with the Port for almost nine years.[15]

In accordance with the mandate given them by the voters, Director Turner and the commissioners moved at once to expand the Port's facilities. They launched the biggest railroad-improvement program ever

---

13 *Ibid.*, January 30, 1957.
14 *Ibid.*, February 1, 1957.
15 "Man of the Month, Jerry Turner," *East Texas* (December, 1965), p. 11.

undertaken by the Navigation District, and on a single day in October, 1957, let contracts for nearly four million dollars for the construction of new wharves and transit sheds. Construction began within a week after the contracts were let, and by the year's end work was well under way on Wharves 18, 19, and 20.[16] The following year, army engineers, again at the instigation of Representative Albert Thomas, recommended a deepening of the channel to forty feet throughout, thus making the Port accessible to the largest vessels.[17]

The future of the Port was further assured by state legislative action. On April 29, 1957, the Texas legislature unanimously passed a bill permitting the Port Commission to issue long-term revenue bonds, thus making it possible to finance the Port's growth from its future earnings. The same act provided that thereafter general tax bonds could be passed by a simple majority of the voters instead of the two-thirds approval previously required. Other legislative action in this year authorized the spending of up to 5 per cent of the Port's gross income in each calendar year for promotion and development, an important provision as the District was engaged in a competitive enterprise.[18]

The expansion program begun in 1957 with tax bonds was continued by revenue bonds issued in 1959 and 1961. The first revenue bonds, in the amount of $12.5 million, were approved by the Port commissioners on January 7, 1959, and earmarked for the construction of a bulk material handling plant, a bulk plant dock, Wharves 21 and 22 with shed, repair and maintenance shops, grain-elevator improvements, and the rehabilitation of Wharf 1. Additional revenue bonds for $9 million were issued in 1961 to continue the expansion. Between 1957 and 1965 a total of more than $37 million was invested in major capital improvements at the Port.

Officials were especially proud of the bulk handling plant completed at Greens Bayou in 1961. Houston was traditionally a great bulk port, handling large amounts of petroleum and grain, but the Port had

16 HCHSCND, Annual Report, 1957, pp. 1–4.

17 "Galveston Harbor and Channel, Houston Ship Channel, and Texas City Channel, Texas," *House Doc.*, 85 Cong., 2 Sess., No. 305. See also, Albert Thomas to John A. Blatnik, July 24, 1956; Thomas to M. E. Walter, March 4, 1957; and Lyndon B. Johnson to Thomas, June 5, 1956, Thomas Papers.

18 HCHSCND, Annual Report, 1957, p. 13.

lacked facilities for handling dry bulk. The new facility filled this lack, permitting the loading and unloading of ores and other dry bulk at the rate of a thousand tons per hour. The plant was fully automatic and was arranged to assure each shipper that his product would remain uncontaminated. Import shipments of ores could be handled through two ten-ton weighing hoppers at the surge bin, while export shipments could be delivered by either rail or truck to the loading pit, there to be moved by belt to shipside. Up to eighty railroad cars could be loaded or unloaded within the plant by means of a highly integrated system of heavy-duty car pullers.[19]

Another proud acquisition of this period was the $3.5 million, twelve-story World Trade Building. Constructed at Texas and Crawford avenues adjacent to the Port Administration Building, this building symbolized the growing importance of world trade in Houston. The facility, the first of its kind in the United States, was designed to be the central point for international trade, international affairs, and international social life in the Houston area. Long before it was officially opened on January 29, 1962, most of the available space had been leased to consulates, steamship agencies, freight forwarders, export-importers, and others interested in foreign trade. The World Trade Club and the offices of the Houston World Trade Association and the Institute of International Education were also located there. In addition, the center offered special services to businessmen—offices for visitors, interpreter and secretarial services, and a library containing trade reference works and trade directories.[20]

At the same time that officials promoted the Port's interests abroad, they sought to make Houstonians more familiar with the Port. In April, 1957, an observation platform was erected at Wharf No. 9, overlooking the Turning Basin, so that visitors could watch Port activities. The following year Houstonians were made more aware of their Port by a contest featuring cartoon strips in the local newspapers and offering tens of thousands of dollars in prizes.[21]

As a further move to show the Port to Houstonians and visitors

19 HCHSCND, Annual Review, 1960, p. 1.
20 Ibid., 1962, p. 1; 1963, p. 15.
21 Ibid., 1957, p. 4; 1958, p. 1.

alike, the Port Commission ordered a new inspection boat, the *Sam Houston II*, in 1957. The first inspection boat, christened the *R. J. Cummins*, had been acquired in 1928 and carried about twenty-four passengers. This boat was replaced in 1948 by the *Sam Houston I*, a converted coast guard cutter that carried between fifty and sixty passengers. Special groups and dignitaries saw the channel from this boat, and the trip proved so popular that the commissioners ordered the lavish new *Sam Houston*, with a capacity of a hundred passengers, as a showcase for the Port. The *Sam Houston II* was christened by Miss Karen Tellepsen on July 30, 1958, and in the next five months it carried 9,031 passengers, more than the old vessel carried in a year's time.[22]

The channel continued to attract industry, and in 1961 the waterway and its industrial complex were decisive factors in bringing to the area one of the most coveted of all governmental installations. The National Aeronautics and Space Administration, popularly known as NASA, chose Houston over some twenty competitors—among them, Boston, Los Angeles, and New Orleans—as the site of a manned spacecraft center to serve as the headquarters for the nation's space program. Houston's Representative Albert Thomas, chairman of the appropriations subcommittee in charge of NASA, ably presented the advantages of Houston, and Lyndon Baines Johnson, then Vice-President of the United States and chairman of the National Space Committee, also promoted the area's interests. "But the truly deciding factor was not political pressure," concluded historian Stephen B. Oates in analyzing the reasons for NASA's choice. "It was the winning combination of advantages which Houston itself had to offer. Chief among these was the fact that Houston's ship channel and port facilities . . . provided an excellent means of transporting bulky space vehicles to other NASA locations, especially to Cape Canaveral."[23] NASA moved into temporary quarters in Houston early in 1962, while permanent facilities were being constructed at Clear Lake, about twenty-two miles from down-

[22] *Ibid.*, 1957, pp. 1–2; 1958, p. 1.
[23] Stephen B. Oates, "NASA's Manned Spacecraft Center at Houston, Texas," *Southwestern Historical Quarterly*, LXVII (January, 1964), 355.

town Houston. Thus the city founded as a way station to the cotton-fields of the Brazos bottom became a way station for men on their way to the moon.

The coming of NASA added a boom on top of a boom to the Greater Houston-Galveston Bay area. The University of Houston Bureau of Business Research predicted that the installation would attract more than 200,000 new residents during the following twenty years, while a survey sponsored by the Texas National Bank predicted almost 8,000,000 people in Greater Houston within fifty years.[24]

In these years of unprecedented growth, several new men were appointed to the Port Commission to help direct the Port's destiny. J. P. (Jake) Hamblen, chairman of the board of the Southern Electric Company, was appointed on June 3, 1958, and served until his sudden death on April 26, 1963. William W. Sherrill, a banker and business-man, completed Hamblen's unexpired term, serving until July 14, 1964. William M. Hatten, a well-known attorney, was appointed August 11, 1960, and served until April 14, 1964. R. H. Pruett, a prominent Baytown civic leader, succeeded John G. Turney, beginning his service on September 3, 1963. In the following year, the year that marked the fiftieth anniversary of deep water, two other new commis-sioners were appointed. E. H. Henderson, president of the Commercial State Bank, took his place on the board on April 14, 1964; and W. D. Haden II, a businessman whose family had long been associated with channel development, began his service on July 15, 1964. In March, 1966, Willie C. Wells, president of Local 1273, International Long-shoremen's Association, became the second representative of organized labor to serve as a Port commissioner. Fentress Bracewell succeeded him in January, 1968.

As the fiftieth anniversary of deep water approached, the incumbent commissioners and all those who had been instrumental in developing the Port could look with pride upon a fantastic achievement. Genera-tions of men had dreamed of the potential of the stream that pointed to the Texas heartland and had turned their efforts to giving body to their

[24] *Ibid.,* pp. 374–375.

dreams. But through the years the stream had surpassed the wildest expectations of the dreamers. The Allen brothers could not have believed
in 1836 that their paper city in the wilderness would one day rank as
the greatest cotton port in the United States; Charles Morgan could not
have envisioned the petroleum development of the 1920's, nor Ross S.
Sterling the petrochemical industry of the 1950's. Nor could those who
struggled with the shortages of the post-World War II period have
envisioned the Port's role in man's probe into space.

By the fiftieth anniversary of deep water the channel and its related
installations represented an investment of billions of dollars in public
and private money, money that had transformed the stream and its
banks so that Sam Houston's men would never have recognized the
meandering, tree-shaded bayou they had followed to San Jacinto in
1836. Indeed, in 1964 there were those still alive who remembered the
stream as it had been fifty years earlier and who had difficulty in relating old landmarks to new ones. The stream had been widened, banks
cut away, and bends removed. In some places islands had been created;
in others, the old bed had been filled in, so that land once on the north
side of the stream was shifted to the south side; in still other places
spoil dredged from the channel had created solid land where none ex-
isted earlier. All along the banks industrial installations had replaced
vegetation. Even the name of the stream had changed. Above the
Turning Basin the old name, Buffalo Bayou, persisted, but below it
was known as the Houston Ship Channel.

In bringing about this transformation, federal and local governments had expended some $92 million—but few public investments
had ever yielded so handsome a return. In 1963 the total tax payments
to all governmental units from economic activities related to the Port
amounted to $148 million, and Dr. Warren Rose of the University of
Houston estimated in a study of the economic impact of the Port that
the total tax payments would reach $200 million annually by 1969.[25]

The federal government collected the larger share of these taxes.
Through the years some $64 million in federal funds had been ex-
pended on channel improvement and maintenance, but in return by

[25] Warren Rose, *Catalyst of an Economy: The Economic Impact of the Port of
Houston, 1958–1963*, pp. 4, 59–62.

1964 the Port complex was paying almost $129 million annually in federal taxes—that is, personal and corporate income taxes, customs collections, and employment taxes.[26] In customs alone the Port collected $317,685,513 between the years 1920 and 1964, a return of five dollars to one on the federal investment.[27]

Local taxpayers as well as federal had invested in the Port, and they too had received handsome dividends. During the twentieth century some $28 million in local tax funds had gone into Port development, but by 1964 Port-related activities were paying almost that amount annually in state, county, and other local taxes. For the five years previous to 1964 the net earnings from Port operations had exceeded $2 million annually. Through the years Port earnings had been reinvested and property values had increased so that by the end of 1963 the taxpayers owned facilities valued at $126 million, well over four times the amount they had invested.[28]

Apart from its production of taxes, the Port of Houston had proved a sound investment. At the beginning of 1964 the industrial complex along the channel was conservatively valued at three billion dollars. The economic impact of this complex could not be precisely measured, but Rose estimated that the direct and secondary income impact accruing from all Port-related activities amounted to $442 million in 1963. At the end of that year some 55,000 persons were employed as a direct or secondary result of Port operations. This accounted for almost one out of every nine, or 11 per cent, of the employed labor force of Houston, and these workers received $314 million in wages. If tertiary employment arising from Port activities were included, the number of workers increased to more than 100,000, one in five or 20 per cent of Houston's labor force, with a consequent increase in wages.[29]

The full economic impact of the Port on the area, state, and nation over the years could not even be estimated in dollars and cents. The Port was largely responsible, however, for the fact that Houston in 1964 was the largest city in the South and the sixth in the nation; that

[26] *Ibid.*, pp. 4, 50–52.
[27] HCHSCND, Annual Review, 1964, p. 34.
[28] Rose, *Catalyst of an Economy*, pp. 15–16, 52–59.
[29] *Ibid.*, pp. 1–2, 31–41.

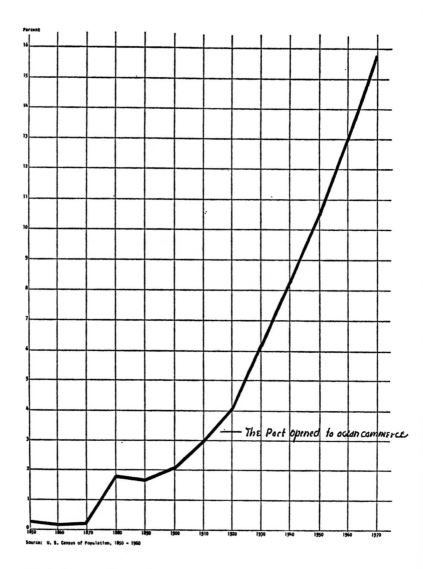

Harris County's Share of the Total Population in Texas, 1850–1960 (With Projections to 1970).

the area was the focal point of a transportation network of highways, railroads, pipelines, and airlines that ranked among the best in the world; that Houston was the location of many home offices, financial institutions, and mercantile establishments. "Actually," commented Dr. J. Edwin Becht in a foreword to Rose's economic study, "the Port is the basis for most of what Houston is today."[30]

In recognition of the importance of the Port, authorities cast about for a suitable means of celebrating the fiftieth anniversary of deep water. The events of the anniversary year in themselves made it a memorable one. Early in February the board together with Humble Oil and Refining Company announced plans for the development of Bayport, a unique industrial project on Galveston Bay near the NASA Manned Space Center. In cooperation with Humble, the District proposed to spend more than $13 million in the following twenty years in the development of a barge-and-ship channel to serve a 7,500-acre industrial site. It was expected that eventually $900 million in capital would be invested in the project and that it would furnish 25,000 new jobs for the area.

Three months after the announcement of the Bayport project, Wharf No. 25 was formally opened by the arrival of the *N/S Savannah* and a ceremony at which Maritime Administrator Nicholas Johnson delivered the principal address. Later in the year the Port played host to the British missile cruiser *HMS London*, and the *Esso Houston*, the largest tanker ever built in the United States. Throughout the year, wheat moved in record-breaking quantities through the Port, so that by the end of the year an all-time high of more than 136 million bushels had been handled. Foreign trade also broke previous records, reaching a total of 12,985,786 tons for the year and bringing in a record of almost $30 million in customs. A grand total of nearly 60 million tons of cargo valued at almost $4 billion passed through the Port during the year, accounting for a record gross revenue of $9,558,614.[31]

To call attention to these impressive statistics as well as to the past, authorities decided to celebrate the Port's fiftieth anniversary of deep water with ceremonies that paralleled those of November 10, 1914.

[30] *Ibid.*, p. i.
[31] HCHSCND, Annual Review, 1964, pp. 1–34.

At that time President Woodrow Wilson had pressed a button in
Washington that discharged a cannon at the Turning Basin. The parallel of this act took on added significance in 1964, for the President
of the United States was Lyndon Baines Johnson, a native Texan who
had taught school in Houston earlier in his career. On the morning of
November 10, 1964, a group of celebrants gathered at the Turning
Basin and heard President Johnson speak from the Texas White House
at Johnson City. "Back in the '30's, when I taught school in Houston,
I remember that some people were still skeptical of the value of the
ship channel," he recalled. "It must be a good feeling today for some
of the early planners of the Port to know that they built not too large,
but too small." At the conclusion of his address, he pressed a button on
his desk that set off a discharge at the Turning Basin—but this act too
was more meaningful than it had been fifty years earlier, for the button
did not merely set off a cannon. Rather it broke ground for three new
docks on the waterfront.

As a further parallel of the earlier occasion, Mrs. George Woods,
nee Miss Sue Campbell, presented her granddaughter, Miss Susan Lee,
who re-enacted her grandmother's role at the christening by tossing a
bouquet of flowers into the channel. The celebration was climaxed by a
banquet at the Shamrock Hilton Hotel with Governor John Connally
as the principal speaker. Where the morning ceremonies had recalled
the past, those of the night emphasized the challenges and opportuni-
ties of the future. "Growth and prosperity today do not guarantee
growth and prosperity tomorrow," warned Governor Connally. "These
are conditions which must be constantly renewed by the initiative and
dedication of people who believe in progress and are willing to work
for it."[32]

Governor Connally spoke to a receptive audience. Indeed, as the
Houstonians paused to celebrate their past achievements they were
looking to the future. Within a few months after the fiftieth-anniver-
sary celebration authorities announced the development of a new industrial park near the Turning Basin; and before the next year ended they

---

[32] Copy of speech furnished by Lloyd Gregory.

had purchased Long Reach Docks. As the Port entered its second half century the words of John Henry Kirby spoken in 1930 still summed up the prevailing spirit along the channel: "We are only getting started!"

APPENDIX A

CITY HARBOR BOARD, HOUSTON, TEXAS, 1913–1922

Name	Date Appointed	Date Service Expired
Jesse H. Jones, Chairman	Dec. 3, 1913	April 23, 1917
Roy M. Farrar	Dec. 3, 1913	April 23, 1917
(Reappointed)	Sept. 17, 1917	March 24, 1922
Thomas H. Ball	Dec. 3, 1913	May 14, 1914
(Reappointed)	March 12, 1919	March 24, 1922
(Chairman May 5, 1921–March 24, 1922)		
John T. Scott	Dec. 3, 1913	Jan. 29, 1921
(Chairman: Sept. 17, 1917–Jan. 29, 1921)		
Camille G. Pillot	Dec. 3, 1913	April 23, 1917
Daniel Ripley	May 4, 1914	April 23, 1917
Jonas S. Rice	Sept. 17, 1917	March 30, 1921
William D. Cleveland, Jr.	Sept. 17, 1917	April 20, 1921
Ben Campbell	Sept. 17, 1917	Nov. 18, 1918
Ross S. Sterling	Nov. 18, 1918	March 30, 1921
Duncan S. Cage	Jan. 21, 1921	March 24, 1922
B. W. Steele	May 5, 1921	March 24, 1922
Robert J. Cummins	May 5, 1921	March 24, 1922

APPENDIX B

NAVIGATION AND CANAL COMMISSIONERS
HARRIS COUNTY HOUSTON SHIP CHANNEL NAVIGATION DISTRICT,
HARRIS COUNTY, TEXAS

Three-man Board (January, 1911–May, 1922)

Name	Date Appointed	Date Service Expired
Charles Dillingham, Chairman	Jan., 1911	July 26, 1916
Ross S. Sterling	Jan., 1911	May 31, 1922
Camille G. Pillot	Jan., 1911	May 31, 1922
Thomas H. Ball	July 26, 1916	May 31, 1922

Five-man Board (after 1922)

Name	Date Appointed	Date Service Expired
E. A. Peden, Chairman	May 29, 1922	Oct. 13, 1924
Roy M. Farrar	May 15, 1922	June 1, 1925
Duncan S. Cage	May 31, 1922	Feb. 8, 1930
Robert J. Cummins	May 31, 1922	July 6, 1946
Ross S. Sterling	May 29, 1922	Oct. 7, 1930
(Chairman Oct. 13, 1924–Oct. 7, 1930)		
Ben Campbell	Oct. 13, 1924	Feb. 8, 1930
William T. Carter, Jr.	June 1, 1925	Sept. 21, 1933
Joseph W. Evans, Chairman	Oct. 7, 1930	March 1, 1945
Stephen P. Farish	Feb. 8, 1930	Jan. 29, 1932
Kenneth E. Womack	Feb. 8, 1930	May 9, 1941
W. A. Sherman	Jan. 29, 1932	May 15, 1942
H. C. Cockburn	Sept. 21, 1933	June 1, 1937
William W. Strong	June 1, 1937	May 14, 1947
Thomas H. Elliott	May 9, 1941	June 30, 1942
Eugene L. Harris	May 15, 1942	July 6, 1946
E. C. Barkley	June 30, 1942	May 30, 1945
J. Virgil Scott, Chairman	March 5, 1945	July 6, 1946
R. Dowman Ernst	May 30, 1945	Sept. 18, 1947

Wilson G. Saville, Chairman	July 6, 1946	July 9, 1950
L. G. Sanders	July 6, 1946	Oct. 30, 1950
W. L. Walker	July 6, 1946	June 29, 1954
Sewall Myer	May 14, 1947	June 16, 1953
Lawton E. Deats	Sept. 18, 1947	Jan. 28, 1953
Warren S. Bellows, Chairman	July 13, 1950	Sept. 30, 1954
Robert Hemphill	Oct. 30, 1950	Dec. 30, 1953
William N. Blanton, Sr.	Jan. 28, 1953	March 9, 1966
John G. Turney	June 16, 1953	Aug. 29, 1963
R. Vernon Whiteside	Jan. 1, 1954	May 14, 1960
M. A. Rowe	June 30, 1954	March 28, 1956
J. S. Bracewell, Chairman	Oct. 1, 1954	Nov. 22, 1955
Howard Tellepsen, Chairman	May 7, 1956	*
H. M. Crosswell, Jr.	Aug. 29, 1956	May 30, 1958
J. P. Hamblen	June 3, 1958	April 26, 1963
William M. Hatten	Aug. 11, 1960	April 14, 1964
William W. Sherrill	May 1, 1963	July 14, 1964
R. H. Pruett	Sept. 3, 1963	*
E. H. Henderson	April 14, 1964	*
W. D. Haden II	July 15, 1964	*
Willie C. Wells	March 9, 1966	Jan. 5, 1968
Fentress Bracewell	Jan. 5, 1968	*

* Member of the board January 15, 1968.

PORT OF HOUSTON TRADE STATISTICS, 1961–1965

Leading Houston Imports* 1961–1965 By Value in Thousands of Dollars

Commodity	1961	1962	1963	1964	1965	% of 1965 Total
Coffee	94,051	112,286	113,756	150,653	120,614	26.7
Steel Mill Products	41,039	42,024	54,946	59,246	80,382	17.8
Motor Vehicles & Parts	22,646	34,519	37,302	40,640	40,844	9.0
Iron & Steel Pipe & Tubes	11,063	13,156	14,007	15,996	22,025	4.9
Machinery & Appliances & Parts	11,970	11,120	9,448	12,310	16,225	3.6
Burlap & Jute Bagging	12,788	12,235	11,294	10,456	12,738	2.8
Liquors & Wines	6,809	8,384	8,945	11,325	11,627	2.6
Distillate & Residual Fuel Oils	17,351	16,382	14,021	9,745	11,324	2.5
Tools, Utensils & Basic Hardware	5,721	6,148	5,642	5,994	10,671	2.4
Plywood & Other Wood Manufactures	5,351	7,387	9,785	11,254	10,072	2.2
Newsprint Paper	5,915	5,640	6,271	7,281	10,029	2.2
Iron Ore & Concentrates	1,240	3,391	4,806	8,923	10,010	2.2
Lead & Zinc Ores & Ingots	2,608	3,583	6,677	6,421	9,213	2.0
Vegetable Fiber Manufactures	6,215	6,010	7,158	8,253	7,276	1.6
Crude Rubber & Rubber Goods	7,697	7,036	6,757	6,991	6,225	1.4

Source: Port of Houston Foreign Trade Statistics 1961–1965

* Commodities selected in order of importance in 1965.

Leading Houston Exports* 1961–1965 By Value in Thousands of Dollars

Commodity	1961	1962	1963	1964	1965	% of 1965 Total
Wheat	177,057	139,842	132,992	237,156	250,300	21.2
Industrial Machinery	46,409	54,292	67,284	78,145	120,208	10.2
Rice	31,605	37,657	42,122	49,221	76,037	6.4
Construction & Mining Machinery	70,958	86,565	76,583	99,541	69,644	5.8
Industrial Chemicals	49,903	44,833	52,390	81,836	68,545	5.7
Cotton	148,672	91,095	82,794	88,163	61,874	5.2
Metal Manufactures	28,381	27,057	27,091	35,992	51,062	4.3
Refined Petroleum Products	40,114	37,075	53,567	55,908	50,173	4.2
Synthetic Rubber	50,970	46,877	42,418	50,542	40,747	3.5
Vegetable Oils	24,613	12,173	22,147	29,528	39,576	3.4
Nonferrous Ores, Metals & Scrap	68,109	34,851	29,526	40,696	38,494	3.3
Synthetic Resins	29,789	31,764	30,005	37,397	37,062	3.1
Chemical Specialties	26,440	29,890	34,913	46,690	31,681	2.7
Wheat Flour	45,937	40,457	33,197	25,890	17,498	1.5
Carbon Black	30,800	25,667	21,588	19,135	14,276	1.3

Source: Port of Houston Foreign Trade Statistics 1961–1965

* Commodities selected in order of importance in 1965.

Leading Suppliers of Houston Imports* 1961–1965 By Value in Thousands of Dollars

Country	1961	1962	1963	1964	1965	% of 1965 Total
Japan	20,142	26,086	39,377	48,949	69,624	15.4
West Germany	36,478	37,435	43,792	55,415	51,257	11.3
Brazil	29,832	41,604	37,813	37,793	30,231	6.7
United Kingdom	19,546	27,250	27,323	29,692	28,163	6.2
Belgium-Luxembourg	22,396	24,698	21,430	19,917	23,909	5.3
France	18,073	14,607	16,827	18,739	20,089	4.4
Colombia	21,724	33,934	30,597	23,708	18,537	4.1
Italy	4,898	7,102	6,651	9,932	17,961	4.0
Mexico	13,169	12,876	13,492	23,103	17,016	3.8
Canada	5,847	5,743	9,316	13,202	16,608	3.7
India	15,136	12,700	11,880	12,766	13,982	3.1
Venezuela	9,522	9,543	7,357	7,573	12,250	2.7
Sweden-Norway-Denmark	7,790	8,704	7,863	9,194	10,136	2.2
Netherlands	14,790	12,899	11,818	13,138	8,385	1.9
Ethiopia	4,448	4,024	4,862	10,149	8,205	1.8

Source: Port of Houston Foreign Trade Statistics 1961–1965

* Countries selected in order of importance in 1965.

Leading Customers of Houston Exports* 1961–1965 By Value in Thousands of Dollars

Country	1961	1962	1963	1964	1965	% of 1965 Total
India	58,122	61,678	73,596	128,590	183,833	15.5
Japan	87,907	46,868	57,550	57,825	70,066	5.9
United Kingdom	59,447	37,265	41,763	43,475	61,383	5.2
Netherlands	43,978	39,596	46,284	60,683	60,728	5.1
West Germany	64,111	41,966	49,913	64,210	50,917	4.3
Venezuela	23,875	29,211	34,097	42,538	41,854	3.5
Yugoslavia	18,102	22,459	16,249	11,462	37,883	3.2
Brazil	65,302	42,672	29,479	50,857	37,381	3.2
France	36,475	33,606	34,807	38,140	34,868	2.9
Argentina	40,936	24,008	19,848	26,660	34,836	2.9
Libya	10,442	21,656	22,856	28,546	28,016	2.4
United Arab Republic	29,618	37,699	25,349	33,653	26,739	2.3
Australia	14,999	17,573	15,943	22,357	26,303	2.2
Italy	59,741	34,573	32,738	29,431	25,811	2.2
Saudi Arabia	6,029	8,209	12,520	14,357	22,066	1.9

Source: Port of Houston Foreign Trade Statistics 1961–1965

* Countries selected in order of importance in 1965.

Value and Weight of Houston Imports and Exports 1961–1965 (Value in Thousands of Dollars; Weight in Short Tons)

	1961	1962	1963	1964	1965
Value of Imports	309,433	357,341	385,513	456,603	451,900
Value of Exports	984,847	857,570	875,843	1,115,725	1,183,025
TOTAL	1,294,280	1,214,911	1,261,356	1,572,328	1,634,925
Import Tonnage	2,787,441	3,435,473	3,492,329	3,794,205	4,107,583
Export Tonnage	7,434,496	6,634,362	6,782,823	9,191,581	9,711,422
TOTAL	10,221,937	10,069,835	10,275,152	12,985,786	13,819,005

Source: Port of Houston Foreign Trade Statistics 1961–1965

Port of Houston 1919–1965
Total Waterborne Commerce

Year	Ship Arrivals	Cargo Tonnage*	Year	Ship Arrivals	Cargo Tonnage*
1919	157	1,287,972	1943	630	15,047,871
1920	165	1,210,204	1944	759	16,956,538
1921	364	2,828,460	1945	1,346	23,869,878
1922	511	3,365,644	1946	2,057	31,837,453
1923	707	4,815,119	1947	2,327	34,323,833
1924	955	7,094,294	1948	2,657	38,904,464
1925	1,193	9,732,731	1949	2,868	36,887,488
1926	1,391	10,359,562	1950	3,271	40,825,048
1927	1,787	12,000,414	1951	3,432	43,774,781
1928	1,973	12,981,113	1952	3,769	46,608,424
1929	2,052	13,917,953	1953	3,598	44,263,704
1930	2,108	15,057,360	1954	3,574	43,244,841
1931	2,092	14,538,452	1955	3,652	47,037,718
1932	2,153	13,296,246	1956	3,754	52,293,262
1933	2,478	17,628,324	1957	4,157	54,945,531
1934	2,489	19,292,629	1958	4,337	55,258,046
1935	2,522	20,572,243	1959	4,558	60,265,293
1936	2,732	23,800,415	1960	4,529	57,132,659
1937	3,018	26,855,739	1961	4,291	56,474,299
1938	3,077	26,737,394	1962	4,276	58,604,886
1939	3,078	28,174,710	1963	3,951	55,895,119
1940	2,809	27,385,598	1964	4,257	59,152,653
1941	2,051	25,623,078	1965	3,851	59,831,766
1942	877	17,661,447			

Source: U.S. Army Corps of Engineers Annual Reports on Waterborne Commerce and Port of Houston statistical records

* Combined barge and ship freight totals.

BIBLIOGRAPHY

Unpublished

Baughman, James P. "The Maritime and Railroad Interests of Charles Morgan, 1837–1885: A History of the 'Morgan Line' " (Ph.D. Thesis, Tulane University, 1962).

Brady Family Papers. Made available by Judge Wilmer B. Hunt, Houston, Texas.

Charles Crotty Collection. Made available by Mrs. Zoe Parsons Crotty, Ingram, Texas, and Mrs. C. M. Wildman, Houston, Texas.

Joseph Stephen Cullinan Papers. Texas Gulf Coast Historical Association Collection, University of Houston.

Deed Records of Harris County, Texas. County Clerk's Office, Houston.

Dickson, John Leslie. "The Houston Ship Channel" (M.A. Thesis, George Peabody College for Teachers, 1929).

Thomas W. House Papers. The University of Texas Archives, Austin.

Harris County Houston Ship Channel Navigation District. Annual Reports and records on file, Administration Building, Houston, Texas. (Cited as HCHSCND.)

HCHSCND. See Harris County Houston Ship Channel Navigation District.

Houston Port and Ship Channel Scrapbook. Houston Public Library.

Jesse Holman Jones Papers. Manuscript Division, Library of Congress, Washington, D.C.

Minutes of the City Council, City of Houston. City Hall.

Minutes of the County Commissioners' Court. Harris County Court House, Houston, Texas.

Muir, Andrew Forest. "The Buffalo Bayou, Brazos & Colorado Railway Company, 1850–1861, and Its Antecedents" (M.A. Thesis, Rice Institute, 1942). Most of this thesis has been published in the *Southwestern Historical Quarterly* articles listed below.

Philips, Lloyd C. "The Houston-Galveston Equalization Agreement: A Basis for the Merging of Houston-Galveston into One Port District for Unified Reporting" (paper submitted for membership in American Society of Traffic and Transportation, Inc., 1963).

Procter, Ben H. "Sidney Sherman" (M.A. Thesis, The University of Texas, 1952).

Scrap Book of the *U.S.S. Houston*. Made available by William A. Bernrieder, Houston, Texas.

Sidney Sherman Papers, 1837–1870. Rosenberg Library, Galveston, Texas.
David A. Simmons Collection. The University of Texas Archives, Austin.
Thibodeaux, Earl Charles. "The New Orleans-Houston Port Rivalry" (Ph.D. Dissertation, Columbia University, 1952).
Albert Thomas Papers. Office of Representative Lera Thomas, Washington, D.C. Mrs. Thomas has announced that these papers will be deposited at Rice University, Houston.
Vandale Collection. The University of Texas Archives, Austin.
J. Russell Wait and Edith Hanner Wait Collection. Kerrville, Texas.
Weinberger, A. L. "The History and Development of the Houston Ship Channel and the Port of Houston" (M.A. Thesis, The University of Texas, 1940).

PUBLISHED

Allen, O. F. *The City of Houston* . . . . Temple, Texas: n.p., 1936.
Allin, Benjamin Casey. *Reaching for the Sea.* Boston: Meador Publishing Company, 1956.
Andrew, James Osgood. *Miscellanies* . . . . Louisville, Kentucky: Morton and Griswold, 1854.
Ball, Thomas H. *The Port of Houston: How It Came to Pass.* Houston: n. pub., n.d.; reprinted from articles appearing in the Houston *Chronicle* and Houston *Post,* August 2–November 1, 1936.
Barker, Eugene C., ed. *The Austin Papers.* Vols. I and II, Washington, D.C.: American Historical Association, 1919–1922; Vol. III, Austin: The University of Texas, 1926.
———, and Amelia W. Williams, eds. *The Writings of Sam Houston.* 8 vols. Austin: University of Texas Press, 1938–1943.
Barnstone, Howard. *The Galveston That Was.* New York: The Macmillan Company, 1966.
Binkley, William C., ed. *Official Correspondence of the Texan Revolution.* 2 vols. New York: D. Appleton-Century Company, 1936.
Board of Engineers for Rivers and Harbors and the Maritime Administration. *The Port of Houston, Texas* (Port Series No. 24). Washington, D.C.: United States Government Printing Office, 1960.
Bollaert, William. *William Bollaert's Texas.* W. Eugene Hollon and Ruth Lapham Butler, eds. Norman: University of Oklahoma, 1956.
Carroll, Benajah Harvey, Jr. *Standard History of Houston.* Knoxville, Tennessee: H. W. Crew & Co., 1912.
City Book of Houston, 1925.
Clopper, Edward N. *An American Family.* Cincinnati: Standard Printing & Publishing Co., 1950.

———, ed. "The Clopper Correspondence, 1834–1838," Texas State Historical Association, *Quarterly*, XIII (October, 1909), 138–144.

———, ed. "J. C. Clopper's Journal and Book of Memoranda for 1828," Texas State Historical Association, *Quarterly*, XIII (July, 1909), 44–80.

Cumberland, Charles C. "The Confederate Loss and Recapture of Galveston, 1862–1863," *Southwestern Historical Quarterly*, LI (October, 1947), 109–130.

De Cordova, Jacob. *Texas* . . . . Philadelphia: E. Crozet, 1858.

Democratic Telegraph and Texas Register.

De Soto [pseudonym]. *Deep Water for Texas.* N. pl., n. pub., 1888.

Dresel, Gustav. *Gustav Dresel's Houston Journal: Adventures in North America, 1837–1841.* Max Freund, ed. Austin: University of Texas Press, 1954.

Farrar, R. M. *The Story of Buffalo Bayou and the Houston Ship Channel.* Houston: Chamber of Commerce, 1926.

Fornell, Earl W. *The Galveston Era* . . . . Austin: University of Texas Press, 1961.

Forney, John W. *What I Saw in Texas.* Philadelphia: Ringwatt & Brown, 1872.

Fortune Magazine, XVI (September, 1937). Special issue on shipping.

Fuermann, George. *Houston: Land of the Big Rich.* New York: Doubleday, 1951.

Galveston *City Directory, 1859–60.*

Galveston *Daily News.*

Galveston *Weekly News.*

Gammel, H. P. N., comp. *The Laws of Texas, 1822–1897.* 10 vols. Austin, Texas: The Gammel Book Company, 1898.

Garwood, Ellen Clayton. *Will Clayton: A Short Biography.* Austin: University of Texas Press, 1958.

Graham, George. "George Graham's Mission to Galveston in 1818: Two Important Documents Bearing upon Louisiana History," Walter Prichard, ed., *Louisiana Historical Quarterly*, XX (July, 1937), 619–650.

Gray, E. N. *Memories of Old Houston.* N.p., n.d.; reprinted from Houston *Chronicle*, April–March, 1934.

Gray, William Fairfax. *From Virginia to Texas* . . . . Houston: Fletcher Young Publishing Co., 1965.

Gregg, Josiah. *Diary & Letters of Josiah Gregg* . . . . Maurice G. Fulton, ed. 2 vols. Norman: University of Oklahoma, 1941.

Gulick, Charles A., and others, eds. *The Papers of Mirabeau Buonaparte Lamar.* 6 vols. Austin: Texas State Library, 1921–1927.

Hardy, Dermot H., and Ingham S. Roberts. *Historical Review of South-East Texas* . . . . 2 vols. Chicago: Lewis Publishing Co., 1910.

Harris County Houston Ship Channel Navigation District. *A Brief Description of the Principal Industries, Port Facilities and Points of Interest Along the Houston Ship Channel.* [Houston, 1965]. Publicity pamphlet.

———. *The Dramatic History of the Port of Houston.* [Houston, 1959]. Publicity pamphlet.

Hatcher, Mattie Austin. *Letters of an Early American Traveller, Mary Austin Holley: Her Life and Her Works, 1784–1846.* Dallas: Southwest Press, 1933.

Herndon, John Hunter. "Diary of a Young Man in Houston, 1838," Andrew Forest Muir, ed., *Southwestern Historical Quarterly*, LIII (January, 1950), 276–307.

Herron, W. W. *Supplement to Sayles' Annotated Civil Statutes of the State of Texas, 1908–1910.* St. Louis: Gilbert Book Co., 1910.

Hill, Charles J. "A Brief History of I.L.A. Local 872," *Personal Telephone Directory and Local History of I.L.A. 872.* Houston: Centaur Publishing Company, 1960.

Hogan, William R. "Henry Austin," *Southwestern Historical Quarterly*, XXXVII (January, 1934), 185–214.

———. *The Texas Republic . . . .* Norman: University of Oklahoma, 1946.

Holley, Mary Austin. *Texas: Observations, Historical, Geographical and Descriptive . . . .* Baltimore: Armstrong & Plaskitt, 1833.

Houston (Chamber of Commerce Magazine).

Houston *Chronicle.*

Houston *City Directory*, 1873.

Houston *Daily Post.*

Houston *Daily Telegraph.*

Houston *Morning Star.*

Houston Port and City.

Houston Port Book.

Houston *Post.*

Houston *Press.*

Houston *Telegraph and Texas Register.*

Houston *Tri-Weekly Telegraph.*

Houstoun, Matilda Charlotte. *Texas and the Gulf of Mexico; or, Yachting in the New World*, 2 vols. London: John Murray, 1844.

Hunter, Robert H. *Narrative of Robert Hancock Hunter, 1813–1902.* Austin, Texas: Cook Printing Co., 1936.

Hutcheson, Joseph C. *Remarks . . . Before the Committee on Rivers and Harbors of the U.S. House of Representatives, March 1, 1898.* n.p.

Ikin, Arthur. *Texas . . . .* Waco, Texas: Texian Press, 1965.

Jacobs, Max H., and H. Dick Golding. *Houston and Cotton*. Houston: Houston Cotton Exchange and Board of Trade, 1949.

Johnston, Marguerite. *A Happy Worldly Abode*. Houston: Cathedral Press, 1964.

Jones, Anson. *Memoranda and Official Correspondence Relating to the Republic of Texas* . . . . New York: D. Appleton and Company, 1859.

Kendall, George Wilkins. *Narrative of an Expedition Across the Great South-Western Prairies from Texas to Santa Fe* . . . . 2 vols. London: David Bogue, 1845.

Lafora, Nicolás de. *The Frontiers of New Spain: Nicolás de Lafora's Description, 1766–1768*. Lawrence Kinnaird, ed. Berkeley, California: Quivira Society, 1958.

Looscan, Adele B. "Harris County, 1822–1845," *Southwestern Historical Quarterly*, XVIII (October, 1914), 195–207; (January, 1915), 261–286; (April, 1915), 399–409; XIX (July, 1915), 37–64.

Lubbock, Francis Richard. *Six Decades in Texas; or, Memoirs of Francis Richard Lubbock*. C. W. Raines, ed. Austin, Texas: Ben C. Jones & Co., Printers, 1900.

"Man of the Month, Jerry Turner," *East Texas*, December, 1965, p. 11.

Moody, W. L. *Galveston Harbor*. N.p., 1884.

Moore, Francis, Jr. *Map and Description of Texas* . . . . Waco, Texas: Texian Press, 1965.

Morphis, J. M. *History of Texas*. New York: United States Publishing Company, 1874.

Morrell, Zachariah N. *Flowers and Fruits in the Wilderness* . . . . Irving, Texas: Griffin Graphic Arts, 1966.

Muir, Andrew Forest. "The Destiny of Buffalo Bayou," *Southwestern Historical Quarterly*, XLVII (October, 1943), 91–106.

————. "Railroad Enterprise in Texas, 1836–1841," *Southwestern Historical Quarterly*, XLVII (April, 1944), 337–370.

————. "The Railroads Come to Houston, 1857–1861," *Southwestern Historical Quarterly*, LXIV (July, 1960), 42–63.

————, ed. *Texas in 1837: An Anonymous, Contemporary Narrative*. Austin: University of Texas Press, 1958.

Murray, Amelia Matilda. *Letters from the United States, Cuba and Canada*. New York: G. P. Putnam & Co., 1856.

Newell, Chester. *History of the Revolution in Texas* . . . . New York: Wiley & Putnam, 1838.

North, Thomas. *Five Years in Texas* . . . . Cincinnati: Elm Street Printing Co., 1871.

Oates, Stephen B. "NASA's Manned Spacecraft Center at Houston, Texas," *Southwestern Historical Quarterly*, LXVII (January, 1964), 350–375.

Olmsted, Frederick Law. *A Journey Through Texas; or a Saddle-Trip on the Southwestern Frontier. With a Statistical Appendix.* New York: Dix, Edwards & Co., 1857.

Ousley, Clarence, ed. *Galveston in Nineteen Hundred . . . .* Atlanta, Georgia: William C. Chase, 1900.

Port of Houston Magazine.

Reed, S. G. *A History of Texas Railroads.* Houston: St. Clair Publishing Co., 1942.

Republic of Texas. *Journals of the House of Representatives,* 1 Cong., 1 Sess.

Rice, Hugh. *Report on the Survey of Buffalo Bayou, San Jacinto River, and Galveston Bay, from the City of Houston to the Gulf of Mexico.* Houston, Texas: Gray, Smallwood & Co., 1867.

Roberts, Merrill J. "The Motor Transportation Revolution," *Business History Review*, XXX (March, 1965), 54–95.

Roemer, Ferdinand. *Texas . . . .* Oswald Mueller, trans. San Antonio, Texas: Standard Printing Co., 1935.

Rose, Warren. *Catalyst of an Economy: The Economic Impact of the Port of Houston, 1958–1963.* Houston: University of Houston, 1965.

Sheridan, Francis C. *Galveston Island; or, A Few Months Off the Coast of Texas: The Journal of Francis C. Sheridan, 1839–1840.* Willis W. Pratt, ed. Austin: University of Texas Press, 1954.

Ship Registers and Enrollments of New Orleans, Louisiana. 6 vols. Baton Rouge: Hill Memorial Library, Louisiana State University, 1941–[?].

Spratt, John S. *The Road to Spindletop: Economic Change in Texas, 1875–1901.* Dallas: Southern Methodist University Press, 1955.

Stansbury, Norwood. "Letters from the Texas Coast, 1875." James P. Baughman, ed. *Southwestern Historical Quarterly*, LXIX (April, 1966), 499–515.

Sterne, Louis. *Seventy Years of an Active Life.* London: [Chiswick Press], 1912.

Stevens, Walter B. *Through Texas.* [St. Louis: General Passenger Department of the Missouri Pacific Railway Co.], 1892.

Stiff, Edward. *The Texan Emigrant . . . .* Cincinnati: George Conclin, 1840.

Sweet, Alexander E., and J. Armoy Knox. *On a Mexican Mustang Through Texas from the Gulf to the Rio Grande.* Hartford, Connecticut: S. S. Scranton & Company, 1883.

Texas Almanac, 1911, 1872, 1858. Galveston, Texas: A. H. Belo & Company.

Timmons, Bascom N. *Jesse H. Jones: The Man and the Statesman.* New York, 1956.

Wait, J. Russell. *Observations Made on a Trip to Japan.* N.p., 1939.

————. "Who Is the Boss?" *Lehigh University Bulletin* (Spring, 1938), pp. 4–6.

Wallis, Jonnie L., and Laurance L. Hill, eds. *Sixty Years on the Brazos: The Life and Letters of Dr. John Washington Lockhart, 1824–1900.* Los Angeles: Dunn Bros., 1930.

Webb, Walter P., and others, eds. *Handbook of Texas.* 2 vols. Austin: Texas State Historical Association, 1952.

Winkler, Ernest W. "The Seat of Government of Texas," *Texas State Historical Association Quarterly,* X (October, 1906), 140–171.

————. "The 'Twin Sisters' Cannon, 1836–1865," *Southwestern Historical Quarterly,* XXI (July, 1917), 61–68.

Young, S. O. *A Thumb-Nail History of the City of Houston, Texas . . . .* Houston: Press of Rein & Sons Company, 1912.

————. *True Stories of Old Houston and Houstonians.* Galveston, Texas: O. Springer, 1913.

Ziegler, Jesse A. *Wave of the Gulf.* San Antonio, Texas: The Naylor Company, 1938.

United States Congressional Documents

"Buffalo Bayou, Tex.," *House Doc.,* 46 Cong., 3 Sess., No. 53 (Serial 1968).

"Buffalo Bayou, Tex.," *House Doc.,* 67 Cong., 1 Sess., No. 93.

"Examination and Survey for a Water Route from the Jetties at Galveston, Texas, through and up Buffalo Bayou to Houston," *Annual Report of the War Department, Report of the Chief of Engineers,* 55 Cong., 3 Sess., Vol. II, Part 2 (Serial 3747), pp. 1515–1527.

"Examination of Buffalo Bayou, Tex.," *Report of the Secretary of War, Chief of Engineers' Report.* 42 Cong., 2 Sess., Vol. II (Serial 1502), pp. 533–537.

"Galveston Harbor and Adjacent Waterways, Tex.," *House Doc.,* 62 Cong., 3 Sess., No. 1390.

"Galveston Harbor and Channel, Houston Ship Channel, and Texas City Channel, Texas," *House Doc.,* 85 Cong., 2 Sess., No. 350.

"Galveston Harbor, Houston Ship Channel, Texas City Channel, and Galveston Channel, Tex.," *House Doc.,* 80 Cong., 2 Sess., No. 561.

"Galveston Ship Channel and Buffalo Bayou, Tex.," *Rivers and Harbors Com. Doc.,* 61 Cong., 2 Sess., No. 35.

"Houston Ship Channel, Tex.," *House Doc.,* 65 Cong., 3 Sess., No. 1632.

"Houston Ship Channel, Tex.," *House Doc.,* 71 Cong., 1 Sess., No. 13.

"Houston Ship Channel, Tex.," *House Doc.*, 76 Cong., 1 Sess., No. 226.

"Houston Ship Channel, Tex.," *House Doc.*, 76 Cong., 1 Sess., No. 256.

"Houston Ship Channel, Tex.," *House Doc.*, 79 Cong., 2 Sess., No. 737.

"Houston Ship Channel, Tex.," *Rivers and Harbors Com. Doc.*, 72 Cong., 1 Sess., No. 28.

"Houston Ship Channel, Tex.," *Rivers and Harbors Com. Doc.*, 74 Cong., 1 Sess., No. 58.

"Houston Ship Channel and Buffalo Bayou, Tex.," *House Doc.*, 75 Cong., 2 Sess., No. 456.

"Improvement of Ship Channel in Galveston Bay, Tex.," *Report of the Secretary of War, Report of the Chief of Engineers*, 48 Cong., 1 Sess., Vol. II, Part 2 (Serial 2184), pp. 1059–1085.

"Red Fish Bar, Galveston Bay, Texas," *House Exec. Doc.*, 43 Cong., 2 Sess., No. 96 (Serial 1646).

"Statement Showing the Importance of Improving the Navigation of Buffalo Bayou . . .," *House Misc. Doc.*, 47 Cong., 1 Sess., No. 32 (Serial 2046).

"Survey for a Ship Channel through Galveston Bay, Tex.," *Report of the War Department, Report of the Chief of Engineers*, 45 Cong., 2 Sess., Vol. II, Part 1 (Serial 1795), pp. 458–466.

INDEX

Adams, First Lieutenant H. M.: on potential of Buffalo Bayou, 94; on canal at Morgan's Point, 95; mentioned, 108
Agricultural and Mechanical College: 144
Ahlers, Henry: 179
Alabama River: 110
Alabama State Docks: 203
Alamo: 23, 28
Albert Gallatin (steamer): 71
Alexander, D. S.: on Buffalo Bayou, 117; mentioned, 135
Alexander Sprunt & Son: 160
Algiers (steamer): 151
Allen, Augustus Chapman: and Galveston, 31; search for city site by, 32; promotional methods of, 33–39, 43; mentioned, 20, 57, 58, 65, 128, 208
Allen, Henry: 48
Allen, H. R.: 92
Allen, John Kirby: search for city site by, 32; promotional methods of, 33–39; in Congress, 35; death of, 47; mentioned, 57, 58, 65, 128, 208
Allen, L. L.: 87
Allen, Sam: 131
Allin, Benjamin Casey: as Port director, 151, 155, 159; arrival of, in Houston, 153; first assignment of, 154; on Ross Sterling, 154; on location of Houston, 155; on tonnage of Port, 161; on Bowie Line, 162; on Galveston, 168; leaves Houston, 172
Almonte, Colonel Juan Nepomuceno: 27, 28
Altemaha (steamer): 151
Alvin, Texas: 84 n. 9
American Association of Port Authorities: 174, 203
American Maid Flour Company: 162
American Petroleum Corporation: 161
Anahuac, Texas: 22, 25, 26

Anderson, Clayton and Company: 160, 201
Anderson, Dillon: 197
Anderson, Miss Susan: 197
Andrew, James Osgood: on Houston, 54; on Texas roads, 61; mentioned, 65
Andrews, John D.: 49, 53
Andrews, Stephen Pearl: 42
appropriations: 68, 96, 100, 104, 107, 108, 153
Ariel (steamboat): 21
Arizona: 30
Arkansas: 10, 180
Armour Fertilizer Works: 148
army: of Texas, 25. SEE ALSO Houston, General Sam, troops of; United States Army
Ashburn, Colonel Ike S.: 169
Atchafalaya River: 98
Atkinson, Captain John J.: 99, 117
Atlantic, Gulf and Pacific Company: 129, 140
Atlantic, Gulf, and West Indies Lines: 148
Atlantic Ocean: 47, 107, 108, 141, 199
Audubon, John James: 45
Austin, Henry: 21
Austin, Stephen F.: on Brazos River, 16; mentioned, 15, 21, 65
Austin, Texas: 46, 55, 63, 64, 81

Bagby, Thomas M.: 87
Bailey, Vernon: 194
Bain, R. M. (Daddy): 179
Baker, Burke: 148
Baker, Captain James A.: 133
Baker, Moseley: 37
Baker, Colonel R. H.: 148
Ball, Tom: terms of, 115, 124, 125; on Rivers and Harbors Committee, 116, 118, 123; on caucus for committee as-